GRUNDLAGEN DER ANGLISTIK UND AMERIKANISTIK

Herausgegeben von Rüdiger Ahrens und Edgar W. Schneider

Band 25

English morphology and word-formation

An introduction

2nd, revised and translated edition

Hans-Jörg Schmid

ERICH SCHMIDT VERLAG

Bibliografische Information der Deutschen Nationalbibliothek
Die Deutsche Nationalbibliothek verzeichnet diese Publikation in der
Deutschen Nationalbibliografie; detaillierte bibliografische Daten
sind im Internet über http://dnb.d-nb.de abrufbar.

Weitere Informationen zu diesem Titel finden Sie im Internet unter
ESV.info/978 3 503 12248 6

1. Auflage 2005
2. Auflage 2011

ISBN 978 3 503 12248 6

Dieses Papier erfüllt die Frankfurter Forderungen
der Deutschen Bibliothek und der Gesellschaft für das Buch
bezüglich der Alterungsbeständigkeit
und entspricht sowohl den strengen Bestimmungen der US Norm
Ansi/Niso Z 39.48-1992 als auch der ISO-Norm 9706.

Druck und Bindung: Danuvia Druckhaus, Neuburg a. d. Donau

Preface

This book is the translated, revised and updated second edition of an earlier book written in German and published in 2005. Like its precursor, it is mainly addressed to students of English and American studies as well as linguistics – in fact first and foremost to German students (which partly shows in the high proportion of German sources referred to).

The purpose of the volume is to introduce students to the field of English morphology and word-formation and assist them in preparing for their intermediate and final exams and in writing term papers and final theses. With these goals in mind, it seems only natural if at least at the outset very little prior knowledge is presupposed which goes beyond what is commonly taught in introductory classes on English linguistics at most universities. Nevertheless an effort has been made not to simplify but to do justice to the complexity of the field.

The analysis and description of morphologically complex words from a structural, sociopragmatic and cognitive perspective takes centre-stage in this book. Questions of a purely theoretical nature, especially those which are only relevant within certain frameworks such as Generative Grammar, receive comparatively little attention. What could nevertheless be of interest to readers who are well-versed in the field anyway, and who are kindly asked to keep in mind that this is meant to be an introductory textbook, is the systematic exploration into sociopragmatic and cognitive issues as well as the empirical corpus-linguistic approach taken.

This book would never have had a chance to be written if it was not for the support and assistance of a large number of people. Wolf-Dietrich Bald, the late co-editor of the series *Grundlagen der Anglistik und Amerikanistik*, prompted me to take the plunge. Carina Lehnen from Erich Schmidt publishers has now had the second opportunity to wait for the final manuscript to materialize. I am greatly indebted to Jens P. Dräger, Ursula Erhard and Sandra Handl for the great competence and stamina which were required for dealing with the intricacies of English morphology and their diligent analysis of the texts which made up the raw material for the corpus used (the *Munich UCL Morphology Corpus*). My heartfelt thanks also go to Bas Aarts, the director of the *Survey of English Usage* at University College London, for giving me permission to use the material.

I am particularly grateful to my father Wolfgang Schmid and my colleagues Wolfram Bublitz, Wolfgang Falkner, Ingrid Fandrych, Sandra Handl, Ursula Lenker, Len Lipka, Edgar Schneider (the series co-editor) and Friedrich Ungerer who read the manuscript of the first edition. A very special thank you goes to Ruth Owen and Sue Bollinger who did an extremely professional job translating and proofreading the second edition. Working together with you was a rewarding experience! Finally, I would like to thank Claudia Höger for formatting the pre-final manuscript and Sandra Handl and Daniela Langer (Erich Schmidt) for their stunningly diligent proofreading. It's hard to imagine how this book would have turned out if it were not for their alertness and competence.

This book is dedicated to my two academic teachers, Len Lipka and Friedrich Ungerer.

Table of contents

1 Introduction

Native speakers of English know a great deal about the structure and composition of the words of their language. For example, on the most mundane level, they know that they can say things like *ten cats, ten dogs* and *ten frogs* but must not say **ten sheeps* or **ten fishs*. They know that they can tell stories about people who *smiled, laughed* and *kissed each other* but cannot say that these people **eated* hamburgers or **drinked* milk. Speakers of English are keenly aware of the fact that words like *apple juice, bus driver* and *paperback* are well-formed, while **juice apple, *driverbus* and **backpaper* are odd, to say the least. They know that if the need arises in discourse they can form words like *unbearability* by adding *-ity* to the adjective *unbearable* or *smasher* by adding *-er* to the verb *smash*. And they know that the kind of objects people have in mind when they are talking about *term papers, newspapers* and *wallpapers* are substantially different in nature, even though all three words seem to refer to types of *papers*. What is more, in addition to being familiar with all these and a host of other facts, regularities and restrictions about words, native speakers feel secure in the knowledge that the other speakers of their language have the same advantages at their disposal and that all of them mutually rely on this shared knowledge when they use words or create or are confronted with new words.

While native speakers do not have any problems in getting things right, 'sticking to the rules' and identifying odd words, it is important to stress that most of them are not consciously aware that they 'know' all these regularities and restrictions. Linguistic knowledge tends, as a whole, to be tacit and implicit rather than conscious and explicit. It is the task of linguists to analyze language systematically in such a way that insights into the kind of knowledge that speakers have and share about their language can be gained. In this endeavour they rely on the close inspection of what seems to be possible or impossible, acceptable or unacceptable, and of what speakers do under certain circumstances and what they never do. These observations allow them to come up with convincing hypotheses and models of how the storage and processing of language, in the case of this book of words and their building blocks and patterns of formation, works. Descriptions of these hypotheses and models are usually couched in terms of linguistic rules, categories and concepts, which are strictly speaking never an end in their own right but serve to capture and illuminate distinctions and regularities that reflect native-speakers' knowledge. So when I now begin by clarifying the terms *morphology* and *word-formation* which occur in the title of this book, I am concerned not only with getting the terminology right, but at the same time with teasing apart different types of linguistic elements and procedures that are processed in specifically distinct ways by speakers of English.

1.1 Morphology and word-formation

The following sentence comes from a sociological text on the subject of the financing of living space for elderly people. It has been taken from the collection of texts (i.e. **corpus**) described in section 1.4.

(1.1)   The future development of government policy towards both institutional care and community care will have significant repercussions upon the housing finance implications of an ageing population.

If we look at the words in this sentence from the point of view of the way they are constructed and the elements they are made up of, we do so from a **morphological** point of view, as **morphology** is concerned with the analysis and segmentation of words into their smallest meaningful parts. From this morphological point of view we can observe firstly that several words in this sentence can indeed be broken down into smaller meaningful components, so-called **morphemes**, e.g. *development* into *develop* and *-ment*, *institutional* into *institution* and *-al* and *repercussions* into *repercussion* and *-s*. A closer look will show that these morphemes are different in nature and fulfil different functions within the words. First of all, morphemes which are at the same time words in their own right can be distinguished from those which can only occur as additions to words: *develop, institution* and *repercussion* belong to the first group, and *-ment, -al* and *-s* to the second. In the next step we can distinguish between those elements in the second group the use of which leads to the creation of a new word and those which merely mark a grammatical form of one and the same word: on the one hand we have *-ment* (*development*) and *-al* (*institutional*), on the other *-s*, which indicates the plural in *repercussions*. We know that these two types of morpheme are sufficiently distinct to warrant being separated into two categories and that they are processed differently, because in speech errors morphemes like the plural ending or the marker of past tense are sometimes inadvertently added to the wrong word (**she look uped the word* instead of *she looked up the word*) while this never happens in the case of morphemes like *-ment* or *-al*.

Two morphological areas can be distinguished depending on which of these two types of morpheme we are dealing with. **Inflectional morphology** includes morphemes of the type *-s* and *-ed*; these are termed **inflectional endings** or **inflectional morphemes**. **Derivational morphology** is concerned with the processes with the help of which speakers of English have formed, and can form if the need arises, new words (e.g. *development*) from words already present in the language (*develop*) by the addition of morphemes (*-ment*). This involves the creation of new words with a complex internal structure, so-called **complex lexemes**. For this reason we regard **derivational morphology** as an important field of **word-formation**, alongside other productive processes such as **compounding** (roughly the juxtaposition of two words as in *community care*) or **conversion** (i.e. the transfer from one word class to another without any visible changes in the morphological form, as in the verb *to age* derived from the noun *age*).

How, in view of these introductory remarks, can the relation between the fields of morphology and word-formation, which are dealt with in this book, be established? What should be emphasized to begin with is that word-formation is not just a part of the wider field of morphology. Word-formation is not only concerned with purely morphological questions but also transcends them, since new words can be created without using morphological components, e.g. when they develop as a result of abbreviation regardless of morpheme boundaries as in *ad* for *advertisement* or *flu* for *influenza* or when only the initial letters of words remain, as is the case with acronyms (*TV, BBC* etc.). Moreover, as already mentioned, the process of conversion traditionally also falls within the scope of word-formation. So morphology includes more than merely word-formation, but word-formation also goes beyond morphology. This relation between the two areas is shown in Figure 1.1.

Fig. 1.1: Relation between the areas morphology and word-formation

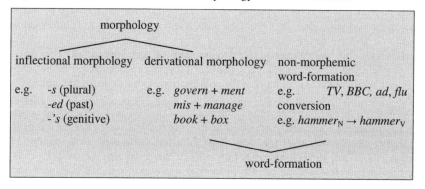

1.2 Objectives and target groups

The aim of this book is to provide an introduction to English morphology and word-formation. The main target group consists of students of English in their second to their final year. While basic knowledge such as is taught in the usual introductory courses to (English) linguistics is not required, there is no doubt that such knowledge would make the reading of this book considerably easier. The reader is led step by step to a degree of competence in the field which should be more than adequate for final examinations and allow for a more in-depth approach to some questions within the framework of final theses.

I would like, however, to offer interested readers more than simply an easily digestible and palatable summary of the present state of research in the field. There are basically two particular aspects of this book which set it apart from the considerable number of textbooks and handbooks already on the market (particularly on word-formation): its theoretical approach (cf. section 1.3) and its data base (cf. section 1.4). The next two sections deal with these two aspects, which might also be of interest to readers already familiar with the area of English morphology and word-formation.

Further reading: to name just a few of the competing introductions and textbooks, **Kastovsky (1982), Bauer (1983, 1988), Cannon (1987), Hansen et al. (1990), Adams (2001), Carstairs-McCarthy (2002), Lipka (2002)** and **Plag (2003).**

1.3 Theoretical framework: broadening the perspectives

1.3.1 Structural perspective

For some considerable time now, morphology and word-formation have been dominated by linguistic theories which focus mainly on the internal structure of words and try to describe and explain their formation with the help of rules which are as precise as possible and allow for no exceptions. The actual usage of words in real social situations, the flexibility with which speakers work with formation patterns and the actual mental processes which take place in the minds of the speakers are of limited interest to the proponents of such approaches. This structure-oriented view of morphology and word-formation is characteristic not only of structuralism but also of most of the contributions in the tradition of Chomsky's generative transformational grammar (see the suggestions for further reading at the end of this section). The main achievement of the structural perspective is that it has produced a detailed description of the inventory of forms and meanings in English morphology and word-formation. Marchand's monumental volume (1st ed. 1960, 2nd ed. 1969) is an exemplary work of this approach; it provides a comprehensive overview of the categories and types of word-formation in English and is likely to continue to be as widely used as a reference book in the next 40 years as has been the case since the publication of the second edition in 1969.

On the other hand, structuralism, and transformational grammar in particular, have raised a considerable number of questions which, since they relate to the specific background assumptions of the theories themselves, have turned out to be of little relevance outside them. For instance, in the late sixties and seventies of the last century a heated discussion broke out about where derivational morphology should be placed in the architecture of grammar and at which point in the course of the generation of a sentence word-formation must come into operation. Was it to be considered as a syntactic rule because derivational morphology creates new words from existing ones with the help of formalizable transformation rules – this was the **transformationalist position** – or does it belong to the lexicon which has been considered to be a "list of basic irregularities" since Bloomfield (1933: 274) and thus cannot be described by rules (the **lexicalist position**)? A second classical contentious issue within generative grammar was the question of whether word-formation works with words or lexemes as basic units (**word-based morphology** as argued for, for example, by Aronoff 1976 and Anderson 1982) or with morphemes (**morpheme-based morphology**, Lieber 1990). Linked to this is the problem of whether complex words are the result of combining morphemes with each other in various ways (**item and arrangement** model, cf. Halle 1973) or whether whole words are simply altered by the processes through which they pass (**item and process** model, Aronoff 1976). Many of these questions are not of great importance today, even within the generative framework, as the general model has developed and changed substantially over the past decades. If one has a different conception of what constitutes language and how it should be analyzed and modelled, one does not necessarily need to tackle all of these problems.

Modern linguistics as a whole has opened up in many new directions since its beginnings in the early 20th century, the heyday of structuralism and the theories which were built on it such as generative grammar. In addition to the structure of the language, the sociolinguistic, pragmatic and cognitive contexts of the use of language and the language system have increasingly come under scrutiny, as they promise important insights into the situation-dependent communicative competence which speakers undoubtedly have in addition to their knowledge about language structures. Against this background my aim in writing this book is to extend the focus systematically beyond the structural description to include socio-pragmatic and cognitive aspects of morphology.

> **Further reading:** classics in the aforementioned debates within generative grammar are **Lees (1966), Chomsky and Halle (1968), Chomsky (1970), Halle (1973) and Aronoff (1976)**, more recently also **Selkirk (1982), Bauer (1988: 122 ff.), Lieber (1990; originally as a dissertation in 1980). Aronoff (2000)** gives a useful overview of generative positions in word-formation. See **Plag (2003: 165 ff.)** on various fundamental theoretical questions in word-formation, *inter alia* a comparison between word-based and morpheme-based approaches in word-formation.

1.3.2 Sociopragmatic perspective

Sociopragmatic considerations are concerned with the **use** of linguistic – in this book, morphological – phenomena in **concrete social** situations **by actual users of the language**. From this point of view it is interesting, for example, to look at the process of the spread of new words in various social groups within a language community. In which social contexts does a new word appear for the first time? In which situations, by which speakers and with which objectives is it used? Consider the word *dog-walker*, for instance. While examples of the word found on the internet suggest that it has become or is gradually becoming established with the meaning 'someone who is paid for taking out other people's dogs', a sign in front of the garden of a house in an English suburb that I came across, which said *Dog-walkers keep off the grass*, suggests that the straightforward sense of 'someone who walks their dog' can also be intended under the right circumstances. This is one small indication that the quality of the linguistic analysis of complex words can be improved if use-related sociopragmatic considerations are taken into account.

Another issue which can be profitably looked at from a sociopragmatic perspective concerns the specific frequencies of appearance of certain morphological phenomena in various kinds of texts or situations. The inflectional morpheme *-ed*, which marks the simple past form of verbs, for instance, is significantly more frequent in narrative texts such as stories than in expository texts, because narratives describe past events (Biber 1988: 135 ff.). Correlations can also be established between word-formation endings such as the aforementioned *-ment* and *-al* as well as endings which form verbs such as *-ize*, *-ify* and *-ate* and certain types of text, namely that they appear more frequently in written texts on abstract subjects than in spontaneous conversation (see p. 181).

Finally, both inflectional morphology and word-formation are important for describing the varieties of English. Peculiarities in inflectional morphology are to be found in many dialects of Great Britain, as the following statement in traditional Berkshire dialect shows:

(1.2)   I sees him every day on my way home. He likes to stop and have a chat, and I generally has the time for that. We often stops in at that pub – you goes there sometimes too, right? – and he has plenty of friends there and they often buys us a drink. (Hughes and Trudgill 1994: 42 f.)

Outside Great Britain, deviations from **Standard English** such as the failure to mark the third person of the verb with *-s* are equally widespread. In the language of many Afro-Americans, for example, so-called *African American Vernacular English*, the copular verb *to be* is used in a morphologically unchanged form (**invariant *be***) to express a habitual aspect, i.e. the habitual nature of a state or an action.

1.3.3   Cognitive perspective

The cognitive perspective introduced in this book is based on approaches from cognitive linguistics and psycholinguistics. These study the mental processes going on during language processing and try to develop psychologically realistic models of language use and the language system. From this standpoint we must, for instance, seek to clarify the question of what takes place in the minds of the speakers of a language when they learn a new compound and begin to set up an entry for it in their **mental lexicons**. Let us take the word *computer virus* as an example. Several years ago, when confronted with the new compound *computer virus* for the first time, many people were uncertain as to the 'true' meaning of the word, even though they were familiar with both parts of the expression, i.e. *computer* and *virus*. From a cognitive point of view, for many speakers the linguistic form at this stage was not associated with one single concept but had to be worked out on the basis of the knowledge of the two constituent concepts. Only with the repeated passive and active use of the word did a more or less specific concept begin to evolve, depending on the extent of the individual's expert knowledge. Both the word-form and the concept were stored in the mental lexicon, and a new, autonomous concept emerged from the initially vague, hazy combination of two well-known concepts.

A further cognitive question to which I dedicate a considerable amount of space in the later chapters of this book is that of the **cognitive functions** of word-formation as a whole and of individual word-formation patterns. What cognitive advantage do speakers gain from coining new complex words or using existing ones? The benefit of a word such as *computer virus* is easy to recognize, since it can express a fairly intricate complex of conceptual content using relatively little linguistic material and we can assume that it will be understood. According to the 5th edition of the *Longman Dictionary of Contemporary English* (LDOCE5) the word *computer virus* denotes a "set of instructions secretly put into a computer, usually spread through emails, that can destroy information stored in the computer".

The old insight, known *inter alia* as the *Sapir-Whorf hypothesis*, that language reflects and influences, or even determines our thinking and perception is revived in cognitive linguistics. The relevance of this hypothesis for word-formation can be demonstrated by reference to nominalization – where nouns are formed from verbs or adjectives by means of word-forming endings, e.g. *development* and *declaration*. In the sentences in (1.3) and (1.4) both the verb *declare* and the nominalization *declaration* occur. Although strictly speaking both the verb and the noun describe a process, they tend to evoke different associations. While the verb in example (1.3) really makes one think of a process, or to be more precise, an action, the noun *declaration* depicts the result or the product of a process. The addition of the suffix *-ation* thus has a reifying effect, which means that it presents an action as if it was a concrete object.

(1.3)   In a recent interview one of them *declared* it's easier to become an astronaut than a pilot for a presidential plane. (ICE-GB: S2b-021 #45)

(1.4)   What's more the meeting produced a joint *declaration* which looks like the start of a compromise between President Gorbachev and his most powerful critic. (ICE-GB: S2b-040 #95)

The application of morphological procedures can therefore bring about differences in the conceptualization of information communicated by means of language, which can be analyzed in the framework of cognitive linguistics.

> **Further reading**: **Aitchison (2003)** provides an introduction to the mental lexicon, **Ungerer and Schmid (2006)** to cognitive linguistics.

1.4   The corpus

The second distinctive feature of this book is its empirical data basis. A corpus encompassing approximately 41,000 words of authentic English present-day conversations and texts was fully analyzed and annotated morphologically, i.e. all the words were broken down into morphemes and then classified in accordance with the criteria defined in sections 2.2.2 and 2.2.3.

The corpus used contains texts of various types, to make the material fairly diverse both thematically and stylistically. In order to be able to make systematic comparisons between texts from different sources, I have made use of pre-selected material from *The British Component* of the *International Corpus of English* (ICE-GB), a computerized corpus of the English language. This data base consists of 500 texts, each comprising about 2000 words, with the entire corpus thus containing about one million words. Sixty per cent of the texts are transcripts of spoken language, the remainder consisting of written texts of various types. With the permission of the *Survey of English Usage*, University College, London, 20 texts were selected from the ICE-GB corpus and subjected to the systematic morphological analysis and annotation mentioned above. This corpus is called the *Munich UCL Morphology Corpus* (MUMC). Unfortunately it cannot be made publicly available due to copyright restrictions.

The MUMC was exploited for this book for two purposes. Firstly it was used as a source of authentic examples from spoken and written texts. This made it possible to focus on word-formations we encounter most frequently in authentic language rather than those which are particularly interesting because they are complex and exotic. Secondly the corpus was utilized for systematic statistical analyses of the frequency of occurrence of morphological phenomena in different text types, which will be presented in the framework of seven empirical corpus studies on central areas of morphology. The data were collected in order to compare the distribution of different English morphemes and word-formation patterns in various text types and serve as both a basis for and proof of hypotheses proposed from the sociopragmatic and cognitive perspectives. The corpus thus constitutes a link between the empirical data base and the theoretical objective of this book, contributing to a consistent research methodology.

The 20 texts are distributed over five text types, with four belonging to each category. Table 1.1 shows an overview of the composition of the MUMC.

Tab. 1.1: Composition of the Munich UCL Morphology Corpus (MUMC)

text code in ICE-GB	length in words	text code in ICE-GB	length in words
spontaneous spoken conversation		personal letters	
S1a-007	2044	W1b-001	2161
S1a-058	2090	W1b-008	2148
S1a-072	1995	W1b-010	2104
S1a-086	1978	W1b-014	2065
total	8107	total	8478
academic writing		press reportage	
W2a-002	2054	W2c-002	2000
W2a-013	2150	W2c-010	2030
W2a-026	2229	W2c-013	2086
W2a-035	2048	W2c-019	1941
total	8481	total	8057
fiction			
W2f-003	2040		
W2f-009	2236		
W2f-011	2189		
W2f-014	2067		
total	8532		
total number of all words in the corpus: 41,655			

1.5 Overview of the structure of this book

This first chapter has served two basic purposes: to identify the subject matter under investigation and to state the fundamental theoretical and methodological assumptions.

Chapter 2 deals with terminological questions concerning the morphological building blocks of English, as a prerequisite for subsequent chapters. The basic concepts will be introduced and defined as prototypical categories with good, less good and marginal examples.

Chapter 3 is devoted to inflectional morphology, treating inflectional morphemes and their formal variants in present-day English and providing an overview of the historical development of the inflectional morphology from Old English to present-day English.

From chapter 4 onwards the focus is on English word-formation. Firstly the development of new, complex lexemes is traced from their emergence to their establishment in the speech community, the English lexicon and the minds of the speakers.

In chapter 5 the most important fundamental issues in word-formation are clarified. Various possibilities for classifying word-formation processes are discussed and a systematic framework for applying the structural, sociopragmatic and cognitive perspectives to the analysis of complex words is introduced.

Chapter 6 investigates the productivity of word-formation processes. Ways of finding out the extent to which speakers still actively use existing word-formation patterns to form new words are discussed here, among other things.

Chapters 7 to 11 address the basic patterns in English word-formation: compounding, prefixation, suffixation, conversion and the non-morphemic word-formation processes of back-formation, clipping, acronym formation, blending and reduplication.

Complex words consisting of more than two constituents are treated in chapter 12 while chapter 13 provides a résumé.

2 The morphological building blocks of English

In section 1.1 morphology was defined as the linguistic discipline concerned with analyzing words into their smallest meaningful elements. The aim of this chapter is to define the nature of the morphological building blocks that can combine to make up English words. First, however, the term *word* itself, the meaning of which has so far not been questioned, even though it is by no means clear-cut, must be clarified.

2.1 Ambiguity of the notion of *word*

2.1.1 Word – word-form – lexeme

Let us start by using the following minicorpus of samples taken from five different text types:

(2.1)

(a)   A: The bit behind the bed.
        B: Yes yes.
        A: Very much like your bedhead.
        B: This is what I'm really saying. (ICE-GB: S1a-086)

(b)   What are your future study plans, and how are your present studies coming along. (ICE-GB: W1b-001)

(c)   Reluctance to regard theory-making or model-making work in AI as respectable can be traced frequently to the mistaken view that the only respectable scientific theories are neat theories. (ICE-GB: W2a-035)

(d)   The news agency, Tanjug, said a parliamentary committee had approved a draft law strengthening the powers of the republic's president to declare a state of emergency. (ICE-GB: W2c-019)

(e)   There were cars strewn on the shag-pile carpet and the baby sat in a yellow high-chair, a soiled bib around her neck and traces of breakfast around her mouth. (ICE-GB: W2f-003)

Faced with the task of determining the number of words in this corpus, one could in principle follow one of three strategies. Firstly one could regard as words any units which are separated from the surrounding text by a space on both sides, or occasionally by a space on the left-hand side and a punctuation mark on the right-hand side. This is how word processing programmes function when counting words, being based on a purely **orthographic concept of the notion of** *word*. In this case its written form is what defines a word. That this method of counting cannot exactly be the ideal solution from a linguistic point of view is obvious from the fact that e.g. *I'm* in (2.1a) is counted as one word even though it is actually two (*I* and *am*). On the other hand, *news agency* is counted as two words, although it would seem sensible to regard it as one word, despite the fact that it is written as two. (We will return to this problem in section 2.1.2.)

A second counting strategy would take into account that some items appear several times in the minicorpus, e.g. frequent function words such as *the*, *yes*, *are*, *your* or *and*, but also content words such as *respectable* and *theories*. One could argue that these occurrences in each case merely represent several citations of one and the same word and should therefore not be re-counted. The linguistic basis for such an approach is the distinction between **token** and **type**. If we count purely orthographically, as described in the previous paragraph, what we are counting are tokens; if we do not re-count any items that we have previously encountered, then we are counting types. It must immediately be obvious that in every text there are more tokens than types. And it should be equally clear, at least after brief reflection, that the relationship between types and tokens, the so-called **type-token-ratio**, can be used to measure the variability of the vocabulary in a text or corpus, since the more types that occur compared to tokens, the more varied is the word stock.

However, we do not have to content ourselves with counting types either, which brings us to the third strategy. It is obvious even to linguistic amateurs that the elements *saying* (in 2.1a) and *said* in (2.1d) are actually only different forms of one 'word'; *study* and *studies* in (2.1b), and *is* in (2.1a), *are* in (2.1b, 2.1c) and *were* in (2.1e) behave in the same way. It is helpful to use the terms **word-form** and **lexeme** to describe such relationships. *Is*, *are* and *were* are described as word-forms of the lexeme *be*; *study* and *studies* are word-forms of the lexeme *study*. Texts always consist of word-forms, irrespective of whether these word-forms differ outwardly from the lexemes that they realize (as in the case of *studies* or *are*) or not (e.g. *study*). In contrast, lexemes are not real components of actual utterances (Saussure's *parole*), but theoretical constructs on the level of the language system (*langue*) and therefore units abstracted from actual use. Yet they appear to be psychologically real entities in the mental lexicons of speakers, as psycholinguistic observations and experiments indicate that the inflectional endings of word-forms, insofar as they are regular, are only added during on-line speech production rather than stored in long-term memory together with their bases (Aitchison 2003: 128 ff., McQueen and Cutler 1998: 418 ff., Stemberger 1998: 440, cf. Booij 2007: ch. 10). The nearest approximation to lexemes that we deal with on a daily basis can be found in dictionaries where as a rule we look for words not under their grammatically marked plural, progressive or past forms, for example, but under their so-called **citation form**, which represents those particular lexemes.

The reference to dictionaries leads us to yet another characteristic of lexemes which must not be overlooked. As a rule, lexemes are abstractions not only from different grammatical word-forms, but also from different word meanings. For example, the entry for the noun *study* in the LDOCE5 (Summers 2009) gives no less than eight meanings, among them: 1. 'piece of work', 2. 'when you spend time learning', 3. 'a subject that people study', 4. 'the work that somebody does in order to learn about a particular subject', 5. 'careful consideration' and 6. 'a room in a house that is used for work or stuy'. The lexeme *study* is therefore polysemous – a characteristic which is entirely typical of lexemes. The meanings of word-forms, on the other hand, are more specific, as they are disambiguated in most cases by their context. In (2.1.b), for example, the first word-form *study (plans)* probably realizes meaning 3, while the second word-form *studies* has the same meaning or possibly meaning 4.

Lexemes thus subsume different grammatical word-forms and different but similar meanings in one idealized lexical unit, which has the status of a linguistic sign. Comparing this with Saussure's well-known idealized model of the sign as an arbitrary linking of a form (*signifier*) with its content (*signified*), it transpires that the lexeme allows for variation on either side of the sign without forfeiting the impression that it is a single conceptual unit.

Further reading: Bauer (2000a), Carstairs-McCarthy (2000).

2.1.2   Typical, less typical and atypical words

As already mentioned in the last section, the distinction between *lexemes* and *word-forms* is not the only terminological problem in the conceptual field surrounding the notion of *word*. We now need to determine what distinguishes *words* – we can keep to the familiar term here – from smaller linguistic units (morphemes and phonemes) and from larger ones (phrases, clauses and sentences). It has to be stressed straight away that a completely watertight definition of the term *word*, which is immune to every counterexample and nevertheless corresponds to what we intuitively envisage as a word, has not yet been proposed. This is not surprising since the category WORD, like other linguistic categories, has no clear boundaries, but overlaps with neighbouring categories just as colour categories such as RED and ORANGE or GREEN and BLUE cannot be separated from one another by clear lines. There is usually agreement on prototypical red, orange, blue or green hues, but in the transition regions classification can be difficult and controversial. It therefore makes sense to start by defining typical representatives of the category WORD using suitable criteria or attributes and only then to assess how less typical members of the category can be described using these attributes.

Typical words are characterized by a set of five attributes on four linguistic levels:

1. Syntactic attributes: Words are the smallest units that can occur alone in certain contexts, e.g. short answers to questions. To be more precise, this criterion – which lies at the heart of what is probably the most well-known definition of the concept of *word* by Bloomfield (1933: 178) as a "minimum free form" – splits into two attributes, a) independence and b) minimality.

2. Orthographical attribute: Words are orthographically uninterrupted units separated on each side by spaces (or punctuation marks).

3. Phonological attribute: Words are phonological units that carry only one primary stress.

4. Semantic-cognitive attribute: A word is associated with a unit of meaning; a word stands for an integrated idea, a conceptual **gestalt**.

Examples of prototypical words in (2.1) are *bed*, *regard* and *declare*. Any deviations from the prototypical examples can now be described with reference to how they fare with regard to these attributes. Table 2.1 gives an overview of them.

Tab. 2.1: Typical and other members of the category word and their attributes

Attributes:	(1a)	(1b)	(2)	(3)	(4)
Typical words: *bed, regard, declare*	+	+	+	+	+
Composite words (compounds):					
– written together (*bedhead, highchair*)	+		+	+	+
– with a hyphen (*theory-making, model-making, shag-pile*)	+		~	+	+
– written separately (*news agency, draft law*)	+			+	+
Idiomatic expressions and phrasal verbs: *come along, get up, put up with*	+				+
Particles and grammatical prepositions: *(reluctance) to, (state) of (emergency)*	~	+	+		
Cliticized forms: *I'm, you're*	+		~	+	

Key to the attributes:
(1) Syntactic: "minimum free form"
    (1a) Independence   (1b) Minimality
(2) Orthographic: separated by spaces on each side
(3) Phonological: one main stress
(4) Semantic-cognitive: one semantic unit
+: the relevant attribute is present
~: the relevant attribute is present with restrictions

The first type of deviation, which has already been mentioned briefly in 2.1.1, is composite word-forms, so-called **compounds**. Since compounds by definition consist of at least two words (see section 7.1.1), the attribute of minimality does not apply. If one differentiates compounds with respect to how they are spelt, which, incidentally, is fairly inconsistent in English (see p. 131), then other attributes no longer apply either: compounds written as one word (e.g. *bedhead, highchair*) fulfil the orthographic criterion, as to a certain extent do compounds written with a hyphen, too (e.g. *theory-making, model-making, shag-pile*); compounds written as separate words such as *news agency* and *draft law*, however, are not regarded orthographically as one word-form and are therefore not typical representatives of the category WORD, even though other criteria, especially the semantic-cognitive one, apply. (The fact that certain types of compounds, e.g. *study-bedroom*, carry more than one main stress, will be disregarded here.)

In a similar but even clearer way so-called **multi-word lexemes** such as idiomatic expressions (e.g. *to get someone off the hook*) and phrasal verbs (e.g. *come along*) differ from typical words, while sharing with the latter the characteristics of independence and semantic-cognitive unity. After all, one of the main characteristics of fixed phrases is that they form a semantic unit. On the other hand, these word-groups neither fulfil the criterion of minimality, nor can they be regarded as orthographic or phonological units.

Particles and **prepositions** with a purely grammatical function, e.g. the forms *to* and *of* in the contexts *reluctance to regard* and *state of emergency* in (2.1), are special cases in a completely different way. Since their function here is to link syntactic elements, they do not evoke a lexical meaning let alone a mental image, which means that the semantic-cognitive criterion is not fulfilled. These forms have no primary stress, presumably as a consequence of or, to look at it another way, as a formal marker of the missing semantic salience; in speech they are pronounced with extremely low intensity like the maximally unstressed syllables of word-forms with several syllables. From an orthographic point of view there is no doubt about their nature as a word-form; syntactically their status as a minimal form is indisputable, though their independence is doubtful.

Finally we must include contracted forms such as *I'm* as well as *you're, don't* or *wouldn't*, which are not documented in example (2.1), and the like in our considerations. These forms contain so-called **cliticized forms**. Semantics, orthography and syntax clearly indicate that in the case of these forms we are not dealing with one but two words. Two separate meanings are combined within these forms and we are aware that the component parts can also be written separately and can occur alone.

In this section we have described the category WORD by putting up a scale ranging from typical to less good representatives. The degree of typicality allocated to individual members of the category WORD was justified by the presence or absence of certain attributes. This seems to be a more suitable strategy for understanding the nature of the notion *word* than attempts to define it unambiguously by means of hard-and-fast criteria. As with many other basic linguistic concepts, the notion of *word* is a collective term for what is, in many respects, a range of similar but by no means identical phenomena. Grading them according to degrees of typicality seems to do justice to this status.

> **Further reading**: On the notion of word: **Di Scullio and Williams (1987), Bauer (1988: 45–55), (2000), Carstairs-McCarthy (2000), Plag (2003: 4 ff.)**; for information on prototype theory, on which the explanation of the notion of word was based, see **Ungerer and Schmid (2006: chs. 1 and 2)**.

2.2 The basic morphological units

In order to describe the meaning-bearing components of words we have basically two competing systems at our disposal. In the terminology of modern linguistics, the notion of **morpheme**, which has already been mentioned in chapter 1, plays a key role. Differences between types of morphemes with regard to the kinds of linguistic environments in which they can occur (their so-called **distribution**, see 2.2.2) and with regard to their **function** (see 2.2.3) are described using morpheme classes such as **bound** and **free**, and **lexical** and **grammatical** respectively. A more traditional terminology, on the other hand, which comes from classical Greek and Latin grammar, and is frequently used in historical linguistics, uses the concepts of **root, stem** and **affix**. Since both terminological systems can be found in the specialist literature, both will be introduced here. The morpheme-orientated terminology will serve as our starting point and frame of reference.

2.2.1 Morpheme and morph

The basic component of words is the **morpheme**, usually defined as the smallest meaningful unit of languages (e.g. Herbst, Stoll and Westermayr 1991: 73). The fact that this definition comprises several aspects or attributes – first and foremost minimality, semanticity and unit status – indicates that with the category MOR-PHEME, as with the concept of WORD, we must expect to see both good and poor examples. And this is indeed the case. In this section I will first treat prototypical manifestations of the category MORPHEME, going on in section 2.3 to deal with the transition area comprising less typical examples and submorphemic components of words.

Let us start our discussion with a short extract from a newspaper report (2.2):

(2.2)   Head teachers are planning to challenge a key part of the government's education reforms ... (ICE-GB: W2c-002).

The passage in (2.2) is shown in (2.3) broken down into morphemes, which are indicated by means of braces, as is common practice in linguistics:

(2.3)   {Head} {teach} {er} {s} (= plural) {are} {plan} {ing} {to} {challenge} {a} {key} {part} {of} {the} {govern} {ment} {s} (= genitive) {educat(e)} {ion} {re} {form} {s} (= plural)

It can hardly be denied that all the elements that have been segmented in this way carry, on the one hand, some sort of meaning and on the other hand cannot be further broken down into smaller meaningful elements. They therefore turn out to constitute the smallest meaningful components of this passage, i.e. morphemes. From a theoretical point of view, however, it is necessary to be slightly more precise. As with other linguistic terms ending in *-eme*, for example *lexeme*, *phoneme* and *phraseme*, the concept of *morpheme* must be interpreted as an abstraction of actually produced language data. Thus the concept of morpheme belongs to the level of the linguistic system (*langue*) and not to actual utterances (*parole*). By analogy with the relationship between *lexeme* and *word-form* as defined in 2.1.1, some linguists (e.g. Lyons 1968: § 5.3.4, Bauer 1983: 15, Bauer 1988: 11–15) make a distinction between *morphemes* (as abstractions on the *langue*-level) and **morphs** (as actual realizations of morphemes). This distinction is not always particularly significant. It comes into operation predominantly when a morpheme formally unites several morphs with the same meaning. This is particularly typical of the field of inflectional morphology. The plural morpheme, for instance, can be realized as /s/ (in *cats*), /z/ (in *dogs*) and /ɪz/ (in *horses*), depending on the ending of the morpheme to which it is affixed (cf. section 3.1). We refer to such cases as **allomorphs** of a morpheme, with this notion being defined as different formal realizations of one morpheme (see section 2.4). In the case of morphemes which only occur in the form of one realization, very few linguists attach any importance to the precise terminological separation of *morph* and *morpheme*. Accordingly there is no consensus on whether morphs – as described above – are generally the realizations of a morpheme on the *parole*-level (a position which is rejected for instance by Mugdan 1986: 33 ff.), whether they are purely phonetic realizations (as in Herbst, Stoll and Westermayr 1991) or whether the use of the term should simply be avoided (as suggested, e.g. by Kastovsky 1986, Hansen et al. 1990 and Lipka 2002). In accordance with the latter position, the term *morph* will only be used in this book in the term *allomorph*.

2.2.2   The distributional classification of morphemes

There are conspicuous differences between the morphemes in (2.3), the most obvious relating to their **distribution**, i.e. the kinds of linguistic environments in which they can occur. To begin with, there is a number of morphemes, e.g. {head}, {teach}, {plan}, {to} and {of}, which are **free**. This means that they can occur alone. Free morphemes are thus at the same time lexemes. Whether they occur alone in a specific context or whether they are part of another word is not the point; what matters is whether they can *potentially* stand alone. The opposite of free morphemes are **bound morphemes**. Examples in (2.3) are {-er}, {plural -s}, {-ing}, {-ment} and {genitive -s}. Bound morphemes can *only* occur in conjunction with other morphemes; they differ strictly speaking from free morphemes – which like {teach} in *teachers* in (2.2) can also occur in conjunction with other morphemes – in that their bound status is *obligatory* (cf. Bauer 1988: 11, Lieber and Mugdan 2000: 406). It is common practice to refer simply to *free* and *bound* morphemes rather than *potentially free* and *compulsorily bound* morphemes.

In English the classification of morphemes with respect to their distribution is to a large extent unproblematic and can be carried out without a comprehensive catalogue of criteria. As a rule the boundaries between classes of free and bound morphemes can be clearly drawn using solely orthographic criteria. Very occasionally cases such as *ism* occur, which was originally a bound morpheme in words such as *socialism* and *realism*, but is also used today according to the LDOCE4 in informal discourse as a free nominal morpheme meaning "to describe a set of ideas or beliefs whose name ends in 'ism', especially when you think that they are not sensible and practical" (s.v. *ism*).

One type of morpheme which is special with regard to its distribution is the small class of so-called **unique** or **blocked morphemes**. This morpheme type describes the elements *rasp-* and *cran-* in *raspberry* and *cranberry*, and the first part of the designations for the days of the week, for example *Tues-*, *Wednes-* and *Thurs-*. Such word elements are granted morphemic status primarily because in each instance the second element *-berry* and *-day* is clearly a free morpheme, which renders it to some extent reasonable to suppose that the first is also a morpheme. The indisputable fact that there is a series of these words ending in *-berry* and *-day* adds weight to this decision. On the other hand, the semantic impact of these **cranberry-morphemes**, as they are sometimes called after one of the examples, is questionable. While they are certainly not prototypical morphemes, they are particularly good illustrations of the structuralist idea that the meaning of linguistic signs does not reside in the signs themselves but emerges from their differences to other signs. We call these elements *blocked* or *unique* morphemes because they can only ever be combined with one other morpheme, namely *-berry* or *-day*. Apart from these two paradigms there do not seem to be any other blocked morphemes in English which actually meet the two criteria of combining with only one other morpheme and being a member of a paradigmatic set.

2.2.3 The functional classification of morphemes

The second fundamental dimension for the classification of morphemes is their function. With regard to this dimension, morphemes with a lexical function – in (2.3) e.g. the free morphemes {head} and {part}, and also the bound {-ment} and

{-ion} – must be separated from those with a grammatical function (e.g. free: {to} and {of}; bound: {plural -s}, {genitive -s}).

Before starting our detailed description of the classification according to function, the morpheme classes arising from the combination of distributional and functional criteria must be translated into traditional terminology. Free lexical morphemes are traditionally described as roots or stems, which must, however, be differentiated even more finely (see section 2.5). Free grammatical morphemes are function words. The group of affixes consists of bound morphemes regardless of their function; if they occur before a free morpheme they are called prefixes, if they are attached to the end of a free morpheme they are suffixes. Bound lexical morphemes are derivational affixes. Bound grammatical morphemes are always suffixes in modern English and are described as inflectional suffixes or inflectional endings. Figure 2.1 shows an overview of these terms:

Fig. 2.1: Classification and terminology of the building blocks of words

function	lexical		grammatical	
distribution	free	bound	free	bound
	root	derivational affix	function word	inflectional affix
position		prefix suffix		suffix

The distinction between lexical and grammatical morphemes can be demonstrated most clearly by comparing free lexical with bound grammatical forms. This can be seen in (2.4) with reference to the morphemes in examples (2.2) and. (2.3):

(2.4)   lexical free: {head}   {key}
        (roots)   {teach}   {part}
                         {plan}   {govern}
                         {challenge} {educate}
                         {form}

        grammatical bound: {plural -s}
        (inflectional endings)   {ing}
                             {genitive -s}

Using these examples we can illustrate two attributes of lexical and grammatical morphemes which are frequently used in the literature in order to distinguish between them:

1. Grammatical morphemes are credited with a relational function – they connect syntactic constituents. The first plural form *teachers*, for example, agrees with the plural verb form *are*; the genitive morpheme relates the noun *government* to *education reforms*. Lexical morphemes, on the other hand, are non-relational, they can fulfil their function largely independently, since they are

31

semantically autonomous. Grammatical morphemes are therefore described as being **synsemantic** (roughly 'having meaning together') and lexical morphemes as **autosemantic** ('having meaning on their own'). Furthermore, lexical morphemes have relatively specific meanings that can conjure up mental images. The meanings of grammatical morphemes, on the other hand, e.g. 'possession' or 'belonging' for the genitive morpheme, 'more than one' for the plural morpheme and 'for a restricted time period' for the {ing}-morpheme, are comparatively abstract.

2. Grammatical morphemes form **closed systems**. The addition of new elements to these systems or the disappearance of existing ones from them takes place only over long periods of time. This assertion is particularly valid in the case of bound grammatical morphemes. Present-day English retains only nine such morphemes, a situation which has not changed for more than 300 years (cf. chapter 3). The stock of lexical morphemes changes – at least in the field of free morphemes – virtually daily. New lexemes are added and existing ones become obsolete. Lexical morphemes therefore form an **open class**.

This means that free lexical morphemes are lexically or semantically autonomous and belong to open classes; bound grammatical morphemes are relational and belong to closed systems. Starting from this observation we can tackle the somewhat trickier distinction between lexical and grammatical morphemes within the two distribution classes of free vs. bound.

Lexically bound vs. grammatically bound – derivation vs. inflexion

Let us start by considering bound morphemes. Examples of bound lexical morphemes in (2.2) are the suffixes {-er} in *teacher*, {-ment} in *government*, {-ion} in *education* and the prefix {re-} in *reform*. Closer examination reveals that these morphemes are not semantically autonomous and that it is difficult to assign them a specific meaning. Although the stock of lexical prefixes and suffixes is relatively stable, we cannot fail to notice that affix-like elements are constantly being added, for example the recent *cyber-* (*cyberspace, cyberpunk, cybernaut, cyberart*), *nano-* (*nanotechnology, nanocomputer, nanocrystal*) and *mega-* (*megastore, megastar, megarich, megahit*). The class of bound lexical morphemes is in principle therefore still open, so a clear-cut distinction between bound lexical and bound grammatical morphemes cannot be made using the two criteria specified above. Instead there are first and foremost four parameters that allow a more accurate division of suffixes into lexical or derivational morphemes.

1. What is the result of adding a bound morpheme to a free one? The examples *teach-er*, *govern-ment* and *educat(e)-ion* on the one hand, and *plan(n)-ing*, *government-'s* and *reform-s* on the other, give an indication of the answer. By adding lexical morphemes, as in the former set, new lexemes are created, whereas adding grammatical morphemes, as in the latter, only produces differ-

ent word-forms of one lexeme. This distinction has two consequences which can be implemented as further distinguishing criteria.

2. Since the addition of derivational suffixes always creates new lexemes, it is also always accompanied by a change in meaning. *Teacher* has a different meaning from *teach*, which is why the two lexemes are listed as separate entries in the dictionary. *Reforms*, which is a word-form of the lexeme *reform*, does not have a separate entry, since the addition of the inflectional suffix does not change the meaning of the lexeme. Closely connected with this parameter is the third aspect which, however, is not as categorical.

3. Inflectional endings always preserve word classes, whereas derivational suffixes, since they invariably determine word class, cause a change in the part of speech in most cases. *Teach* is a verb, *teacher* a noun; the same holds for *govern – government* and *educate – education*. It is only in rare cases, such as the suffix {-ish} in *greenish* for example, that the word class remains unchanged following the addition of a derivational suffix.

4. Lexical suffixes precede grammatical suffixes. Since derivational suffixes determine the word class while the addition of inflectional suffixes is dependent on the word class, it is obvious that the grammatical morphemes usually have to be positioned further from the stem than the lexical ones. This is confirmed by the order of the morphemes in *teach-er-s*, lexically free – lexically bound – grammatically bound.

While these four criteria are undoubtedly very helpful, it should be emphasized that, as in other cases treated above, there is essentially a gradient from typical derivational to typical inflectional morphemes (cf. Bybee 1985). The adverb-forming suffix *-ly* is a good example of an element straddling the boundary between derivational and inflectional morphemes since it changes the word class but does not have a noticeable semantic effect. Leaving aside theoretical considerations, however, the identification of bound grammatical morphemes in modern English – i.e. the historical period since *c.* 1700 – is considerably facilitated by the fact that, as already mentioned, it is more or less indisputable that only nine morphemes of this type are still in existence, namely {plural -s} and {genitive -s} for nouns; {3rd person -s}, {ing}, {ed$_1$} (= simple past) and {ed$_2$} (= past participle) for verbs; {er} (comparative) and {est} (superlative) for adjectives; and the {th} (ordinal morpheme) as in *fourth* in numerals. When carrying out a practical morphological analysis and classification, we can therefore more or less rely on a process of elimination in case of doubt, treating all suffixes not covered by this list as lexical. (In the analysis itself, however, the problem of allomorphs must be kept in mind; see chapter 3, which gives an overview of inflectional morphology.)

The forms *-ing*, *-ed* and *-er* are somewhat problematic, but also of particular interest, since they can occur with a grammatical as well as a lexical function (cf. Adams 2001: 6 ff.). Examples of these functions are contrasted in (2.5) to (2.7).

(2.5.a) Australia and Canada *had issued* an invitation to informal talks ... (ICE-GB: W2c-019)

(2.5.b) ... as a contribution to more effective community care "for what the report calls" adults who are mentally ill, mentally *handicapped*, elderly or physically *disabled* and similar groups ... (ICE-GB: W2a-013)

(2.6.a) I was *telling* you about that, wasn't I? (ICE-GB: S1a-086)

(2.6.b) ... Mr John Major [...] would raise the issue with the United States president, Mr George Bush, at their summit *meeting* in Bermuda on Saturday, in the hope of *softening* US opposition to forced repatriation ... (ICE-GB: W2c-019)

(2.7.a) Especially when I was *younger* he was boring ... (ICE-GB: S1a-072)

(2.7.b) And although the Gulf crisis may have attracted more newspaper *readers* around the world ... (ICE-GB: W2c-013)

In all three examples marked (a) it is obvious from the context that in each case the forms *-ed*, *-ing* and *-er* fulfil a grammatical function. They are clearly instances of the morphemes {ed$_2$}, {ing} and {er}, i.e. morphemes with the functions of perfect participle, present participle and comparative respectively. This is not the case with the examples marked (b). *Handicapped* and *disabled* are not simply word-forms of the verbs *handicap* and *disable*, but lexemes in their own right. Both are given separate entries in dictionaries since their meanings do not concur entirely with those of the verb on which they are based. In these instances the form *-ed* does not function as an inflectional ending, but as a derivational suffix. The suffix *-ing* in *meeting* in (2.6.b) behaves in a similar way in that it also creates a discrete lexeme rather than a word-form of the verb. The gerund *softening* in (2.6.b) adopts an interesting midway position between the word-form of a verb and a noun. Syntactically it functions as a noun, but it would be going too far to regard it as an autonomous lexeme since *softening* is clearly not a stable part of the lexicon but constructed on-line in context. *ing*-forms of this type are therefore traditionally considered to be a syntactic rather than a lexical phenomenon; the *ing*-form here is thus a grammatical morpheme.

The two manifestations of the form *-er* in (2.7.a) and (2.7.b) differ much more from each other than the two cases discussed in the previous paragraph. The derivational suffix {er} in (2.7.b), which is attached to a verb, has no semantic similarity with the comparative adjectival morpheme {er}. Hence, while it is possible to envisage treating the forms *-ing* and *-ed* as one **polysemous** morpheme, i.e. a morpheme with several meanings, which can operate with either a lexical or a grammatical function, in the case of *-er* we must assume that there are two distinct but formally identical morphemes {er}$_1$ and {er}$_2$, the first with a grammatical and the second with a lexical function. Their relationship is thus a **homonymic** one.

Lexically free vs. grammatically free – content words vs. function words

Free morphemes are simultaneously lexemes. In consequence, their functional classification depends on whether the lexeme in question has a lexical or a grammatical function. This question can be answered quite satisfactorily in practice by implementing the two criteria mentioned above, 'relational vs. autonomous' and 'closed vs. open'. A helpful additional dimension is to ascertain whether a morpheme can be inflected, i.e. whether bound grammatical morphemes can be added to it or not. Further theoretical discussions will not be undertaken here (for more details, see further reading).

Members of the classes of nouns, adjectives and adverbs are indisputably content words and hence, insofar as they are monomorphemic (i.e. consist of only one morpheme), also free lexical morphemes. These word classes are constantly being extended and are therefore open; their members are semantically autonomous and inflect (except for adverbs). Finer divisions must be made within the class of verbs: primary auxiliary verbs (*be, do, have*) and modal verbs (e.g. *must, will, shall*) form a closed class and fulfil grammatical functions; they should therefore be regarded as grammatical morphemes. Since the primary auxiliary verbs can also function as full verbs, in the case of forms such as *is, are* and *had* we must clarify in each individual instance, for the purposes of morphological analysis, whether they are functioning syntactically as an auxiliary or a full verb. Full, main or lexical verbs such as *eat, teach* and *please* constitute an open class; they are semantically autonomous and inflect. Hence it follows that monomorphemic main verbs are free lexical morphemes.

The application of the two criteria explained above – i.e. semantic autonomy and class openness (cf. p. 31 f.) – assigns the status of free grammatical morphemes to the English articles *the* and *a(n)*, the particle *to*, all morphologically simple pronouns (e.g. *she, him, why, which*), prepositions (e.g. *of, in, at*) and conjunctions (e.g. *and, or, after*). Since the class of morphologically simple numerals (*one* to *twelve, hundred, thousand, million* etc.) is closed, and their members are semantically only autonomous to a limited extent, it seems sensible to regard them also as grammatical morphemes. The final part of speech that is generally distinguished, the class of interjections, though not as comprehensive as the other typical open classes, is nevertheless subject to clearly recognizable changes influenced by fashion. It is therefore open rather than closed. Furthermore, interjections such as *ouch, damn, blimey, goodness* and *heavens* are semantically, syntactically and even discursively completely autonomous, since they can convey adequate information even when they occur in isolation. Everything speaks in favour of categorizing them as lexically free, even though they are more likely not to belong in this category if one takes into account the criterion of inflection.

2.2.4 Corpus study I: overview of morpheme classes and their frequencies in texts

Table 2.2 gives an overview of the morpheme types illustrated in sections 2.2.2 and 2.2.3, their most important attributes and some examples. Blocked or unique morphemes are not included in the table.

Tab. 2.2: Overview of morpheme types with examples

morpheme class	attributes	examples	
lexically free (lexemes, roots)	• semantically autonomous • open class • inflecting (except for interjections)	N: Adj: Adv: V lex: Interj:	{head}, {key}, {part} {green}, {pale}, {nice} {fast}, {well}, {here} {plan}, {teach}, {pass} {ouch}, {damn}
grammatically free (lexemes, function words)	• not autonomous, relational • closed class • not inflecting	V aux: Pron: Prep: Conj: Num:	{will}, {must}, {have} {she}, {which}, {why} {of}, {in}, {at} {and}, {that}, {as} {one}, {thousand}
lexically bound (derivational affixes)	• (more or less) open class • create lexemes with discrete meaning • usually change word class (suffixes) • closer to the stem	prefixes: {re-}, {dis-}, {post-} suffixes: {-er}, {-ify}, {-ment}	
grammatically bound (inflectional suffixes)	• closed class • create word-forms with unchanged meaning • always maintain word class • further away from the stem	for Ns: {plural}, {genitive} for Vs: {3rd pers. pres. sg.}, {ing}, {ed$_1$}, {ed$_2$} for Adjs: {er}, {est} for Nums: {th}	

From a sociopragmatic perspective it is remarkable that the frequency of occurrence of individual morpheme types in texts is significantly dependent on the text type and register investigated. As I have already explained in the introduction, the corpus used for this book, the MUMC, permits an investigation into five different registers: spontaneous spoken conversation, personal letters, fiction, newspaper reporting and academic writing. Comparing the characteristics of the words in the various registers, the first thing we notice is an obvious correlation between text types and the morphological complexity of words as measured in the number of morphemes per word.

Table 2.3 shows that the internal word complexity increases continuously from spontaneous conversation to letters, fiction, newspaper reports and academic writing. Words in scientific texts contain on average 0.3 morphemes more than those in oral conversation.

Tab. 2.3:   Average number of morphemes per word in the five MUMC registers

	conversation	letter	fiction	newspaper	academic
morphemes per word	1.17	1.22	1.32	1.38	1.48

As shown by the distribution of lexical and grammatical morphemes in Table 2.4, this can be ascribed to the relatively high frequency of lexical morphemes in the text types with a more formal style and a more abstract content.

Tab. 2.4:   The relative distribution of lexical and grammatical morphemes in the five MUMC registers

	conversation	letter	fiction	newspaper	academic
lexical	44 %	47 %	47 %	54 %	59 %
grammatical	56 %	53 %	53 %	46 %	41 %

While the relative frequency of lexical morphemes steadily increases as we go from left to right in the table, the number of grammatical morphemes decreases. In order to discover what lies behind this distribution it is worth taking a closer look at the distribution of the morphemes. As shown in Table 2.5, the high proportion of lexical morphemes in reports and academic writing is the result of the comparatively high frequency of bound lexical morphemes. As will be shown in chapters 8 and 9, these occur in prefixations and above all suffixations which frequently produce abstract lexemes, especially nouns.

Tab. 2.5: Relative distribution of free and bound lexical and grammatical morphemes in the five MUMC registers

	conversation	letter	fiction	newspaper	academic
lexical free	38 %	40 %	38 %	40 %	35 %
lexical bound	5 %	6 %	8 %	12 %	19 %
gramm. free	43 %	41 %	37 %	31 %	29 %
gramm. bound	13 %	13 %	15 %	15 %	12 %

The complementary distribution of grammatical morphemes, on the other hand, has its roots in the occurrence of free grammatical morphemes. The high proportion of morphemes of this type found in conversations, personal letters and fictional texts is largely due to pronouns, particularly personal pronouns, which are used to refer to people and states of affairs in texts, both exophorically (i.e. directly to persons) and anaphorically (i.e. to information previously mentioned in the text). In contrast to specialist scientific texts, which are largely written in an impersonal style and tend to be dominated by references to abstract ideas, conversations, letters and fictional texts deal with people and what they do and say.

What is striking in the case of the bound grammatical morphemes, which are not listed individually in the table, is the distribution of the morpheme {ed$_1$}, which marks the simple past. The largest number of occurrences of this inflectional morpheme can be found in the fictional texts (7.08%), followed by conversations (4.06%), newspaper reporting (3.66%), letters (2.65%) and, a long way behind, academic writing (0.89%). This distribution confirms the well-known finding that the frequency of simple past forms in texts correlates with the extent to which these texts are narrative (Biber 1988: 135 ff.).

The corpus analyzed, with its approximately 41,000 words, is naturally far too small to be able to make representative statements about the distribution of morpheme types. On the other hand, the present results converge internally on the various levels so well and are so clearly consistent with earlier corpus-based observations that even this limited material enables us to come to interesting and relatively reliable conclusions about the register-dependence of the relative frequency of occurrence of different morphological building blocks from a sociopragmatic perspective.

Further reading: On the difference between inflection and derivation: **Bauer (1988: 73 ff.), Dressler (1989), Plank (1994), Booij (2000), Bybee (1985), (2000), Croft (2000), Plag (2003: 14 ff.).** On the register-dependence of inflectional morphemes: **Biber et al. (1999: 456–465).** On psycholinguistic aspects of inflectional morphology: **Aitchison (2005), Booij (2007: ch. 10).**

2.3   From prototypical morphemes to submorphemic units

Let us now move to discussing other building blocks of words which are more or less morpheme-like. As stated above, prototypical morphemes are commonly defined by the handy expression "smallest meaningful unit of a language". Morphemes are therefore also **minimal** or **atomic linguistic signs**, since they link linguistic forms which cannot be broken down any further with meanings. If we take this symbolic nature of morphemes seriously, then we have to add two further attributes (to minimality and semanticity, both of which are contained in the short definition): typical morphemes must have a formal substance, i.e. a phonological or graphic realization; and like lexemes (which they sometimes are, of course), typical morphemes link *one* form with *one* meaning or *one* set of related meanings rather than several different ones.

For the purposes of morphological word analysis and depending on how one approaches the segmentation, it can be necessary to add two more external criteria to these four internal attributes of morphemes. Firstly, it is often stipulated, for instance by linguists of the influential American structuralist school (Bloomfield, Harris, Nida among others), that it should always be possible to break down words completely into morphemes without leaving any word components that do not have the status of morphemes. Secondly, and this goes back to the traditional assumption that words always consist of at least one root, every word should contain at least one free morpheme. No provision is made for words comprising solely bound morphemes. All in all, then, typical morphemes can be characterized by four internal properties (minimality, semanticity, formal substance and semantic unity) and two external ones (words can be exhaustively segmented into morphemes and every word contains at least one free morpheme; cf. the overview in Table 2.6).

The vast majority of English lexemes and word-forms can easily be broken down into morphemes exhibiting the aforementioned four internal and two external attributes – but not all. Consider, for instance, the word *necessary*. It does not seem unreasonable to split this word into the two morphemes {necess-} and {-ary}, since the component *necess-* carries a clearly definable meaning, cannot be divided further and also occurs in the noun *necessity*; moreover {-ary} and {-ity} are common adjectival and nominal suffixes respectively. However, if one adheres to the stipulation that at least one morpheme must be free, then this plausible analysis breaks down, since neither *necess-* nor *-ary* are potentially free. The only other possibility would be to regard *necessary* and *necessity* as separate words consisting of one morpheme, in other words as monomorphemic lexemes or **monemes**, which is also not entirely satisfactory. This indicates that there are word components that may fulfil one or more of the criteria for 'morphemehood' but not all of them, and can therefore only be classified as atypical or poor representatives of the category morpheme. These morpheme-like elements, which also have linguistic labels of course, are explained individually below. Table 2.6 gives an overview of the extent to which prototypical morphemes and other morpheme-like units display the attributes of the category MORPHEME.

Tab. 2.6: Typical and less typical representatives of the category MORPHEME and their attributes

attributes	morpheme-internal				morpheme-external	
	mini-mal	meaning-bearing	formal substance	one form-meaning pairing	at least one free morpheme per word	word exhaustively segmentable into morphemes
prototypical morpheme	+	+	+	+	+	+
bound root	+	+	+	+	–	+
combining form	+	+	+	+	~	~
portmanteau morpheme	+	+	+	–	?	?
zero morpheme	+	?	–	–	+	+
Fugenelement/formative	+	–	+	–	+	+
phon-aestheme	+	~	+	~	–	–

Bound roots

Word components such as the aforementioned *necess-*, as well as, e.g., *spec-* (in *special, specific, specify, specialty*), *ident-* (in *identity, identical, identify*) and *sculpt-* (in *sculptor, sculpture*) are described as **bound roots**. They display all the attributes of prototypical morphemes except the one requiring every word to contain at least one free morpheme (Stockwell and Minkowa 2001: 61 ff.). It is important to emphasize that bound roots must only be postulated if they appear in several lexemes and therefore form word families, and if the other word components in each case clearly possess the characteristic of affixes that can be added to a variety, rather than just one type, of roots. The concept of bound roots acknowledges the fact that native speakers tend to be able to ascribe a meaning to all the word components, irrespective of whether one of them can occur alone or not. For this reason the usual stipulation that roots must be potentially free is waived (cf. section 2.5). The reason for the existence of these bound roots in the English language is historical. As a rule, these forms are Latin or Greek roots which have been borrowed as parts of complex lexemes from Latin or French, often in larger word families. The roots themselves, however, were either not borrowed or have become obsolete in the course of the history of the English language.

Combining forms

The term *combining form* has gained currency chiefly as a result of its use in the influential *Oxford English Dictionary* (OED; Simpson and Weiner 1989). Combining forms also have their origin in the rich history of borrowings in the English language. They are effectively the counterpart to bound roots, since in contrast to the latter combining forms were borrowed in isolation (not as complete words) and then combined with other combining forms or morphemes to form English or even international words.

Accordingly combining forms occur in so-called **neo-classical compounds** such as *biography, democracy, microscope* and *photograph*. I will have more to say about them in the chapter on compounds (see section 7.1.3). For the time being I am only trying to clarify how combining forms differ from prototypical morphemes. As with bound roots, the problem can arise with combining forms that no free morpheme emerges from segmentation. Neither *bio-* nor *-graphy* are free forms, nor are *demo-* or *-cracy*. The form *scope* is potentially free (e.g. in a phrase like *the scope of the theory*), but obviously with a meaning that is completely different from the one it has in *microscope*.

In contrast to bound roots, which can only be posited if the element remaining after analysis is an affix, in the case of combining forms there is an added complication in that *neither* word component is a typical morpheme. While *-ary* and *-ity* in *necessary* and *necessity*, for example, are clear instances of bound lexical morphemes, this cannot be claimed for either *demo-* or *-cracy*. In fact, there are often hardly any indications as to which of the two elements is more of a root and which is more like an affix, since combining forms occupy a borderline position between free and bound forms with regard to their distribution. On the one hand, they resemble bound morphemes in that they cannot occur in isolation; on the other hand, their content is lexical to such a high degree that they are more comparable to free morphemes than to bound ones. These uncertainties in the field of segmentation have rendered the term combining form unattractive for many linguists. In its favour, the term expresses linguistically (particularly historically) and psycho-logically real phenomena in a theoretically relatively unloaded and neutral form.

Portmanteau morphemes and suppletion

Forms such as *had*, *first* and *best* differ from prototypical morphemes in a differ-ent way. Their hallmark is that they carry several meanings, each marked by indi-vidual forms in comparable words. *Had* for instance carries the lexical meaning 'have' and the grammatical meaning 'simple past' or 'past participle'. From a semantic point of view, *had* thus consists of the morphemes {have} and {ed$_1$} or {ed$_2$}, depending on its use; from a formal point of view, however, it cannot be segmented. *First* ({one} plus {-th}) and *best* ({good} plus {-est}) behave in the same way. In all cases of this type – which are regarded grammatically as *irregu-lar forms* or *exceptions* – there is no agreement (**isomorphy**) with regard to the complexity of form and content, since a simple form represents two (or more) grammatical meanings. That the attribute 'one form corresponds to one semantic complex' does not apply in these cases becomes clear if we compare these mor-phemes to isomorphic 'regular' forms such as *laugh-ed*, *four-th* and *nice-(e)st*.

Terminologically one can distinguish two forms of these deviations from proto-typical morphemes. In the case of so-called **portmanteau morphemes**, a formal similarity with the root is visible. The term was coined by Lewis Carroll, the author of *Alice in Wonderland*: "It's like a portmanteau [i.e. suitcase]: there are two meanings packed up in one word." **Suppletions**, also called **replacive mor-phemes**, are not formally related to the root. Accordingly, *had* (cf. *have*) is classi-fied as a portmanteau morpheme while *first* (cf. *one*) and *best* (cf. *good*) are sup-pletions. Further examples of portmanteau morphemes are the past forms *did*, *sang* and *got*; further cases of suppletion are *was*, *went* and *better*.

Zero morphemes

Zero elements are postulated in morphology in order to explain semantic and grammatical differences between words which are not formally marked. This is required principally for two types of phenomena: the **zero allomorph** and the **zero morpheme**. The aim of morphological analysis to be systematic and consistent plays a decisive role in both cases.

The first case, the zero allomorph, belongs to the field of inflectional morphology and is related to the issue discussed in the last section. Apart from portmanteau and suppletive forms, English also has 'irregular' forms of the type *put* (simple past) – *put* (past participle) and *sheep* (singular) – *sheep* (plural). If the context clearly shows that the form *put* refers to the past tense, for instance, then a com-parison with forms such as *laughed* or *kissed* shows that from a semantic point of view the inflectional morpheme {ed$_1$} must be involved. Since this morpheme has no formal counterpart it is often falsely classified as a *zero morpheme*. However, what we are dealing with here is a *zero allomorph* of the {ed₁}-morpheme.

The theoretical construct of a zero morpheme in word-formation allows for the observation that while in the verb *darken* (from the adjective *dark*) the change in word class is marked by the suffix {-en}, the same change is not marked at all in the case of the verb *clean* (derived from the adjective *clean*). It is argued that in order for a change of word class to take place a morpheme must also be added in the case of *clean*. Since this morpheme can be neither heard nor seen, i.e. does not have a formal (phonetic or graphemic) substance, the existence of a zero morpheme is postulated. (See chapter 9 for further discussion.)

Even if one is prepared to recognize the convenience of this theoretical construct, it has to be admitted that zero morphemes are not exactly good examples of the category morpheme since, as we have seen, zero morphemes have no formal substance. They are also problematic with regard to their meaning, as the zero morpheme is held responsible for changes from adjectives to verbs (as in *clean*), from nouns to verbs (as in *cash*), from verbs to nouns (as in *cover*) and for further types of derivation. The only common denominator which could be considered as a 'meaning' or function of the zero morpheme is the triggering of a change in word class (see section 10.2.3). Hence, it is questionable whether in the case of the zero morpheme it is really plausible to claim that there is a connection between a meaning complex and a form. Even though the term *morpheme* itself is contained in the expression *zero morpheme*, ultimately it has to be concluded that zero morphemes represent an extremely atypical type of morpheme in several respects.

Linking elements (*Fugenelemente*) and formatives

The counterpart to zero morphemes are word components that have formal realizations but no meaning. Such "empty" morphs are extremely rare in English. In German they exist in the form of so-called **Fugenelemente**, or **linking elements**, such as the *-s-* in *Wiederaufbereitungsanlage* ('recycling-s-plant') and the *-n-* in *Augenbraue* ('eye-n-brow'). The closest we get to such elements in English is in compounds such as *craftsman* and *statesman* in which the phoneme /s/ also has no meaning or at best a very vague one. Historically these phonemes are genitive morphemes (analogous with *driver's seat* and *bull's eye*), but their meaning in the case of *craftsman* and *statesman* is no longer identifiable.

A special instance of the morphological segmentation problem arises in idiomatic expressions such as *blow one's top* and phrasal verbs such as *get by* and *make up for*, whose meanings cannot be derived from the individual components. As in the case of portmanteau morphemes, there is no isomorphy between the form and the content. Although all the parts of such idiomatic phrases clearly have the form of familiar morphemes, a simple morphemic analysis fails since the forms cannot each be assigned an individual content. Kastovsky and others use the term **forma-**

tive to refer to such elements. According to Lipka (2002: 87), formatives are "minimal formal units without identifiable meaning, which are only relevant on the phonological or syntactic level".

Phonaesthemes

In English, as in other languages, there are word paradigms that begin, (or less commonly, end) with similar or identical sounds and share certain meaning components. Many verbs beginning with /fl-/ for example have something to do with movement. The MUMC cites *fly, flow, flick, flicker* and *flinch*; Marchand (1969: 412) gives several further examples (*flee, float, fling, flip* etc.). There is evidently an association here between form and meaning which is definitely comparable to that found in morphemes or signs. New words which are immediately understandable are coined now and again on the spur of the moment in accordance with such patterns. The reason for the success of these sounds, so-called **phonaesthemes,** is presumably their sound symbolism, which also accounts for well-known onomatopoeic lexemes such as *cuckoo, crack* and *splash*, whose motivation is clearly of an imitative nature. Although phonaesthemes fulfil the criteria of semanticity and minimality, they are extremely questionable members of the category MOR-PHEME, since their meaning is difficult to define and as a rule any element left over after segmentation (*-y, -ow, -ick, -icker, -inch* in the case of the phonaestheme /fl/) would not be eligible for morphemic status.

> **Further reading:** On the definition of the notion of morpheme: **Mugdan (1986), Luschützky (2000)**; on zero elements in morphology: **Bergenholtz and Mugdan (2000)**; on combining forms: **Bauer (1983: 213 ff., 270 ff.), Warren (1990)**; on suppletion: **Mel'čuk (2000)**, on submorphemic units: **Dressler (1990), Kubrja-kowa (2000)**; on phonaesthemes: **Käsmann (1992), Adams (2001: 121–132)**.

✓ 2.4 Morphemes and allomorphs

I have mentioned several times that linguistic units exhibit considerable variability without forfeiting the property of being perceived as some kind of unit or *conceptual gestalt*. Let us take the example of lexemes once more. Although in actual usage they occur with different meanings and in varying word-forms, they are nevertheless perceived as linguistic units. Put the other way round, lexemes are abstractions of actual word-forms that are so similar with regard to meaning and form that they can be regarded as different uses, instantiations or realizations of one abstract unit. The same holds true for morphemes. They are also variable with regard to meaning and form. This fact can be seen most clearly in the case of free lexical morphemes, which at the same time, of course, are also lexemes. These morphemes do not stand for the same meaning each time they are used but are polysemous. Since it is fundamental to the nature of polysemy (by contrast to homonymy) that these meanings are perceived as being related to each other, both morphemes and lexemes are characterized by semantic unity. For this reason morphemes were referred to in the previous two sections as being associated with sets of meanings or semantic complexes. The realizations of morphemes can be very different not only in a semantic but also a formal sense. Different formal, i.e. phonetic or graphic, realizations of a morpheme are referred to as **allomorphs**.

Free and bound morphemes differ with regard to whether variation tends to be found in particular with regard to the form or to the meaning. Variation in free morphemes is more likely to occur in the meaning whereas in bound morphemes it is usually formal. This last point can be explained by the fact that the form of bound elements is influenced by the free elements they are attached to, for instance when phonetically conflicting sounds meet. In order to avoid this situation additional sounds can be inserted (e.g. when the vowel /ɪ/ is inserted in *matches* as the plural of *match*), existing sounds can be removed (e.g. when the /d/ is severed from the base form *decide* in *decision*) or sounds can be adapted (*assimilation*; e.g. in *irresponsible* instead of **inresponsible*). In each instance the phonetic adjustments result in one morpheme being realized by different allomorphs. In the case of *matches* we have the allomorphy of the plural morpheme, with *decision* the root allomorphy of the root *decide/decis-*, and with *irresponsible* the allomorphy of the prefix *in-*, which is realized in the forms *in-* (*infinite, informal*), *il-* (*illegal, illiterate*) and *im-* (*impossible, impeachable*).

Tab. 2.7:   Illustration of the allomorphy of various morpheme types

morpheme type	examples	allomorphs
lexically free	{able} {deep} {explain}	/ˈeɪbl/, /əˈbɪl-/ (*ability*) /diːp/, /dep-/ (*depth*) /ɪksˈpleɪn/ /ˌekspləˈn-/ (*explanation*)
prefix (lex. bound)	{in-}	/ɪn/ (*informal*), /ɪr/ (*irregular*), /ɪl/ (*illegal*), /ɪm/ (*immoral*)
suffix (lex. bound)	{-ion}	/-ʃən/ (*collection*), /-ˈeɪʃən/ (*explanation*)
gram. bound	{plural}	/z/, /s/, /ɪz/, /ən/, Ø-allomorph, *ablaut* (cf. section 3.1)
gram. free	{a}	/ə/ (*a book*), /ən/ (*an idea*), /eɪ/ (hesitating and emphatic)
	{the}	/ðə/ (*the book*), /ðɪ/ or /ðiː/ (before vowel, e.g. *the idea*, as well as hesitating and emphatic)

Allomorphic variation can be observed as a basic principle in all types of morphemes, as is shown in the overview in Table 2.7. Nevertheless inflectional morphology is usually, and justifiably so, quoted as a prime example of allomorphy, since a systematic description can be applied to allomorphy in this field. Since inflectional allomorphy will be described in detail in section 3.1, Table 2.7 contains only a selection of data.

2.5   Summary: overview of morphological building blocks

The morphological building blocks described in sections 2.2 and 2.3 can be characterized as a continuum from typical morphemes via intermediate forms through to relatively clear cases of submorphemic units. The following morphological elements are proposed as the terminological and theoretical basis of this book. As demonstrated by the practical segmentation carried out when analyzing the MUMC, these morphological units are both necessary and sufficient to describe and explain the morphology of English vocabulary systematically. (Cf. also the sample analysis in section 2.6 below):

- **morphemes:** minimal meaningful units that have a formal realization. These formal realizations are referred to as **allomorphs.**
- **bound roots:** morpheme-like word components with an identifiable meaning and a close functional similarity with free morphemes (having distinct semantic content and forming word families) which only occur in bound distribution together with bound morphemes (affixes).
- **combining forms:** morpheme-like word components with an identifiable meaning occupying an intermediate position between free and bound morphemes which occur together with free morphemes and other combining forms.
- **portmanteau morphemes and suppletions:** forms realizing several semantic components which are expressed by means of several formally identifiable morphemes in comparable words (e.g. *sang* vs. *laughed*, both V + {ed$_1$}).
- **zero morphemes:** morpheme-like theoretical constructs with no formal representation which are attributed with a meaning or function.
- **formatives:** minimal formal units to which no identifiable meaning can be attributed.

Since linking elements and phonaesthemes are clear cases of submorphemic units they will no longer feature in this book.

Finally, this chapter must clarify the use of traditional terminology in the field of morphology. This applies to the terms *root*, *stem* and *base*.

- **root**: in principle we refer to a root as being that part of a word-form which remains when all bound morphemes have been removed. In the word *disclaimers*, for example, *dis-*, *-er* and *-s* are bound, so *claim* is the root. As a rule, the root is a free lexical morpheme. If we operate with the concept of bound roots, then the root is the element remaining after all clearly identifiable affixes have been split off. In this case we can posit so-called **root morphemes** (cf. e.g. Hansen et al. 1990: 15, Carstairs-McCarthy 2002: 20), which can be free or bound. In *disruption*, for instance, the component *rupt* remains when one has removed the productive affixes *dis-* and *-ion*. Since the form *rupt* is also separable as a root e.g. in *erupt(ion)* and *interrupt(ion)*, it is reasonable to categorize it as a bound root in accordance with the considerations discussed in 2.3. If we accept that words can be made up solely of combining forms (e.g. *demography* from the combining forms *demo-* and *-graphy*), then it is ultimately impossible to identify a root.
- **stem**: the stem of a word-form is the component remaining when all the bound grammatical morphemes, i.e. all the inflectional morphemes, have been removed. Stems can consist of a root or a free lexical morpheme, in which case they are **monomorphemic** or **simple** (in the technical morphological sense). They can also be **polymorphemic** or **morphologically complex**, if they are composed of several lexical morphemes. Accordingly the word-form *disclaimers* has a complex stem *disclaimer*, whereas the word-form *claimed* has a morphologically simple stem *claim*, which is simultaneously the root.
- **base**: while the term *stem* belongs to inflectional morphology, the concept of *base* operates in the field of derivational morphology. Any form to which lexical affixes can be attached is called a base. The concept of a base is therefore relational. *Claim* is the base in the prefixed form *disclaim*, which is in turn the base for the suffixed *disclaimer*.

Figure 2.2 gives an overview summarizing the traditional terms explained here.

Fig. 2.2:   Illustration of traditional morphological terminology

dis	*claim*	*er*	*s*
stem			inflectional suffix/ending
base		suffix	inflectional suffix/ending
prefix	root	suffix	inflectional suffix/ending

2.6 Morphological segmentation and classification: sample analysis

In order to illustrate the categories described in this chapter, a short extract from the ICE-GB will be analyzed below with regard to the function and distribution of the morphological building blocks. The passage is part of a specialist text on Freud's psychoanalysis (ICE-GB: W2a-002).

(2.8) Freud also entirely ignores the death wish in Hanold's first and third dream whilst he is enchanted with the metaphor of archaeology for memory unevenly buried in an unstable mental terrain (a metaphor which was to become one of his most creative models of the mind); he ignores the potential violence of Jensen's images of burial, flattening, cutting, measuring.

The analysis in (2.9) presents a version of the passage in (2.8) segmented into morphemes and morpheme-like components with the functional analysis above and the distributional analysis below the elements in each case. Following the analysis a few explanatory comments are given.

(2.9) Analysis: segmentation and classification

lex	lex	lex	lex	lex	gr	gr	lex	lex	lex
Freud	*also*	*entire*	*ly*	*ignore*	*s*	*the*	*dea(d)*	*th*	*wish*
fr	fr	fr	bd	fr	bd	fr	fr	bd	fr

gr	lex	gr	gr+gr	gr	gr+gr	lex	gr	gr
in	*Hanold*	*'s*	*first*	*and*	*third*	*dream*	*whilst*	*he*
fr	fr	bd	fr+bd	fr	fr+bd	fr	fr	fr

gr+gr	lex	gr	gr	gr	lex	gr	lex
is	*enchant*	*ed*	*with*	*the*	*metaphor*	*of*	*archaeo*
fr+bd	fr	bd	fr	fr	fr	fr	CF

lex	gr	lex	lex	lex	lex	lex	gr	gr
logy	*for*	*memory*	*un*	*even*	*ly*	*bur(y)*	*ed*	*in*
CF	fr	fr	bd	fr	bd	fr	bd	fr

gr	lex	lex	lex	lex	gr	lex	gr	gr+gr
an	*un*	*stable*	*mental*	*terrain*	*a*	*metaphor*	*which*	*was*
fr	bd	fr	fr	fr	fr	fr	fr	fr+bd

gr	lex	lex	gr	gr	gr	lex	lex	lex
to	*become*	*one*	*of*	*his*	*most*	*creat(e)*	*ive*	*model*
fr	fr	fr	fr	fr	fr	fr	bd	fr

gr	gr	gr	lex	gr	lex	gr	gr	lex
s	*of*	*the*	*mind*	*he*	*ignore*	*s*	*the*	*potential*
bd	fr	fr	fr	fr	fr	bd	fr	fr

lex	lex	gr	lex	gr	lex	gr	gr	lex
violen(t)	*ce*	*of*	*Jensen*	*'s*	*image*	*s*	*of*	*bur(y)*
fr	bd	fr	fr	bd	fr	bd	fr	fr

lex	lex	lex	gr	lex	gr	lex	gr
al	*flat*	*en*	*ing*	*cut*	*ing*	*measure*	*ing*
bd	fr	bd	bd	fr	bd	fr	geb

Explanatory notes:

- *death*: In a strictly synchronically orientated analysis this lexeme would not be segmented into morphemes, since the derivational suffix is no longer productive (cf. chapter 6). The present analysis acts on the maxim that one should segment complex-looking words as long as it makes sense, morphologically and semantically, to do so.

- *enchanted*: The same maxim is decisive here, too. However, since the semantic connection between the forms *chant* and *enchanted* (which incidentally was borrowed in this form) no longer holds, I have not segmented *enchant*.

- *first*, *third*: suppletive forms which are split into *one* and *three* respectively (in each case gr, fr) and *-th* (gr, bound; ordinal numeral morpheme)

- *is*, *was*: suppletive forms which are split into *be* (gr, fr, since here they are functioning as an auxiliary) and *s* (gr, bound, 3rd person sg.) or *-ed* (gr, bound, simple past, although strictly speaking the singular form should be segmented as well)

- *archaeo-*, *-logy*: CF = combining forms

- *burial*, *flattening*, *cutting*, *measuring*: While the *-al* in *burial*, being without doubt a word-forming suffix, must be classified as a lexical morpheme, the ending *-ing* of the words *flattening*, *cutting* and *measuring* must be treated as a gerundive inflectional ending and consequently classified as a grammatical morpheme.

3 Inflectional morphology

Inflectional morphology plays an important role in all languages. With its help categories are expressed that are essential for our understanding of the world and its linguistic description: the number of people or objects being spoken about (above all one as opposed to many), the point in or period of time of an event being described, and the perspective on the event. Since such cognitively fundamental ways of looking at objects, people and events must be described through language very frequently, it is worth anchoring them in grammatical rules, i.e. in a regular system. This is why grammatical categories such as NUMBER, TENSE and ASPECT exist. English grammar, for instance, not only enables but actually forces speakers in most cases to specify whether they want a noun phrase to refer to a single object or multiple objects (*the girl* vs. *the girls*). It only allows for a neutral form for 'one or many' in the case of non-countable nouns such as *milk* or *butter*.

speakers have no choice

Which of these categories are expressed by inflectional morphology and how many values are possible per category varies considerably from language to language. There are, for instance, languages in which the category NUMBER not only allows the values singular and plural (as in English and German), but also dual (for two units).

A relatively superficial comparison between English and German shows straight away that the inflectional morphology of German is much more complex. Whereas in German, even in the present tense of regular verbs, paradigms with four different inflectional endings are the general rule (*ich geh-e, du geh-st, er/sie/es/ihr geh-t, wir/sie geh-en*), in present-day English only the base form *go* and the *-s* marking the third person singular present (*he/she goes*) are found. This difference was not always so strongly pronounced, however. In earlier phases of its history English possessed a system of inflectional morphemes and allomorphs comparable in complexity to that of present-day German. In contrast to German, the English language has lost the majority of its inflectional morphemes and allomorphs since Old English was spoken (450–1100). This was only possible because the formerly free word order in sentences was replaced by the *subject-verb-object* pattern ensuring that the syntactic status of constituents remained marked. It is therefore generally acknowledged that English has undergone a transformation from a **synthetic language** – in which a high degree of grammatical information is encoded in inflectional morphemes – to an **analytic language** with very little inflection, in which grammatical information is expressed strongly through the word order in sentences and through complex, so-called **periphrastic** constructions. Examples of this will be given later.

The aim of this chapter first of all is to provide an overview of the inflectional morphemes of present-day English (3.1.1) and their allomorphs (3.1.2). Based on this, a short excursion into the history of the language will describe the decline of the previously rich inflectional morphology (3.2).

3.1 The inflectional morphology and allomorphy of present-day English

3.1.1 Overview of inflectional morphemes

As already mentioned, an overview of the inflectional morphemes still in existence in present-day English is rapidly achieved if we disregard a few peculiarities in the verbs *to be* and *to have* and the pronouns (see Table 3.1).

Tab. 3.1: Inflectional morphemes in present-day English[1]

word class	morpheme	functions/meanings
noun	{plural}	marking of plural
	{genitive}	marking of genitive; possession, part-of etc.
verb	{3rd person}	3rd person singular present
	{ing}	present participle
	{ed₁}	simple past
	{ed₂}	past participle
adjective	{er}	comparative
	{est}	superlative
numerals	{th}	ordinal number

In two areas in modern English there are inflectional morphemes that go beyond the overview in Table 3.1. On the one hand, these are to be found as suppletive forms. For the verb *to be* the forms *am*, *are*, *was* and *were* still exist, expressing the grammatical categories NUMBER and PERSON which have become lost for all the other verbs:

- *am*: {1st person} {singular} {present}
- *are*: {2nd person} {singular} or {plural} {present}
- *was*: {1st person} or {3rd person} {singular} {preterite}
- *were*: {2nd person} {singular} {preterite} or {plural} {preterite}

---

[1]   In the sources influenced by American structuralism we find the following abbreviations for the inflectional morphemes, derived from the voiced realizations in spoken English: {Z1} = plural, {Z2} = genitive, {Z3} = 3rd person sg., {D1} = simple past, {D2} = past participle.

On the other hand, in the area of personal and possessive pronouns, grammatical categories that are no longer marked in nouns, i.e. CASE, GENDER and PERSON, have survived. Since not even pronouns formally allow a distinction between the accusative and dative cases, modern descriptive grammars of English only distinguish three cases according to syntactic function, subjective case, objective case and genitive or, better, possessive case. The first two are also referred to as *common case*. These three cases are still marked for the relative pronoun *who* (*whom*, *whose*). Table 3.2 gives an overview of the forms based on the description by Quirk et al. (1985: 336).

Tab. 3.2: Overview of the forms of personal pronouns

PERSON	1st		2nd	3rd				rel. pron
GENDER				masc.	fem.	neut.		
NUMBER	sg.	pl.	sg./pl.	sg.	sg.	sg.	pl.	sg./pl.
subjective	I	we	you	he	she	it	they	who
objective	me	us		him	her		them	who(m)
possessive det. head	my mine	our ours	your yours	his	her hers	its	their theirs	whose

The overview shows that in the form *us*, for example, the morphemes {1^{st} person} and {objective case} have merged, and in the form *it*, the morphemes {3^{rd} person}, {neuter} and {common case}. For most possessive forms a distinction must be made between whether the pronoun functions as a determiner in a noun phrase (i.e. before a noun) or itself represents the head of a noun phrase substituting a noun.

The remaining part of this section will be devoted to describing first the grammatical functions and meanings of the morphemes listed in Table 3.1 and then their formal realizations.

{Plural}

The plural morpheme comprises a referential function, i.e. one based on the relationship to the extra-linguistic world, and a grammatical function. It shows that the noun phrase in question refers to several entities, and it establishes the agreement between a plural subject and a verb which is not marked for the 3rd person.

{Genitive}

The genitive morpheme sets up a relationship between two nouns. Depending on the context this relationship can be of a range of types including possession, part-of, origin, attribute and others that will not be discussed further here. The genitive morpheme in present-day English grammar is in competition with a periphrastic form, the *of*-genitive, which is generally used for inanimate nouns, while the genitive morpheme (with decreasing frequency) occurs in the types of noun groups shown in Table 3.3.

Tab. 3.3: Genitive morpheme and noun types

referents of nouns	examples
individual persons (proper names)	*Freud's repression of his own vocabulary of parapraxis* (ICE-GB: W2a-002)
persons	*... trying to take her eyes off the baby's cheeks* (ICE-GB: W2f-003)
animals	*I steal the food from the cats' bowls* (ICE-GB: W1b-001)
collectives	*the government's education reforms* (ICE-GB: W2c-002)
places and countries	*other countries in Asia have followed Hong Kong's lead* (ICE-GB: W2c-019)
time	*Mr Mandela arrived for yesterday's hearing* (ICE-GB: W2c-019)

{3rd person}

The morpheme marking the third person singular of the verb also indicates the number agreement between the subject and the verb phrase. The frequency of this morpheme is dependent on the text type, since its use not only depends on the number of the subject but is also influenced by the categories of time and aspect, which in turn are dependent on the text type. Looked at from this perspective, the {3rd pers.}-morpheme can be said to mark verb phrases as neutral with respect to progressive and perfective aspect as well as tense.

{ing}

From a formal grammatical point of view, the function of the {ing}-morpheme is to form the present participle of verbs. This form serves two functions. Firstly, in combination with the auxiliary verb *to be* it expresses the progressive aspect and therefore contributes to the encoding of the meaning 'ongoing activity of a limited duration'. (The continuous form can also have other meanings, e.g. reference to the future, but at present we are not concerned with details of this nature.) Secondly, the same form is used to form participles in participial clauses or verb complements (e.g. *he started talking to me*). The first *ing*-form in example (3.1) illustrates its use in participial clauses and the second the progressive aspect.

(3.1) *Having* said that, some of the greatest stresses **are coming** in the UK and Scandinavia. (ICE-GB: W2c-013)

Three further uses of the *ing*-form – not of the {ing}-morpheme, however – have already been mentioned in section 2.2.3: as an adjective-forming suffix (*an interesting book*), as a noun-forming suffix (*the meeting, the building*) and as an *ing*-form with a hybrid nominal-verbal function (*the hope of softening US opposition*). The first two uses are clear instances of lexical morphemes, which are therefore irrelevant to the current discussion of inflectional morphemes. Forms like *softening* are much more difficult to assess, since their similarity to participles give them verbal features, whereas when they are used syntactically in nominal functions (e.g. following articles and prepositions) they appear to be more of nouns. What remains clear, however, no matter whether these forms are more verbal or more nominal (such as traditional *gerunds*), is that they serve grammatical rather than lexical functions. (cf. p. 34).

{ed₁}

The morpheme {ed$_1$} marks the simple past with the core meaning of 'point or limited period in the past with no effect on the present'. This morpheme occurs without other inflectional morphemes with almost all verbs, the only exception being the verb *to be* (as an auxiliary or main verb), where the morpheme {ed$_1$} and the marking of number agreement are merged in the suppletive forms *was* and *were*.

{ed₂}

Like the {ing}-morpheme, the morpheme {ed$_2$}, commonly called *past participle*, is instrumental in various grammatical constructions and fulfils several functions. Combined with the auxiliary verb *to have* it expresses the perfective aspect (cf. 3.2), and combined with the auxiliary verb *to be* it forms the passive (as in 3.3); analogously with the {ing}-morpheme it also occurs in participial clauses (3.4).

(3.2) I haven't *seen* her for a while but will be doing so on Wednesday (ICE-GB: W1b-014)

(3.3) … a large house *was demolished* on Westmoreland Hill (ICE-GB: S1a-007)

(3.4) Moro was on the way to Parliament *with the deal fixed* when he was kidnapped. (ICE-GB: W2c-010)

The forms *-ing* and *-ed* also share the function of serving as adjective-forming derivational suffixes (as in *dark-haired, half-dressed, semi-detached*). In such instances the form is treated as a lexical morpheme.

{er} and {est}

The comparative morpheme {er} and the superlative morpheme {est} are used to grade adjectives and a few adverbs, most of which – an exception is *soon* – are formally identical to their adjectives: *fast, hard, late, long* and *quick*. With regard to this semantic function both these morphemes compete with the periphrastic construction using the adverbs *more* and *most*. The possible choice – whether an inflectional morpheme or a periphrasis occurs – is determined by the length of the adjective:

- Monosyllabic adjectives usually form their comparatives by means of inflection, although the periphrastic form is occasionally also chosen.
- Two-syllable adjectives ending in *-er* (e.g. *proper, eager*) do not allow inflection at all; others are nearly always inflected, particularly those ending in *-y* (*early, happy*), and *-ow* (*narrow, shallow*); a third group (*quiet, common*) can occur with an inflectional ending but can also express comparison periphrastically, depending on the style.
- Adjectives of three or more syllables use only the periphrastic form, unless they are derivations of adjectives ending in *-y* using the prefix *un-* (*unhappier, untidier*).
- The comparative of participles which have been turned into adjectives (e.g. *interesting, wounded*) is expressed using periphrasis.

{th}

The morpheme used to form ordinal numbers, {th}, is often overlooked when setting up an inventory of the inflectional morphemes in present-day English, although it meets all the important criteria for inflectional morphemes (cf. 2.2.3). It produces a word-form of a lexeme and keeps the word class as well as the meaning intact. As is well known, its function is to turn cardinal numbers into ordinals.

3.1.2 The formal realization of morphemes: phonological and morphological conditioning of allomorphs

On the face of it, the forms *seen* (in 3.2) and *demolished* (in 3.3) have nothing in common. And yet, due to the similarity of their functions, both being participle forms, they can be said to contain the same morpheme, viz. {ed$_2$}. This shows that morphemes can be realized more or less systematically by different forms, so-called **allomorphs**. The choice of the allomorphs of inflectional morphemes is governed by the linguistic environment, first and foremost by the stem to which they are attached.

There are principally two possible ways of selecting allomorphs. Firstly, the choice of allomorph can depend on phonetic factors, i.e. the final sound of the stem to which the inflectional morpheme is attached. This is referred to as **phonological conditioning**. Alternatively, allomorphs can be **morphologically conditioned**, which means that the choice of allomorph depends on the whole morpheme to which the inflectional morpheme will be attached and not just on its final sound. Since the conditioning morpheme is frequently also the only morpheme in the word stem, the word is taken to be the conditioning factor. For this reason some linguists (e.g. Bauer 1988: 14, 240) use the term **lexical conditioning**. The choice of the allomorph /t/ in *demolished* is phonologically conditioned by the unvoiced final sound /ʃ/ of the stem *demolish*; the allomorph /n/, attached to *see*, on the other hand, is morphologically (and lexically) conditioned by the whole verb.

Not all inflectional morphemes are subject to formal variation to the same extent. The form of the morpheme {ing} for instance is invariable; it has only one realization: /ɪŋ/. It might be commonly pronounced /ɪn/ (*walkin'*, *runnin'*) in colloquial English, but this is not an allomorph of the morpheme, only a **free variant**, since it has not been conditioned by the phonetic or morphological environment. Its selection is in fact a preference on the part of the individual speaker. This demonstrates that 'true' allomorphs cannot be defined simply in terms of 'possible formal realizations' but, like allophones, are determined by the linguistic environment; in addition, their distribution is complementary. This means that only one of the available allomorphs can occur at a given time.

The morphemes {er}, {est} and {th} have no phonologically conditioned, but only morphologically conditioned allomorphs which are treated by traditional grammars as irregular forms. In morphology they are categorized as suppletive forms or suppletions, as already mentioned in section 2.4. These are forms that are not formally related to the stem or the base. The suppletive forms of {er}, {est} and {th} are listed in Table 3.4.

Tab. 3.4: Suppletive forms of the inflectional morphemes {er}, {est} and {th}

morpheme	stem/base form	suppletive forms
{er}, {est}	*good*	*better – best*
	bad	*worse – worst*
{th}	*one*	*first*
	two	*second*
	three	*third*

The remaining inflectional morphemes have both phonologically and morphologically conditioned allomorphs.

Allomorphs of the inflectional morphemes {plural}, {genitive} and {3rd person}

The phonologically conditioned allomorphs common to the {plural}, {genitive} and {3rd pers.} morphemes are /s/, /z/ and /ɪz/. For all three morphemes the voiced allomorph /z/ occurs after vowels and all voiced consonants except for the voiced sibilants /z/, /ʒ/ and /dʒ/; the voiceless variant /s/ occurs after all voiceless consonants except for the voiceless sibilants /s/, /ʃ/ and /tʃ/; and the allomorph /ɪz/ occurs after the six sibilants (/z/, /s/, /ʒ/, /ʃ/, /dʒ/ and /tʃ/).

An exception to this system which applies to the genitive morpheme is an additional phonologically conditioned zero allomorph (Ø), since there are contexts in which the genitive is not phonetically marked. The most frequent case of this is the genitive of a regular plural noun ending in -s. Although the genitive is indicated graphically by the apostrophe, it is not realized phonetically (cf. 3.5).

(3.5)   … a boys' grammar school in Birmingham (ICE-GB: W2c-002)

Further environments for the zero allomorph – which are so rare that they do not appear in the MUMC – are firstly proper nouns ending in /z/. Apart from the use of the allomorph /ɪz/ (*Dickens's*, *Burns's*), the genitive can also be realized as Ø (*Dickens'*, *Burns'*). Secondly, and this is a combination of phonological and morphological conditioning, the zero allomorph occurs in Greek polysyllabic proper nouns ending in -s, such as *Socrates'* or *Euripides'* (cf. Quirk et al. 1985: 320).

These three morphemes – {plural}, {genitive} and {3rd person} – behave differently with regard to their morphologically conditioned allomorphs. This type of allomorphy is most noticeable with the plural morpheme, which can be realized by three such allomorphs. By far the most common of them, at least from the point of view of the number of tokens, is **Umlaut** (or **i-mutation**), i.e. a change of the vowel in the word stem (historically caused by the influence of an open vowel in an unstressed syllable following the stressed one). The discourse frequency of this allomorph is due first and foremost to the lexemes *man* (pl. *men*) and *woman* (pl. *women*, /ˈwɪmɪn/); the other five lexemes of this type *mouse – mice, louse – lice, goose – geese, tooth – teeth* and *foot – feet* are comparatively rare.

Secondly, the zero allomorph can also be morphologically determined, particularly when used for the names of classes of animals (*sheep – sheep, deer – deer* and *cod – cod*), but also for other individual words such as *aircraft* and designations of nationalities ending in -ese (e.g. *Japanese, Portuguese*). Thirdly, three lexemes still exist as a remnant of the Old English weak plural forms (see section 3.2) which form the plural in /ən/: *ox – oxen, child – children* and, but only in the religious sense of the lexeme, *brother – brethren*.

For the genitive morpheme there is only the above-mentioned marginal form of morphological conditioning: the zero allomorph in Greek proper nouns of several syllables ending in -s. The verbal morpheme for the 3rd person sing. has no morphologically conditioned allomorphs apart from the suppletive form *is*.

Allomorphs of the inflectional morphemes {ed₁} and {ed₂}

The phonologically conditioned allomorphs of {ed₁} and {ed₂} behave to a certain extent analogously to those of the {plural}, {genitive} and {3^{rd} pers.}. The allomorph /ɪd/ occurs with stems ending in /d/ and /t/, (*wanted, nodded, started, ended* etc.); the allomorph /d/ occurs after stems ending in a vowel or a voiced consonant except /d/ (*seemed, called, changed*); and the allomorph /t/ occurs after stems ending in a voiceless consonant except /t/ (*looked, used, asked, stopped*).

The morphologically conditioned allomorphs of both morphemes are numerous and confusing, as learners of English realize when they are studying the irregular forms. This is why most grammar books attempt to sort the irregular verbs into classes. However, as a rule these classes are orientated towards the degree of agreement between the base form, the simple past and the past participle and what type of purely formal differences occur (cf. e.g. Quirk et al. 1985: 105 ff.). A morphological description must, by contrast, focus on forms that are formally segmentable and endeavour to establish systematic similarities to their base forms. If we adhere to this requirement, the following types of allomorphs can be identified:

- The zero allomorph is postulated for all simple past and past participle forms that are identical with the base, e.g. *bet, cast, cut, hit, let, put, set* (where the base form is formally identical with {ed₁} and {ed₂}); and *come, become* (where the base form is formally identical with {ed₂}).
- Vowel gradation/ablaut, that is a change of the vowel in the stressed syllable, e.g. *got, came, began, took, drank, sat, held, gave, knew, became, wrote, spoke, fell* for {ed₁}; *begun, got* (in British English), *drunk* for {ed₂}; and *held, sat* and *won* for {ed₁} and {ed₂}.
- The allomorphs /ən/ and /n/ for {ed₂} e.g. in *taken, eaten, given* and *beaten*. Both occur frequently combined with a vowel change, which impedes segmentation, e.g. *spoken, written, broken, driven, trodden, woken, woven* and *gotten* (in American English).
- Suppletion (*was, were, went*) and other portmanteau forms, which can be formally combined into groups (e.g. *send – sent – sent, bend – bent – bent, lend – lent – lent*, and *catch – caught – caught, teach – taught – taught, seek – sought – sought*); to describe them as allomorphs is hardly sensible, however, because it is impossible to segment them with regard to their form.

The entries towards the bottom of this list in particular show clearly that the concept of the allomorph is more successful when applied to the field of phonological than morphological conditioning. Indeed, the notion of morphologically conditioned allomorphs could be viewed as a not altogether successful attempt at integrating special cases which are the result of historical development into a systematic set of rules that can be formalized. And this is only possible, at least theoretically, because the number of 'irregular' verb forms is fairly limited.

To conclude this section, Table 3.5 once more shows a summary of the phonologically and morphologically conditioned allomorphs of the inflectional morphemes of present-day English. For the reasons already mentioned – i.e. historically developed 'irregular' forms – it is difficult, particularly in the area of morphological conditioning, to reach the degree of linguistic systematicity that linguists tend to strive for. This is particularly true for frequent verbs, for which irregularity is far more likely to be the rule than the exception. We will now turn briefly to the origin of this disorder, the history of English inflectional morphology.

Further reading: Neef (2000a), (2000b).

3.2 The history of English inflectional morphology

I have already mentioned that English was not always so lacking in inflectional morphemes as it is today. The system of inflectional endings was far more complex earlier on in the history of the English language. It is characteristic of Old English in particular – i.e. the period from 450 or 700 (depending on whether one reckons from the settlement of the Angles, Saxons and Jutes or from the first written records) to 1100 – that there is not only an abundance of grammatically bound morphemes, but also that these morphemes are realized by numerous allomorphs.

In addition to the grammatical categories that are still part of today's inflectional system, CASE and GENDER were marked in nouns, adjectives, the definite article and the demonstrative pronoun. In Old English nouns had grammatical GENDER (masculine, feminine, neuter), as in present-day German. Apart from singular and plural the personal pronouns could distinguish a third numeral, the *dual* for two people (e.g. *wit* 'we two' and *git* 'you two', both in the nominative). Old English verbs took inflectional endings expressing NUMBER, PERSON, TENSE and MOOD (indicative, subjunctive and imperative). In contrast, whereas present-day English comprises a progressive and a perfective aspect, ASPECT had not yet been developed in Old English. A good example of the well developed range of allomorphs in Old English is the plural morpheme of nouns, which was realized *inter alia* as *-as, -an, -n, -u, -a, -e, -r,* Ø as well as *i*-mutation (Faiß 1989: 116, Mitchell and Robinson 1992: 19–30).

Tab. 3.5: Overview of the allomorphs of the inflectional morphemes in present-day English

morpheme	phonologically conditioned			morphologically conditioned	
	form	environment; stem ending in	examples	form	examples
{plural}	/z/	vowel or voiced consonant[1]	*cars, dogs, worries*	Ø	*sheep, aircraft, fish*
	/s/	unvoiced consonant[1]	*cats, ducks, rips*	i-mutation (*umlaut*)	*men, mice, geese*
	/ɪz/	sibilant (/z/,/s/,/ʒ/,/ʃ/,/dʒ/,/tʃ/)	*houses, matches*	/ən/	*oxen*
{genitive}	/z/	vowel or voiced consonant[1]	*dog's, John's*	Ø (polysyllabic Greek names ending in /z/)	*Socrates', Xerxes'*
	/s/	unvoiced consonant[1]	*cat's, Pat's*		
	/ɪz/	sibilant (/z/,/s/,/ʒ/,/ʃ/,/dʒ/,/tʃ/)	*George's, Jones's*		
	Ø	after /z/ (and gen. plural in general)	*Dickens', the boys'*		
{3rd pers.}	same as {plural}			suppletion	*is*
{ing}	no allomorphs				
{ed₁}, {ed₂}	/d/	vowel or voiced consonant[2]	*loved, remembered*	Ø	*put, let, hit, cut*
	/t/	unvoiced consonant[2]	*kissed, stopped*	gradation (*ablaut*)	*sang/sung, began/began*
	/ɪd/	dental (/d/,/t/)	*founded, rented*	/ən/ (often with gradation)	*taken, spoken, been*
				portmanteau forms	*did, taught, told, stood*
				suppletion	*was, were, went*
{er}	no phonologically conditioned allomorphs			suppletion	*better, worse*
{est}	no phonologically conditioned allomorphs			suppletion	*best, worst*
{th}	no phonologically conditioned allomorphs			suppletion	*first, second, third*

Explanatory notes: 1) except voiced (/z/,/ʒ/,/dʒ/) and voiceless sibilants (/s/,/ʃ/,/tʃ/) respectively
2) except voiced (/d/) and voiceless dental (/t/) respectively

61

In view of the marked abundance of the forms of Old English inflectional suffixes, this section can only offer a glimpse of the history of English inflectional morphology, using selected examples and focussing on the wealth of forms in Old English and the decline in inflection in Middle English; the more recent and less drastic changes in Early Modern English will be largely excluded since they can be deduced by comparing the situation in Middle English with that of Modern English.

3.2.1 The richness of forms in Old English

To give an impression of the abundance and diversity of inflections in the morphology of Old English, Table 3.6 shows the forms of the nominal phrase *sē wīsa cyning* ('the wise king'). The lexeme *cyning* is masculine and belongs to the *a*-declension. The affiliation of Old English nouns to declensions can be traced back to Indo-European. Stems ending in a consonant are declined weakly while those ending in a vowel are strong. There are four subclasses, *a*, *ō*, *i* and *u*.

Tab. 3.6: Old English paradigm of the nominal phrase *sē wīsa cyning*

	singular		plural	
	weak	strong	weak	strong
Nom.	se wīsa cyning	wīs cyning	pa wīsan cyningas	wīse cyningas
Gen.	pæs wīsan cyninges	wīses cyninges	para wīsena cyninga	wīsra cyninga
Dat.	pǣm wīsan cyninge	wīsum cyninge	pǣm wīsum cyningum	wīsum cyningum
Akk.	pone wīsan cyning	wīsne cyning	pa wīsan cyningas	wīse cyningas

The table shows that there are different forms for the definite article, which at that time was still more like a type of demonstrative pronoun, the attributive adjective and the noun, depending on the CASE. Furthermore, the adjective also distinguishes between a weak and a strong form, as does German (*der weise König* vs. *weiser König*), this being determined by the position of the adjective. The weak form occurs after the definite article, after demonstrative pronouns, and in the comparative or superlative, while the strong form occurs attributively without the definite article and in predicative function.

This paradigm represents only a small proportion of the wealth of forms in the area of nouns, since both the other two genders and the other declensions (which are linked with the genders) require different forms. This is the reason for the numerous allomorphs of the plural morpheme mentioned above. The modern *s*-plural, for example, comes from the form *-as* in the nominative and accusative masculine of the *a*-declension (see Table 3.6), while the allomorph /ən/ (see Table 3.5) is a remnant of the nominative and accusative plural of the (weak) *n*-declension (*-an*). The origin of the modern genitive *-s* is the Old English form

-es, which marked the genitive singular masculine and neuter of the strong *a*-declension.

Nevertheless we cannot fail to see that not every case is clearly marked but that some forms collapse, a phenomenon known as **syncretism**. This also applies to the other declensions and to a certain extent to other morpheme classes. In the *a*-declension of nouns, the nominative and accusative singular forms are identical, and the same goes for the plural forms; in fact, the nominative and accusative plural forms are the same in all declensions, which means that the subject and the object cannot be distinguished. The genitive, dative and accusative singular morphemes for the weak declension of adjectives are also the same. The greatest variety of forms can be found in the demonstrative pronouns and the definite article, of which only *the, this, these, that* and *those* still remain today.

The inflectional morphology of verbs in Old English is also extremely complex. Table 3.7 provides an idea of the wealth of forms. The table shows that during this period of the English language there was still a large number of morphemes in the present and preterite marking PERSON, NUMBER and MOOD. Furthermore, one can glean from the table that the difference between strong and weak paradigms only occurs in the preterite. It is typical of the strong paradigms that the allomorphs of the morphemes for the preterite are marked by gradation (*ablaut*).

Tab. 3.7: Inflectional morphemes of Old English verbs

			strong		weak	
stem			*sing-*		*dēm-*	
infinitive			*sing*	*-an*	*dēm*	*-an*
present indicative	sg.	1st pers.	*sing*	*-e*	*dēm*	*-e*
		2nd pers.	*sing*	*-est*	*dēm*	*-est*
		3rd pers.	*sing*	*-eth*	*dēm*	*-eth*
	pl.		*sing*	*-ath*	*dēm*	*-ath*
subjunctive	sg.		*sing*	*-e*	*dēm*	*-e*
	pl.		*sing*	*-en*	*dēm*	*-en*
imperative			*sing/sing*	*-ath*	*dēm/dēm*	*-ath*
participle			*sing*	*-ende*	*dēm*	*-ende*
preterite indicative	sg.	1st pers.	*sang*		*dēm*	*-de*
		2nd pers.	*sunge*		*dēm*	*-dest*
		3rd pers.	*sang*		*dēm*	*-de*
	pl.		*sung*	*-on*	*dēm*	*-don*
subjunctive	sg.		*sung*	*-e*	*dēm*	*-de*
	pl.		*sung*	*-en*	*dēm*	*-den*
participle			*ge- sung*	*-en*	*ge- dēm*	*-ed*

These gradations are also responsible for the pronounced allomorphy of certain verbal morphemes. The fact that these numerous forms are usually divided into seven classes of strong verbs can also be traced back to Germanic.[2] If we disregard variations within these classes – for details see e.g. Mitchell and Robinson (1992: 35 ff.) – the important forms, i.e. the infinitive, the 1st and 3rd person singular of the preterite, the plural of the preterite and the past participle, are shown summarized in Table 3.8.

Tab. 3.8: The forms of strong Old English verbs (after Mitchell and Robinson 1992: 37)

Class	Infinitive	Pret. Sg.	Pret. Pl.	Part. Pret.
I	*scīnan* ('shine')	*scān*	*scinon*	*scinen*
II	*crēopan* ('creep')	*crēap*	*crupon*	*cropen*
	brūcan ('enjoy')	*brēac*	*brucon*	*brocen*
III	*findan* ('find')	*fand*	*fundon*	*funden*
IV	*beran* ('bear')	*bær*	*bǣron*	*boren*
V	*tredan* ('tread')	*træd*	*trǣdon*	*treden*
VI	*faran* ('go')	*fōr*	*fōron*	*faren*
VII	*healdan* ('hold')	*hēold*	*hēoldon*	*healden*
	hātan ('command')	*hēt*	*hēton*	*hāten*

As with the nouns, analogies with present-day German are very obvious (cf. e.g. German *finden – fand – gefunden* and *treiben – trieb – getrieben* etc.). Indeed, Old English and Modern German are much more similar with regard to the variety of their inflectional morphological forms than Old English and Modern English.

3.2.2 Inflectional decline in late Old English and Middle English

Starting in the late Old English period and intensifying in early Middle English (1100–1500) the system of inflectional morphemes was eroded until, after a few further minor changes in Early Modern English (1500–1700), it finally reached its current state.

In late Old English all the nominal inflectional morphemes except {plural} and {genitive} disappeared, presumably as a result of the weakening of the unstressed suffix vowels (i.e. a, e, u, o) to /ə/. The graphic marking of the genitive morpheme by means of the apostrophe appeared in the singular occasionally in the 14th and 15th centuries, but was not consolidated until towards the end of the 17th century. If we neglect dialectal variations, the inflected forms of the demonstrative pro-

---

[2]   Strong verb classes 1 to 6 have *ablaut* forms while class 7 contains the formerly reduplicating verbs.

nouns and the definite article were abandoned as early as the 12th and 13th centuries. Today's lack of inflection of the adjective has been in place since the first half of the 15th century (Lass 1992: 112 ff.).

The noun phrase suffered drastic losses to its inflectional morphological marking. In noun phrases consisting of a determiner, a premodifier and a head noun, only the plural and the genitive morphemes of the noun survived in Middle English. In order to compensate for the disappearance of morphological markers for CASE, which serve to indicate syntactic constituents such as subject (nominative), direct object (accusative) and indirect object (dative), word order within the sentence became increasingly fixed.

The decline in inflection took place more slowly with verbs than with nouns. As a result, Middle English retains more verbal inflectional morphemes than Modern English. The reasons for this are probably phonetic. As we have already seen, most verb endings consist of obstruents (-p, -s, -t or -d), which resist phonetic reduction for longer than the vowels and nasals in nouns (Welna 1996: 80). Table 3.9 gives an overview of examples for the Middle English period; however, it should be taken into consideration that it does not take into account the variation caused by ongoing historical change during this period and dialectal differences (see the references below for further details).

Tab. 3.9: Inflectional morphemes of Middle English verbs

stem = infinitive = imperative			strong		weak	
			sing		deem	
present indicative	sg.	1st pers.	sing	-e	deem	-e
		2nd pers.	sing	-est	deem	-est
		3rd pers.	sing	-eth	deem	-eth
	pl.		sing	-en/-eth	deem	-en/-es
subjunctive	sg.		sing	-e	deem	-e
	pl.		sing	-en	deem	-en
participle			sing	-ing	deem	-ing
preterite indicative	sg.	1st pers.	sang		deem	-de
		2nd pers.	sunge		deem	-dest
		3rd pers.	sang		deem	-de
	pl.		sung	-en	deem	-den
subjunctive	sg.		sung	-e	deem	-de
	pl.		sung	-en	deem	-den
participle			i- sung	-en	i- deem	-d

The most salient changes compared to Table 3.7 are the loss of the infinitive and imperative endings and the replacement of the Old English participial ending *-ende* by *-ing* and of the present indicative plural ending *-ath* by *-en*. The precursors of the three verbal inflectional morphemes still extant in Modern English {3rd pers.}, {ed$_1$} and {ed$_2$} are more easily recognizable in this table than in Table 3.7. All other forms were lost in late Middle English or Early Modern English; the function of the *ing*-form, on the other hand, gained substantially in significance as a result of the strengthening of the progressive aspect during the 18th and 19th centuries.

In principle there are two types of loss of form that distinguish Old English from Middle English and Early Modern English: one on a morphemic level and the other on the level of allomorphs. On the one hand, the stock of morphemes marking MOOD, NUMBER and PERSON is reduced by forms merging. For instance, in Middle English there is no way of distinguishing between the indicative and the subjunctive in the present and the preterite by means of morphological marking. In the case of the strong verbs, the morphological distinction between the two preterite forms (1st and 3rd pers. sing. vs. 2nd pers. sing. and plural) is lost. On the other hand, strong verbs move into the weak class resulting in a significant reduction in the number of *ablaut* allomorphs. This trend is reinforced by the disappearance of half of the strong Old English verbs, particularly those which were already unusual in Old English and/or which had difficult paradigms (Görlach 2002: 61).

3.2.3 Summary

The historical development of the basic morphological and grammatical categories of English has been described as a contrast between the strengthening of some categories and the weakening of others (Leisi and Mair 2008: 112 ff.). The strengthened categories include ASPECT, TENSE, infinite verb forms (gerunds, participles and infinitives) and WORD ORDER. The most important development in the area of inflectional morphology is the strengthening of the progressive aspect, resulting in a significantly higher discourse frequency of *ing*-forms, and the semantic differentiation of the preterite (*simple past*) as opposed to the perfective aspect.

Conversely, the weakened categories are grammatical GENDER, CASE, MOOD and to a limited extent, NUMBER, affecting the bulk of Old English inflectional morphemes:

Grammatical GENDER no longer exists. If, for instance, feminine pronouns are used in present-day English to refer to ships or cars (e.g. *she's a beauty* about a veteran car), this may not have much to do with the grammatical gender but reflects emotive and affective factors (Siemund 2008).

With regard to CASE, for nouns only one unmarked case (common case) and the genitive remain. Articles, demonstrative pronouns and adjectives are no longer marked for CASE. Personal pronouns still have case forms but these should be categorized today according to their syntactic function as *subjective* or *objective* rather than as reflecting traditional cases.

As for MOOD, in present-day English the imperative is formally identical with the equally unmarked infinitive or base form. The subjunctive has survived only in fixed expressions such as *God save the Queen*, in conditional sentences (*if I were you*) and particularly in American English in so-called mandative *that*-sentences (*I demand that the manager resign*; see Quirk et al. 1985: 155 ff.). With the exception of the verb *to be*, the subjunctive is formally identical with the base form and hence not marked by an openly realized morpheme. Finally, morphemes marked for number have disappeared from articles, demonstrative pronouns, adjectives and verbs (except for {3rd pers. sing. present}).

The loss of many Old English morphemes and allomorphs has led to a significant simplification and hence to an increase in the economy of the English language (Leisi and Mair 1999: 152). At the same time the functional burden has been shifted from the individual word including its inflectional morphemes to word combinations, as can be seen *inter alia* from the complex forms used to express ASPECT and TENSE, the periphrastic *of*-genitive and the periphrastic comparative forms of the adjective.

Now that we have completed this short excursion into the history of the English language, we shall leave the field of inflectional morphology and turn to word-formation. Our first task is to outline the developmental process of the emergence and establishment of new complex lexemes.

Further reading: Brunner (1965: 194 ff.), Faiß (1989), Mitchell and Robinson (1992: ch. 3), Lass (1992), Welna (1996), Leisi and Mair (1999: ch. IV), Obst and Schleburg (1999: chs. 5 and 6), Görlach (2002: ch. 6).

4 The origin, development and establishment of complex lexemes

4.1 New words: possibilities for extending lexical resources

The word stock (or *lexicon*) of every living language is constantly changing. On the one hand, words are no longer used, become obsolete and drop out of the collective lexicon of the speakers of a particular speech community. The Old English word *niman*, for instance, which is formally and semantically related to the German word *nehmen*, was displaced by the Scandinavian loan word *take*. Its meaning as 'take' went out of use during the late Middle English period, and other meanings such as 'steal', to which it had reverted, went out of use later on. Other Old English lexemes suffered a similar fate, such as *weorpan* (the German *werfen*, replaced by *cast*), *wyrt* (Ger. *Wurzel* replaced by *root*) and *steorfan* (Ger. *sterben*, relegated to the meaning 'starve' and replaced by *die*; cf. Leisi and Mair 2008: 42).

On the other hand, new words are continually being added to the lexicon, generally because new objects are being invented and new ideas are arising, all requiring a designation. In addition, words which are not strictly speaking 'required' for naming purposes are created to encapsulate new trends and social practices. A good example is the recent coinage *overparenting*, which refers to the practice of parents who are overprotective about their children and prevent them from doing things independently due to worry. Creations of this type often reflect business interests, e.g. when the launch of new products, practices or services is supported by the invention of trendy new words.

Essentially the following procedures are available to name new objects, ideas and social practices:

* **Word creation (word manufacture, root creation, creatio ex nihilo).** One possibility is to invent new words totally from scratch, i.e. words that originate neither formally nor semantically from morphological material that already exists. However, the chances of success for such new creations, i.e. the probability that they will gain a firm place in the lexicon, are comparatively small, simply because they do not relate to anything already known. They are completely arbitrary, non-deducible, and therefore linguistically and cognitively uneconomical. Bauer (1983: 239) names six examples of such words known to him (not counting invented product names, such as *Kodak*, *Teflon*, *frisbee* and *yo-yo*): *grok*, *wampeter*, *foma*, *grandfalloon*, *quark* and *scag*. Only the words *quark* (an elementary particle) and *scag/skag* ('heroin') are listed in the 4th edition of the

LDOCE, which suggests that the others no longer belong to the current word stock of present-day English.

- **Borrowing**. It is very much more common for words to be borrowed from other languages than for them to be created *ex nihilo*. With regard to the origin of its words, English is renowned for having a very mixed vocabulary as a result of its changeable history (see Scheler 1977, Leisi and Mair 1999: 41–77). This does not mean that what is adopted are always whole words, however. Even today new English words are still being formed from the building blocks of the dead languages Latin and Old Greek, in particular in the sciences, for example, *euro-sceptic, cyberspace, cyberpunk, bovine spongiform encephalopathy* (or *BSE*) or *paleo-conservative* (examples taken from Knowles 1997). Words are often borrowed from the language from whose culture the new idea originates. We only have to think of the massive borrowing influence English has had on German in the field of computer technology (e.g. the German words *Laptop, Notebook*, and the word *Computer* itself) and in business and economics (e.g. *just-in-time, Broker, outsourcen*, etc.). The number of German words borrowed into English is relatively modest in comparison, although a considerable number can be found in certain scientific fields such as e.g. mineralogy, geology, psychology and psychiatry (cf. Pfeffer and Cannon 1994). Some of the more common examples are *kindergarden, rucksack, zeitgeist* and *angst*.

- **Semantic transfer**. Novel objects and ideas can also be named by giving existing lexemes a new meaning. The process behind this is called **semantic transfer**, which most often occurs in the form of **metaphor**. The meaning of a lexeme is transferred from one cognitive domain into another as a result of more or less objective similarities. A typical example of a metaphor is the transfer of the lexeme *mouse* from the domain of mammals into that of computer accessories. The advantage of semantic transfer lies in the fact that from both the cognitive and the speech-economy point of view the similarity motivating the transfer often renders the figurative meanings deducible. Furthermore, only the content is new and thus basically no new word has been created, only a new meaning. Strictly speaking, it is not the word stock that has been extended here, only the 'meaning stock'.

- **Word-formation**. Finally, the lexicon is being expanded continually through the formation of new lexemes from already existing morphological material, i.e. by means of word-formation. The results of word-formation processes are **complex lexemes** (cf. p. 14 above). I will discuss the developmental progress of such additions to the lexicon in more detail in what follows.

Regardless of its type of formation, a new lexeme must always pass through certain stages before it can be considered as having become 'part of the language'. Every new lexeme has either been spoken or written down for the first time (phase 1) at a particular point in time. If the lexeme is subsequently taken up and used by an increasing number of other speakers (phase 2), then it can eventually become a member of the general word stock of a language (phase 3). In this book these three phases are called **creation**, **consolidation** and **establishment**. The aim of this chapter is to describe the three-stage process of establishing new words in the lexicon.

> **Further reading:** On word-creation and other creative processes: **Hohenhaus (1996: 125 f.), Baldi and Dawar (2000), Lipka (2007), Munat (2007)**. On identifying and monitoring new words on the internet: **Stegmayr, Kerremans and Schmid (forthcoming)**.

4.2 Three perspectives on the establishment of complex lexemes

A useful method for describing the process of the establishment of complex lexemes is to apply the three perspectives already introduced in section 1.3.

- **Structural perspective**: Viewing the internal structure of the word itself with regard to changes in its form, meaning and dependence on the immediate linguistic context.
- **Sociopragmatic perspective**: Viewing the word in the speech community with regard to the extent of its spread and diffusion, i.e. the degree of use and familiarity among the members of the speech community.
- **Cognitive perspective**: Viewing the word in the minds of the speakers with regard to its entrenchment in the individual mental lexicons of the speakers and the conceptual status it has achieved there.

These three perspectives are summarized in Figure 4.1.

Fig. 4.1: Perspectives on the processes involved in the establishment of complex lexemes

structural perspective			sociopragmatic perspective		cognitive perspective	
the word itself			the word in the speech community		the word in the minds of speakers	
form	meaning	context dependence	use	familiarity	mental lexicon	conceptual status
lexicalization			institutionalization, conventionalization		entrenchment	

The actual phases of establishment and the perspectives on the progress of establishment have to be kept separate. As can be seen from Table 4.1, the terms **lexicalization, institutionalization** and **entrenchment** have been used to describe the three perspectives. In later chapters (see p. 85), where the sociopragmatic perspective is widened beyond the institutionalization of individual words to include that of word-formation patterns, the notion of **conventionalization** will be introduced. Institutionalization is then a special form of conventionalization pertaining to the spread of new lexemes. The term **establishment** functions as the generic term for the whole process of becoming, and the final state of having become, established.[3]

In the following, the three phases of creation, consolidation and establishment are used for purposes of classification. Each phase is defined from all three perspectives (cf. the summary given in Table 4.2, p. 83). In each case we begin with the sociopragmatic perspective, since it is always the speakers of a language who are responsible for the formation of new lexemes. The following extract from a newspaper article about Angola in the ICE-GB serves as a source for illustrations. Complex lexemes are highlighted in italics:

(4.1)   Rains have failed for four years and, says the *United Nations*, 1.9m people are on the brink of *starvation* in the nine provinces where fighting has been fiercest and drought most severe. Ganda is a vivid example of how the famine is feeding off a war the world has largely forgotten. Both the rebels and *government forces* have destroyed villages, *commandeering* what food they can find, and both sides have a history of *press-ganging* recruits, snatching men and younger women. Their *indiscriminate* scattering of *land mines* has caused further agony. Angola is said by *Africa Watch*, the *human rights group*, to have suffered the highest number of *civilian landmine casualties* in the world – up to 50,000. *Amputees* are common.

In recent weeks it rained in some areas, but there are no seeds left to plant. *Relief workers* know that if they bring in fresh seeds, they must bring in food too, *otherwise* the seeds will *simply* be eaten. Ganda, like other *government-held* towns, has been inundated with *refugees* from the *countryside*. Joaquim Silva, a 73-year-old *farmer*, told a familiar story: "We came to the town because we couldn't stay in our village. Unita had stolen all our cattle and *belongings*. We started farming here, but now Unita has stolen our *farming implements* and taken all the food we had." Getting aid through, *however*, is a nightmare. While the *government* holds the towns, Unita controls much of the *countryside*, its troops equipped with *Ameri-*

---

[3]   It is important to note that these concepts are used by other authors in different ways. The present use of *institutionalization* and *lexicalization* agrees largely with that of Lipka (e.g. 2002: 110 ff.). Bauer (1983: 42 ff.), on the other hand, uses the terms to describe stages in the development of establishment (similarly to Quirk et al. 1985: 1515 ff.)

can-supplied ground-to-air missiles to deter *air transport.* A visit involves a *50-minute treetop-hugging* flight in a *military helicopter* from a *government airfield* at Benguela; *low altitude flying* minimises the time Unita has to react. (ICE-GB: W2c-002)

4.3 The development towards establishment

4.3.1 Creation

Sociopragmatic perspective. Words do not arise of their own accord, out of the blue so to speak. New complex words can only appear in a speech community if they are initially uttered or written down at a given time by a speaker. We shall call this initial use (the process of) **ad-hoc formation**. Another term frequently found is **nonce formation**, which, however, emphasizes the idea that a word is only used once in a given situation but never taken up again.

It is not the case that speakers always intend to initiate the establishment of a new lexeme when they use an ad-hoc formation. More often than not speakers come up with a previously unknown word for other reasons – because of problems in finding the right word, i.e. because an existing word for the idea they want to express does not occur to them, or because they want to express something in a particularly concise, pithy, original or humorous way. In press articles such as (4.1), the use of new words is often motivated by the need for brevity. These words are not here to stay but first and foremost to reduce syntactic complexity. Examples of this type of nonce formation in (4.1) are *50-minute* and *American-supplied*. Like many other nonce formations of this type, both of these examples have more of a syntactic and co-textual function than a lexical, naming one (see p. 101); both can be regarded as abbreviations and compressions of potential relative clauses (… *which lasts 50 minutes* and *which have been supplied by the US* respectively).

The only good candidate in text (4.1) for a new complex word for which the author may have had big ambitions, is *treetop-hugging* (third line from the end), an adjective that gives a metaphorical description of flying with very low altitude. In press reports, in which new lexical creations are also often used to increase the originality of the style, ad-hoc formations and very 'young' words are often additionally marked as such by the use of inverted commas. An example taken from the book blog of the online edition of the *Guardian* newspaper (www.guardian.co.uk) is the headline "Is 'crowdfunding' really the way ahead for author advances?" (posted 16 February 2010, downloaded 23 September 2010; *crowdfunding* can be defined as the 'use of the web or another online tool to get a group of people to finance a particular project').

Structural perspective. The new word itself, which is also referred to as a (product of an) *ad-hoc formation*, constitutes a previously non-existent combination of existing morphemes. In contrast to the new word itself, the word-formation pattern according to which it was created is, as a rule, well known and transparent. We can therefore say that ad-hoc formations are **type-familiar**, because we can identify them as a new instance of a known word-formation type, but not **item-familiar** (Lipka 2002: 112).

From the point of view of meaning, it is typical of ad-hoc formations that when taken out of context they can often be very ambiguous. This indicates that their interpretation is significantly dependent on the linguistic and situational context, both of which can be instrumental in their disambiguation. This statement is only valid for the recipients of a new ad-hoc formation, however. Their 'coiners', at the moment of creation, usually have a very specific concept in mind of what they mean or want to describe with their ad-hoc formation. Since, due to the rules of word-formation, they can only make use of a limited amount of morphological material in order to put their intended meaning into words, the entire meaning, although fully conceptualized by the coiner, is underdetermined for the recipient.

The potential ambiguity of many ad-hoc formations for their recipients is illustrated by the above-mentioned example, *treetop-hugging flight*. Significantly, the meaning of this expression is taken up again in the following sentence by the established lexeme *low altitude flying* and thus explained and as it were 'glossed'. Without this additional information and the rest of the context, an interpretation such as 'crash landing ending up embracing the treetop' would be just as plausible as the one intended in the text.

Cognitive perspective. By definition ad-hoc formations have no entry in the mental lexicons of the speakers of the speech community in question, whereas the morphemes from which they are composed **are** already stored and accessible for the hearers or readers and can be identified more or less immediately (cf. Aitchison 2003: 165 ff.). Readers of the article in (4.1) are undoubtedly able to retrieve the meanings of the morphemes, {tree}, {top}, {hug} and {ing}, and they have no other choice than to form a plausible hypothesis about its meaning as a whole on the basis of these meanings. As its significance must be computed rather than retrieved, the form *treetop-hugging* does not have the status of a **concept** or a **cognitive category**, since concepts are characterized by a stored association in the memory of the individual speaker between **one** form and **one** conceptual complex. This association is enhanced by knowledge about the attributes of concrete objects or abstract states-of-affairs which belong to the cognitive category associated with the form. Taking up a notion introduced by the Russian psychologist Vygotsky (1962) to describe a phase in onotological development, I will refer to this preliminary stage in the conceptual creation of complex lexemes as a **pseudo-concept**. In the usage represented here pseudo-concepts are characterized by two properties: their content must be computed by the hearer through analysis of the individual word elements and cannot be recalled as a whole, but the very fact that one word is used suggests that this lexical item stands for one conceptual unit, or concept.

4.3.2   Consolidation

From a **sociopragmatic perspective** the consolidation of a new lexeme is characterized by its **spread** and **diffusion** in the speech community. The word is used by a growing number of speakers, gains currency in more and more social groups and is recognized by ever increasing sections of the speech community as a familiar item, i.e. an individually known word. In the initial phase of its diffusion, when new complex lexemes are still perceived as new, they are referred to as **neologisms**. Neologisms are thus not simply new words, as the Greek roots of the word suggest (*neo* = 'new', *logos* = 'word'), but new words that have succeeded in surviving beyond a one-off use in an ad-hoc situation (cf. Hohenhaus 1996: 19, Fischer 1998: 3–6).

As already discussed in section 4.2.1, not all ad-hoc formations are used with the intention of helping them along the road to consolidation. Many instances are syntactically motivated and do not serve a naming function. But even many of the lexically motivated coinages do not progress beyond the stage of creation, simply because they are not spread among and by the members of the speech community. For example, judging from its declining spread on the internet, the recent coinage *sodcasting*, a blend from *sod* and *podcast* referring to the irritating practice of playing music on a mobile phone in a public place, does not seem to be catching on.

The chances of an ad-hoc formation being successfully diffused, institutionalized and thus conventionalized are dependent on a range of semantic, sociolinguistic, pragmatic, cognitive and ultimately also phonological factors, of which only the most important can be briefly addressed here (cf. Bauer 1983: 43 ff., Ungerer 1991, Fischer 1998: 15 ff.). New words naming rapidly and widely spreading new objects, such as trendy gadgets in media technology, obviously have a better chance than those whose referents are only relevant for individual people or professions. A good example of a word which managed to spread literally globally within a few days because of the salience of its referent is *vuvuzela*. If words are coined and used by people in the public eye with prestige and influence in the media, e.g. politicians, media celebrities, managers, journalists and the like, then their chances of diffusion, consolidation and establishment are better than if they are coined by a private individual. Depending on the circulation of the medium in which the word first appears, it reaches a much larger number of speakers, and there is a higher probability that a word is not just reused but also becomes the topic of a metalinguistic discussion, which in turn contributes considerably to its diffusion. Today, the internet and the increasing interactivity in blogs, forums and social networks is instrumental in the fast diffusion of new words. The existence of word-watch, word-spy or new-word websites is more than a superficial symptom of the interest many people have in recent additions to the lexical stock of their language (cf. e.g. *New Words* by *Merriam-Websters* at http://www.merriam-webster.com/info/new_words.htm, *UrbanDictionary* at http://www.urbandictionary.com), and *WordSpy: Dictionary of New Words* at http://www.makeuseof. com/dir/wordspy-dictionary-of-new-words-and-phrases). Another factor that can be crucial for determining whether a word is accepted by the speech community and diffused is the appeal of the external form or the originality of the idea described. And finally, of course, cognitive aspects such as the ease of segmenting and computing the meanings of new words play an important role in their spread (cf. Schmid 2008).

From a **structural perspective** the consolidation stage can be described as the stabilization of form and meaning. Occasionally, for a variable period following the creation of a new word, formal variations in the pronunciation or the orthography are observed. For example, the now well established word *email* is still spelt in the variants *email, e-mail* and even *E-mail*, but unlike less institutionalized *e*-prefixed words like *e-book* or even *e-government*, there is a distinct tendency to omit the hyphen. This indicates that the extent of this variation is usually reduced in the course of a word's diffusion, and the form stabilizes. Semantically the original potential ambiguity for the recipients can be seen to be reduced. If the form *treetop-hugging flight* were to catch on and begin to become stabilized for instance, then the probability of its being understood literally as 'crash landing ending up embracing the treetop' would decrease. The reduction in ambiguity is accompanied by a reduction in context-dependence.

From a **cognitive perspective** the consolidation of a complex lexeme means two things. On the one hand, the word is tentatively assigned an entry in the mental lexicon of an individual speaker and begins to be linked with other entries in a multitude of associative connections, which, on the one hand, can be the type of classical structuralist paradigmatic sense relations (such as synonymy, antonymy, hyperonymy and hyponymy). On the other hand, syntagmatic relations such as collocations start to develop when the possible combinations of, e.g., a new noun with verbs or adjectives become fixed.

As for its conceptual status, the components of the pseudo-concept begin to merge into an integral (or *holistic*) concept. An associative link between the form and **one** concept, which differs from the combination of the concepts represented by the morphemes involved, begins to become entrenched in the minds of the speakers. Simultaneously the conceptual contribution of the individual morphemes gradually fades so that, for instance, in processing the expression *treetop-hugging flight* the mind focusses less on treetops and embraces and more immediately and directly on low-altitude flying. These two converging processes – construction of a conceptual unit and fading of the prominence of the individual elements – lead to the formation of a conceptual **gestalt** in the sense used in gestalt psychology, i.e. a unit whose meaning as a whole differs from the sum of the meanings of its components. At the consolidation stage new words thus begin to achieve their own conceptual gestalt and substance.

4.3.3 Establishment

Although establishment marks the theoretical end point of the consolidation process, it must be stressed that in the course of constant language change further diachronic developments take place and can cause further changes in the word.

A lexeme can be said to be fully **institutionalized** from a **sociopragmatic perspective** when it is known and used by the majority of speakers. The vague allusion to the "majority" shows that no clear line can be drawn between the diffusion stage and the state of being institutionalized. While lexemes in (4.1) such as *government, starvation, United Nations, landmines* and of course *however* and *otherwise* are familiar to all adult native speakers of English and are therefore fully institutionalized, we can assume that *commandeer, press-ganging, ground-to-air missile* and *relief worker*, at least as regards their active use, are limited to a smaller circle of users and hence can be regarded as being institutionalized to a lesser degree. While there can be no doubt that frequency of use and degree of familiarity are important indicators of institutionalization, it is also obvious that they are quite difficult to measure objectively. Quantitative investigations of usage frequencies in recently compiled corpora and particularly on the internet are very helpful tools.

According to Bauer (1983) and Quirk et al. (1985), a lexeme is accepted as fully **lexicalized** from the **structural perspective** when it exhibits formal properties that are not explicable using the rules of word-formation and/or has semantic features that cannot be deduced from the meanings of its components. A detailed discussion of these formal (i.e. principally phonological, orthographic and morphological) and semantic indicators of lexicalization is provided by Bauer (1983: 50 ff.). Instances of the various types of formal lexicalization processes are rarer than semantic ones, and there are no examples of them in the text in (4.1). Examples of phonological lexicalization found in the literature (and in the ICE-GB corpus) are the lexeme *holiday* and the names of the days of the week (*Sunday, Monday, Tuesday* etc.). The pronunciation of the first part of *holiday* has changed from /ˈhəʊli/ to /ˈhɒli/; the diphthong in the constituent -*day* /deɪ/ of weekdays can occur in the reduced monophthong form /di/ (e.g. /ˈfraɪdi/). Many examples of phonological lexicalization can be found in products of the word-formation pattern of prefixation. For instance, as a rule lexemes prefixed with *non-* carry the main stress on the stressed syllable of the base, while the prefix carries a secondary stress (cf. ˌnon-ˈviolent). The lexicalized lexeme *nonsense*, in contrast, which is formed according to the same pattern, carries the main stress on the prefix. In words beginning with the prefix *re-*, lexicalized formations can be identified by the fact that the prefix does not carry secondary stress and that the vowel is reduced, (cf. the non-lexicalized *re(-)count* /ˌriːˈkaʊnt/ 'count again' as opposed to *recount* /rɪˈkaʊnt/ 'tell (in detail)' (Hansen et al. 1990: 71; see also p. 156). The lexeme *nonsense*, which does not follow the rule of the pattern whereby *non-* is written with a hyphen, can also be used to illustrate orthographic lexicalization.

Further examples are words such as *welcome, welfare* and *fulfil* (AmE *fulfill*), in which the double consonants of the simple forms *well* and *full* no longer occur.

It is of greater interest with regard to the examples in text (4.1) to investigate semantic lexicalization. The point here is to establish whether complex lexemes are **compositional** or not. This means that we have to determine whether the established sense of a complex lexeme can be fully explained with recourse to the meanings of the morphemes it consists of and the 'meanings' of the pattern on the basis of which they are formed. Lexicalized lexemes fail to fulfil this principle of semantic compositionality. We say that their meaning is not, or at least not completely, *compositional* or *transparent*, and that they are **demotivated** or **idiomatized**, like idioms whose meanings can also not be deduced from the meanings of the words they are made up of. The highest degree of lexicalization and loss of motivation is reached in obscured compounds, e.g. *lord* (from Old English *hlāfweard*, 'loaf keeper') and *gospel* (from Old English *gōd spel*, 'good news'). Today these lexemes are neither formally nor semantically identifiable as compounds.

Let us consider the lexeme *airfield* as an example of a less strong form of semantic lexicalization. It is easy to see that not even the core meaning, 'a place where planes can fly from' can be immediately deduced from the morphemes {air} and {field} and the knowledge that noun-noun compounds of this type often express the semantic relation of 'location', since the relation between the concepts of AIR and PLANE is not explicitly specified in the compound. Furthermore, in contrast to *airport* the lexeme *airfield* is used typically when referring to military airports (cf. LDOCE: "… especially one used by military planes"). This non-obligatory, but nevertheless characteristic semantic component is clearly part of the meaning of the compound, although not inherent in the compositional meaning of *air* and *field*. It is not part of the set of features or attributives associated with the two separate nouns and must therefore be assessed as an indication of semantic lexicalization in the sense described above. Note that here, as in many, or arguably even most cases of lexicalization, we can assume that the lack of motivation is not, or not necessarily, the result of a diachronic process, but has been established from the outset at the stage of ad-hoc formation (Schmid 2008: 4 f.). Lipka (1981: 122) describes this phenomenon as *instantaneous coining*.

Further examples of semantic lexicalization in text (4.1) are the noun *refugee* and the verb *to press-gang*. In addition to the largely transparent meaning 'someone who takes refuge', according to the LDOCE *refugee* has acquired the attributes 'in another country' and 'especially during a war'. The verb *to press-gang* has drastically extended the original meaning of the noun *press-gang*, "a group of sailors employed in the past to take men away by force to join the navy", which was also semantically lexicalized. The verb is described as having the much wider meaning "(*informal*) to force someone to do something". This shows that in the course of lexicalization, meanings can not only become restricted or change altogether but can also be extended (cf. Lipka 1977: 160, Bauer 1983: 55 ff.).

What are the reasons for lexicalization? Firstly, as was just explained, newly formed complex lexemes tend to underspecify the intended meanings and rely on the situational or linguistic context for disambiguation. As a result, it is usually from the very moment of the ad-hoc formation of new words onwards that there is a divergence of their compositional meaning vis-à-vis the individual meanings of their components, because the morphological material used by the coiner does not exhaustively specify the intended meaning. In the further development following the act of ad-hoc formation, principally three types of reasons for lexicalization taking place can be distinguished: cultural, linguistic and cognitive.

The classic case of a cultural cause for semantic lexicalization is a change in the designated object. These days boards are usually green rather than black. However, the English lexeme *blackboard* has remained in its original form with the result that the meaning of the lexeme as a whole and the compositional meaning have moved apart. Interestingly, when whiteboards were introduced, this was accompanied by a new word, presumably because other accompanying props were also replaced, like felt pens instead of chalk. Other lexemes which became lexicalized as a result of a change in the referent include *cupboard*, *shoemaker* and *watchmaker* (cf. Lipka 1983: 927).

The main linguistic cause of lexicalization is the mirror image of the cultural one. While the extralinguistic referents of a lexeme remain on the whole relatively stable, the meaning of the lexeme changes. Changes in meaning caused by extension, narrowing and shift of meaning are everyday processes in living languages affecting all words, not just complex lexemes. However, simple and complex lexemes differ with regard to the extent to which these changes are traceable from a synchronic perspective. Since most simple lexemes are not motivated but arbitrary, changes in meaning cannot generally be determined synchronically. Speakers who are not familiar with the history of English, for instance, will not be aware that the word *nice*, which these days is almost devoid of meaning, at the time of Jane Austen used to have the quite specific meaning 'fine' (Leisi 1985: 134), which only remains in collocations such as *a nice point*. Complex lexemes, on the other hand, are relatively motivated, since their components have been combined as determined by a specific idea and since their parts form associative links to related words. If the word-form that reflects this idea remains in existence but the meaning changes, then the linguistic change will also be visible synchronically because of the discrepancy between the compositional meaning and the meaning of the whole word. We can illustrate this using the lexeme *holiday*, already mentioned in connection with phonological lexicalization, which in the Old English period did indeed still mean 'holy day'. The semantic extension to the meaning 'day on which a break is taken from work' and eventually 'extended period in which a break is taken from work' led to a divergence of the compositional meaning and the meaning as a whole. However, in contrast to the simple lexeme *nice*, this divergence is also perceptible synchronically and hence is traceable by speakers who are not aware of the history of the language.

An even more fundamental cause of semantic lexicalization is the power of words to form concepts or more generally, the cognitive tendency towards gestalt-formation (Lipka 1977: 161, 1981: 122). This leads us to the **cognitive perspective** on the stage of establishment.

It is evidently more economic for the human cognitive system not to process clusters of stimuli that satisfy the principles of gestalt, such as proximity, closure and similarity, individually but as conceptual units and to combine them into one gestalt. We perceive two vertical lines connected in the middle by a horizontal line not as the combination of the three separate visual stimuli l – l but as a holistic perceptual unit, an H. Likewise, a series of tones, e.g. ♫♫ ♪, is not perceived as a sequence of individual tones but holistically as a melody. There is every reason to believe that the same process of **gestalt-formation** takes place when morphemes are combined, particularly if they frequently recur and their cognitive processing is repeated. Thus, the chances of individual stimuli being perceived and conceptualized as an integrated whole increase not only according to the extent to which they satisfy the gestalt principles mentioned above, but also with the frequency of their co-occurrence. In the case of morpheme combinations this means that the probability of conceptual gestalt-formation increases with the degree of diffusion and institutionalization. The more frequently a speaker encounters and processes a complex word, the greater is the probability that it becomes a holistic form for him or her, disconnected from the concepts or ideas associated with the word constituents. In cognitive grammar, the frequency-dependent process of gestalt-formation is metaphorically perceived as **entrenchment** (Langacker 1987a: 59, 100; cf. also Schmid 2007, 2008). Langacker explains the entrenchment and concept-formation of composite words with the help of the scaffolding metaphor. In this image, the morphological components are a sort of scaffolding for the complex lexeme that can be dismantled once the complex unit has been established as a self-sufficient entity (Langacker 1987a: 461). The final stage of conceptual gestalt-formation is a fully entrenched concept, which has acquired its own conceptual substance and plasticity.

The psychological plausibility of the processes of lexicalization, entrenchment and concept-formation has been empirically demonstrated by Ungerer and Schmid (1998) using so-called **attribute listing tasks**. They confronted groups of students separately with compounds and their constituents and asked them to write down the characteristics that all the referents of the lexemes had in common. The aim of the test was to ascertain the conceptual contribution made by the two constituents to the overall concept of the compound. Semantic lexicalization and concept-formation were considered to have taken place if there was only a slight agreement between the concept of the compound and the concepts of its component parts. The experiments showed that with regard to their degree of lexicalization there are different types of compounds. Compounds that are not lexicalized – but are definitely fully institutionalized – such as *apple juice* and *kitchen chair* draw their entire attribute inventory and hence their entire conceptual content from their constituent nouns, *apple* and *juice* or *kitchen* and *chair*. This is not so with lexicalized compounds such as *newspaper* and *wheelchair*. In these cases, a large number of attributes appeared in the attribute lists of the compounds which were not found in the lists of the simple nouns, e.g. 'photos/pictures' and 'articles' for *newspaper* and 'disabled' and 'not deployable everywhere' for *wheelchair*. This shows that these complex lexemes have broken away conceptually from the meaning of their constituent parts.

It is characteristic of entrenched concepts that they can be accessed and retrieved directly from the mental lexicon, i.e. without having to make a detour via the morphemes of which they are composed. Metaphorically speaking, the relevant word has firmly set up its own entry in the mental lexicon and has established multiplex and dense associative links to other nodes in the network. For the example *treetop-hugging flight*, this means that in the case of full entrenchment as an autonomous concept the associative connections with treetops and embraces would be reduced in salience, and in return those with low altitude, danger and the possibility of enemy fire would be strengthened. This kind of storage of an expression in the mental lexicon has repercussions on the nature of the concept. Since the meaning of what is read or heard does not have to be computed from the meanings of the separate morphemes and since there are many associations with other nodes in the conceptual network, the concept is also enriched with connotations beyond the pure denotative or referential meaning.

4.4 Summary

An overview summarizing the three perspectives on the establishment of complex lexemes and its three stages can be seen in Table 4.2. Looking at this table, one should keep in mind that the three stages do not always run parallel with respect to the three perspectives as the systematic representation in the table would suggest. Complex lexemes can reach different stages of development depending on the perspective, and this is what justifies the somewhat tedious and seemingly unnecessarily complex division into three stages and three perspectives. There is no doubt that complex lexemes such as the previously mentioned *apple juice* and *kitchen chair* have been fully institutionalized and entrenched, as Ungerer and Schmid's tests (1998) have shown; however, they do not seem to have lexicalized significantly. Complex lexemes in specialist literature, on the other hand, e.g. *mechanoreceptor*, *motor end-plate*, *denervation*, *axon death* and *peripheral innervation density*, which can be found in a text from the field of psychiatry in the ICE corpus (ICE-GB:W2a-026), have only been partially institutionalized, but nevertheless, as far as the speakers who know how to use them are concerned, they have been fully entrenched and lexicalized, which in turn makes understanding them even more difficult for the uninitiated.

Tab. 4.2: Overview of the stages of the establishment of complex lexemes from three perspectives

criterion / phase	structural perspective: the word itself			sociopragmatic perspective: the word in the speech community		cognitive perspective: the word in the mind	
	lexicalization			institutionalization		entrenchment	
	form	meaning	context-dependence	use	familiarity	mental lexicon	conceptual status
creation	(product of) ad-hoc formation			(process of) ad-hoc formation		pseudo-concept	
	new combination of forms	highly ambiguous	highly context-dependent	first use by a speaker	the word itself is not familiar; type-familiarity	no entry in the mental lexicon	new combination of concepts
consolidation	stabilization			diffusion		process of entrenchment	
	form becomes stabilized	reduction of ambiguity	reduction of context-dependence	use by parts or sections of the speech community	item-familiarity in parts or sections of the speech community	preliminary entry and incipient networking in the mental lexicon	concept-formation; merging into a holistic concept
establishment	lexicalized lexeme			institutionalized lexeme		entrenched concept	
	additional orthographic, phonological and/or morphemic features	additional semantic components	minimal context-dependence	use by the majority of the members of the speech community	item-familiarity for the majority of the members of the speech community	full-fledged entry with multiplex links in the network	holistic concept, autonomous conceptual gestalt

Further reading: On lexicalization and institutionalization**: Bauer (1983: 42–61), Lipka (1992), Hohenhaus (2005)**. On ad-hoc formation and neologisms: **Hohenhaus (1996), Fischer (1998), Lipka (1999), Stegmayr, Kerremans and Schmid (forthcoming)**. On gestalt-formation and entrenchment: **Langacker (1987a: 59, 100), Ungerer and Schmid (2006: 34–44), Schmid (2007) and (2008)**.

5 Fundamental issues in English word-formation

So far we have looked at the nature and types of morphological building blocks which can be used to form complex lexemes (chapter 2) and provided an account of the stages that newly-formed words typically go through on their way from ad-hoc formation to establishment in the lexicon (chapter 4). In this chapter I will turn to the patterns that guide speakers when they coin new words, and have guided those in the past who coined new words still existing today. Following a brief survey of the major types of word-formation patterns (5.1), different ways of accommodating these in coherent systems will be discussed (5.2) and fundamental questions which must be addressed in the linguistic investigation of word-formation will be introduced.

Before we embark on this, it is important to clarify the status of these word-formation patterns. I regard patterns as moulds or blueprints for the creation of complex lexemes, which are stored by individual speakers and tacitly agreed upon by the members of the speech community. In short, they are **entrenched** (stored individually) and **conventionalized** (shared and tacitly agreed upon). While language users seem to be able to extract or distill these blueprints from their constant exposure to existing complex lexemes (see section 5.2.5, pp. 93 ff.), they are clearly not consciously aware of the rules or restrictions governing acceptable new products of word-formation. It is the job of linguists to discover these regularities and restrictions, and in this endeavour they rely on the systematic observation of existing products of word-formation, just as native speakers do essentially. So if, e.g., the layperson and the linguist notice that in English compounds the modifying element generally precedes the modified element – since we have *barman*, *pay rise* and *night shift* rather than **manbar*, **rise pay* and **shift night* – this yields knowledge about a word-formation pattern which is as valuable for the layperson creating a new compound as it is for the linguist on the hunt for generalizations about word-formation rules. It is in this sense that the word-formation processes 'discovered' and described by linguists in terms of patterns, types or rules are not just weird theoretical constructs but actually represent the tacit knowledge that lay speakers are likely to have of their language.

5.1 Overview of English word-formation patterns

In order to provide a systematic description of English word-formation patterns we must first make a fundamental distinction between patterns that use morphemes or morpheme-like building blocks and those which do not. The first group is referred to as **morphemic**, the second as **non-morphemic word-formation patterns**. The two following sections will outline first the morphemic and then the non-morphemic word-formation patterns of English. More detailed discussions of the individual patterns follow in chapters 7 to 12.

5.1.1 Morphemic word-formation patterns

If we assume the idealized case of a complex lexeme consisting of not more than two morphemes, then the core area of prototypical morphemic word-formation patterns can be described by specifying (a) the types of morphemes involved and (b) the way they are ordered. As in the area of syntax, in word-formation elements that participate directly and exhaustively in the formation of larger units are referred to as **immediate constituents**. Table 5.1 gives an overview of the type and order of the immediate constituents of the three basic morphemic word-formation patterns, compounding, prefixation and suffixation.

Tab. 5.1:   The three basic morphemic word-formation patterns

pattern	first immediate constituent	second immediate constituent	examples
compounding	free lexical morpheme	free lexical morpheme	*boatpeople*, *showroom*, *timetable*
prefixation	bound lexical morpheme	free lexical morpheme	*dislike*, *inside*, *rebuild*
suffixation	free lexical morpheme	bound lexical morpheme	*attachment*, *harmless*, *owner*

Within these patterns there are a number of variations and modifications which considerably extend the possibilities for creating new words:

- Words can consist not just of morphemes but entirely or partly of morpheme-like, meaning-bearing constituents. This is the case when a free morpheme combines with a preposed combining form (see p. 41) (e.g. *neuromuscular*, *endoneural*), or when a word is made up of two combining forms (e.g. *bio-logy*, *demo-cracy*, *psycho-logy*).

- Suffixations can contain bound roots instead of free morphemes, as in *necessary* or *special*, for instance (see p. 165).

- Traditionally word-formation also deals with a process the effect of which is similar to suffixation in as far as a change of word class takes place but different because the change is not marked by a visible morpheme. For example, while the suffix *-ment* is seen to be responsible for the transposition of the verb *attach* into the noun *attachment*, the noun *knife* has also been turned into a verb (*to knife*), but here the change is not marked on the morphological surface. Depending on the theory subscribed to, this change is considered to be the result of a so-called **conversion** from one word class into another or understood as **zero-derivation** or **derivation by means of a zero morpheme** (see section 10.2).

- Finally there is the comparatively rare and special case in which a change of word class is caused not by the addition but by the elimination of lexical building blocks. This process is described as **back-formation**, an example being the verb *to baby-sit*, which did not originate from the combination of the free morphemes *baby* and *sit*, but was derived from the noun *babysitter*.

This leaves us with **compounding, prefixation** and **suffixation** as basic morphemic word-formation patterns, and **conversion/zero-derivation** and **back-formation** as less typical ones. It is important to point out that in the course of practical analysis of the existing products of word-formation – which, as was mentioned above, is the basis of the linguistic study of word-formation – one repeatedly encounters further variations of these fundamental patterns. As with other areas of linguistics, the field of word-formation is not characterized by categories that can be clearly separated from one another, but by a co-existence of relatively clear, prototypical cases with an abundance of borderline phenomena. It is for this reason that we shall have to address the issue of transition phenomena and classification problems repeatedly in each of the chapters dealing with word-formation patterns (chapters 7 to 11). From a cognitive point of view, this is just an indication that the entrenched and conventionalized word-formation patterns and blueprints do not have the status of binding, hard-and-fast rules but are guidelines which speakers usually follow if they want their new coinages to be comprehended. A speaker who violates the conventional order of modifying and modified element mentioned above by producing an ad-hoc compound like *phone chocolate* (rather than *chocolate phone*) to refer to a phone that is smeared with chocolate is of course free to do so but clearly runs the risk of not being understood.

5.1.2   Non-morphemic word-formation patterns

Strictly speaking, back-formation should be regarded as a borderline case between morphemic and non-morphemic processes, since it is not only 'genuine' morphemes that are separated but also word components that were obviously considered to be morphemes although – at least historically – they never had this status. The verbs *to burgle* and *to peddle*, derived from the nouns *burglar* and *peddler*, are often quoted as examples of the fact that the detached part is mistakenly understood as being a manifestation of the morpheme {-er}.

Clear-cut cases of non-morphemic word-formation processes are **clipping** e.g. *photo* from *photograph*, *phone* from *telephone*; **blending** or **blend**, e.g. *brunch*, *chunnel*, *infotainment*; **acronymy** and **abbreviation**, e.g. *USA, UK, UNESCO, radar*; and **reduplication**, e.g. *willy-nilly, girly-girly*. Since for current purposes the examples given adequately illustrate the respective patterns, nothing more will be said about these processes at this point. For more detailed information see chapter 12.

5.2 Different approaches to the classification of English word-formation patterns

In the previous section I outlined the basic principles of English word-formation in a way that was as neutral and independent of specific theories as possible. Nevertheless, this account cannot be described as objective. Despite the fact that the database of linguistic phenomena is shared by all researchers, every description and classification is inevitably biased, since it is based more or less explicitly on certain theoretical assumptions and pursues specific goals. For instance, even the decision to describe the basic patterns of compounding, prefixation and suffixation by means of the morpheme types they consist of rather than using concepts such as *word*, *stem* and *affix*, is potentially controversial. The same applies to the path we have already taken in labelling bound roots and combining forms *morpheme-like meaning-bearing constituents*.

Since classifications in linguistics reveal a great deal about the theoretical background assumptions, the main focus and the goals of an approach, it is worthwhile comparing different attempts at classifying English word-formation patterns. In so doing I will restrict myself largely to the field of morphemic patterns.

5.2.1 The 'traditional' approach

The classification of word-formation patterns in the appendix of Quirk et al.'s *Comprehensive Grammar* (1985) can serve to represent the traditional school, as it is a well-established classification method. The system can be summarized as shown in Figure 5.1.

The distinguishing features of this classification method are its orientation towards the morphological form and independence of the constituents of complex lexemes and the adoption of the notions of *base* and *affix*, i.e. *prefix* and *suffix*. Prefixation and suffixation are regarded as types of affixation, since both consist of a base plus an affix. Conversion and compounding are independent patterns, the former

being characterized as a base which changes its word class but "with no change of form" (Quirk et al. 1985: 1520), the latter as the addition of one base to another.

Fig. 5.1: Classification of word-formation patterns according to Quirk et al. (1985: 1520)

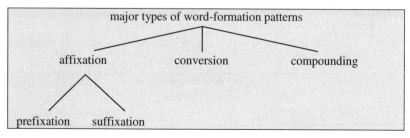

Hansen et al. (1990: 41 ff.) take a similar approach. However, since, in accordance with Marchand's tradition, they interpret the formally non-marked change of word class as *derivation by means of a zero morpheme* rather than *conversion* (see section 10.2.3), they propose a two-way division into compounding and affixation, with affixation being split into prefixation, suffixation, derivation by means of a zero morpheme and back-formation.

5.2.2 The syntagma approach

The most prominent representative of the syntagma approach is Marchand (1969). While for Quirk et al. (1985) the issue of a change of word class is important but not crucial for their classification, this criterion is of paramount importance to Marchand, as can be seen from the depiction of Marchand's system in Figure 5.2.

In contrast to Quirk et al., Marchand sees a closer relationship between prefixation and compounding than between prefixation and suffixation. This is due to his ideas on the internal structure of complex lexemes, which he regards as *word-formation syntagmas*. The term s*yntagma* is based on a concept proposed by Saussure and his student Charles Bally and has been taken over by Marchand and his followers (cf. Marchand 1969: 2 f., Kastovsky 1982: 21 f., 152, Lipka 2002: 95 f.). Word-formation syntagmas are considered to be shortened grammatical constructions or sentences. The underlying structure of word-formation syntagmas is the so-called **determinant-determinatum relationship**, meaning that one element modifies another. In English this usually means that the first element (*determinant* = 'determining') modifies the second (*determinatum* = 'determined'). This relationship is a specific variant of the *modifier-head* principle, according to which grammatical units such as noun phrases are generally composed of a dependent, modifying constituent, the *modifier*, and a more autonomous constituent, the *head*. Marchand transfers this principle to word-formation, referring to it as the *determi-*

nant-determinatum relationship. In this book we will adopt the principle as such but use the terms *modifier* and *head*, as they are also established outside Marchand's system. From a grammatical point of view, the head is always the dominant element because it can replace the whole structure. According to Marchand, in English complex words the head is invariably the right-most, i.e. final, lexical morpheme.

Fig. 5.2:   Classification of word-formation patterns according to Marchand (1969: 2 ff.)

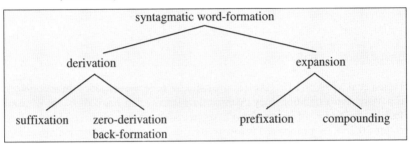

This claim is also Marchand's (1969: 11–13) main motive for the classification depicted above. In compounds and prefixations, the final morpheme typically belongs to the class of free morphemes which also serve as heads in grammatical constructions, e.g. *people* in *boatpeople* and *book* in *e-book*. The term *expansion*, which functions as a superordinate term for prefixation and compounding, captures the common denominator that in both processes a morphological extension by means of a modifier takes place while the word class of the head remains the same. This is not the case with the processes subsumed under derivation; here the position of the head, which also determines the word class of the complex lexeme as a whole, is occupied by a bound morpheme, or in the case of zero-derivation by a zero morpheme. The word class is therefore not determined by the morpheme which grammatically would be more suitable for the function of the head. This is why Marchand claims that there is a transposition of a free morpheme to the atypical role of *modifier*. He thus defines *derivation* as a form of transposition in which the role of the head is assumed by a bound morpheme (Marchand 1969: 13).

5.2.3 Tournier (1985) and (1988)

The French linguist Tournier (1985) puts his classification on an entirely different basis: the question as to which of the two sides of the linguistic sign undergoes changes during productive lexical processes. The following diagram of his system and the subsequent discussion are based on Lipka's summary (2002: 108 ff.):

Fig. 5.3: The classification of word-formation patterns and other productive lexical processes according to Tournier (1985: 47 ff., 1988: 18–24, based on Lipka 2002: 108 ff.)

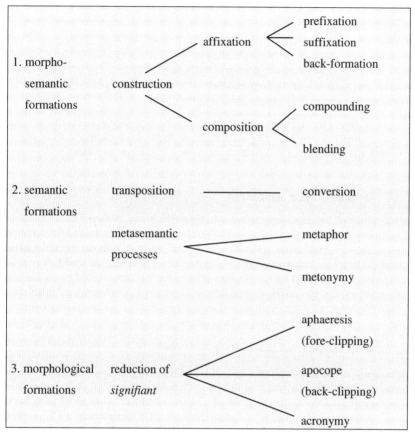

There are broadly three types or macro-mechanisms depending on whether the changes affect both the form and the content (*morpho-semantic formation*), only the content (*semantic formation*) or only the form (*morphological formation*). The individual processes represented on the right-hand side of the chart are regarded by Tournier, just as they are here, as blueprints which speakers can use creatively. Since I am only aiming at a general approach to classification, I will not discuss the individual patterns of this classification but only its fundamental characteristics.

The first point of interest is that in addition to the classic word-formation patterns it is not only the semantic transfer processes of metaphor and metonymy that fit naturally into the system of productive lexical processes, but also the non-morphemic patterns which shorten the form. For Tournier, actual word-formation is restricted to areas 1 and 3, i.e. those patterns in which changes in form take place, which is unusual, since this decision excludes conversion from word-formation.

Furthermore, it is remarkable that conversion is separated from suffixation as the former is a form-preserving process while the latter is not. In contrast to Marchand and others, who direct their attention to the power of conversion to change word classes and who regard it as a process with far-reaching grammatical effects, Tournier puts semantic changes centre-stage.

Finally it should be emphasized that Tournier's classification reflects the obvious similarity between *compounding* (in our terminology) and *blending*, both of which combine free morphemes and create a semantic relation between them.

5.2.4   Onomasiological approaches

The essence of onomasiological approaches to the study of linguistic meaning is that, in contrast to the semasiological, it does not start with the linguistic elements by asking what they mean and what they stand for, but with the extralinguistic world of things, or rather the cognitive concepts we have of this world. A typical semasiological question about word-formation, for instance, would be, 'what are the meanings that the suffix -*er* can denote?'; an equivalent onomasiological one would be, 'what are the morphological means for creating complex lexemes referring to people?'. Since onomasiological approaches are interested in the encoding of cognitive concepts, there is a close affinity between them and a cognitive treatment of language (see section 5.2.5).

According to Fleischer (2000: 887 ff.) onomasiological approaches to word-formation have a longer tradition in Slavic Philology than in English studies (see also Štekauer 1998: 7). In the field of English word-formation there have been three relatively recent attempts at contributing to the understanding of complex lexemes from the onomasiological perspective proposed by Szymanek (1988), Štekauer (1998), (2000) and (2005), and Ungerer (2002). All three approaches have in common that they are based on the fundamental cognitive categories that enable us to understand the world around us, e.g. PERSON, SUBSTANCE, OBJECT, ACTION, PROCESS and QUALITY. The enormous cognitive and linguistic importance of these categories is reflected in the fact that they correlate with the basic word classes found in many languages: people and objects are typically denoted by nouns, actions by verbs, and qualities by adjectives. Moreover, there are fundamental relationships between these categories, which are part of our experience of the world, such as the knowledge that the ACTIONS of PERSONS are carried out with the aid of OBJECTS. These important cognitive categories and the relationships between them constitute the starting point for word-formation studies from an onomasiological point of view. For example, a lexeme such as *truck driver* (Ště-kauer 1998: 15–17) encodes – to put it simply – conceptual and semantic knowledge about a PERSON with certain attributes, an OBJECT with certain attributes and the relationship between the two, namely that the PERSON carries out an ACTION with the OBJECT.

Viewed from this perspective, derivational morphological processes not only change the word class of words, but also have the function of transferring concepts into other conceptual categories. Hence one of the functions of {-er}-suffixations as in *baker* and *driver* is to construe PERSON concepts derived from the ACTION concepts *bake* and *drive*. According to Ungerer (2002), word-formation types such as *personizers, actionizers, qualitizers, object creators* and, when creating abstract words, *domain creators* can be distinguished on a relatively general level against this background. Conversion is described as onomasiological or conceptual recategorization in such a framework (Štěkauer 1998: 11, Ungerer 2002: 560).

The chapters on prefixation (chapter 8) and suffixation (chapter 9) below will be organized according to the categories suggested by the onomasiological approach.

5.2.5 Cognitive approaches

A cognitive perspective on word-formation has been called for for some time (Lipka 1994: 13 ff.) and has now begun to take shape in the form of a number of more or less programmatic papers and applications. Surveys of the existing body of work are presented in Tuggy (2005), Ungerer (2007), Onysko and Michel (2010b) and – for compounds – Heyvaerts (2009). A number of studies applying cognitive approaches are collected in Onysko and Michel (2010a).

From a general perspective, we can say that there are three central features that characterize cognitive approaches to the classification (and investigation) of word-formation patterns.

Firstly, cognitive linguists share with those colleagues pursuing an onomasiological approach a keen interest in the effects of word-formation processes on **conceptualization** and **concept-formation**. From this perspective, a fundamental distinction separates word-formation patterns that combine several more or less richly structured concepts (i.e. compounding, prefixation and blending) from those which mainly serve the purpose of re-categorizing conceptual content in terms of conceptual types (i.e. suffixation and conversion). This will be discussed in greater detail in later sections (see pp. 182 and 190).

Secondly, cognitive approaches do not see word-formation patterns as neatly separated categories defined by categorical features and hard-and-fast rules but regard the knowledge about types and classes of word-forming processes, which language users have stored in their brains, as variable, flexible and dynamic. Essentially, this approach provides the foundation for the way morphology and word-formation are represented in this book and underlies the account of word-formation patterns provided at the outset of this chapter (see p. 85). A key concept encapsulating the idea of flexible blueprints introduced there is the notion of **schema** (cf. Ryder 1994, Kemmer 2003, Tuggy 2005, Booij 2010: 82 f., Lampert and Lampert 2010: 37 ff.). Generally speaking, "schemas are essentially routinized, or cognitively entrenched, patterns of experience" (Kemmer 2003: 78). This means that just as we know from experience that a house consists of (at least) walls and a roof, we know that certain words consist of say a verb and the suffix *-er*, and that these words have certain semantic characteristics in common. If we build a new house we automatically follow this stored structural pattern, and the same applies if we produce or come across a new word consisting of a verb and *-er*. The knowledge stored in the form of schemas can be fairly abstract and unspecific – meaning that our schema of a house does not need to contain specific information of the types of walls and the roof – but they can also be more specific, as in the case of the schema for *log cabin*, which specifies that the walls are built from logs and leaves little room for variation in that respect. Analogously, we have stored linguistic schemas on different levels of abstraction, e.g. ones representing fairly general knowledge like 'free morphemes can be combined with bound morphemes' and more specific ones like 'verbs can be combined with *-able* to convey certain meanings'.

Thirdly, many cognitive approaches agree on how we acquire these schemata. This has also already been hinted at above (p. 85). As Kemmer puts it, "[a] schema is a cognitive representation consisting of perceived similarities across many instances of usage" (2003: 78). Roughly speaking, if children come across a sufficient number of words ending in *-er* and referring to people who do things more or less regularly and habitually (*driver, baker, teacher* etc.) they abstract some kind of schema from the perceived morphological and semantic similarity. That this process of schema-formation is not restricted to the early stages of language acquisition is demonstrated by the process of **secretion** (cf. p. 130) which gradually turns non-morphemic parts of words into productive morphemes. Elements like *-aholic, -gate* or *-burger* are cases in point. What these examples also show is that schemas can start their development from few or even single but sufficiently prominent words like *alcoholic/workaholic, Watergate* and *hamburger*. The idea that grammatical knowledge is formed and stored on the basis of experience with input from language use – which casts doubt on the strictness of the venerable disctinctions between *langue* and *parole* or *competence* and *performance* respectively – is known as the **usage-based approach** (cf. Bybee 1985, 1995, 2006).

Cognitive approaches have so far not presented a genuinely new classification of word-formation types but mainly focussed on investigating how these basic insights can help us to understand the obvious flexibility and heterogeneity of morphological processes (cf. Lampert and Lampert 2010).

5.2.6 Summary

> The approaches discussed here differ with regard to essential basic assumptions and objectives. Quirk et al.'s classification represents a more traditional, descriptive approach based on the notions of stem, base and affix. Marchand's classification is more strongly influenced by grammatical considerations; the analogy between full grammatical syntagmas and shortened word-formation syntagmas takes precedence with him. Tournier rejects the prevalent focus on morphological i.e. formally visible changes, turning his attention systematically to the two sides of the linguistic sign. We could therefore describe his approach as being semiotically orientated. The onomasiological approaches discussed are characterized by a reversal of the perspective of linguistic form and mental concept. The claim that word-formation patterns are flexible and variable and serve cognitive functions, the notion of *schema* and the idea that knowledge about word-formation schemas is acquired by extracting commonalities from observed usage are hallmarks of the cognitive approach.

Further reading: A concise survey of English word-formation processes is provided by **Lieber (2005)**. Other classification systems can be found e.g. in **Algeo (1978, 1980)**, **Bauer (1988: 89 ff.)** and **Cannon (1987)**.

5.3 Questions and methods in word-formation analysis

Having surveyed the basic patterns and various ways of classifying them, we will now proceed to suggesting the contents of a toolbox which are helpful for the analysis of complex lexemes and the resultant description of word-formation patterns. As will be shown, the differences between formations and patterns can only be described adequately if we study them from various angles.

Even in early studies on English word-formation such as Koziol (1937) and Jespersen (1942), it was common practice to describe complex lexemes from two perspectives, namely according to their formal composition and their semantic structure. Marchand refines word-formation analysis considerably by explicitly suggesting a multi-level pattern for the analysis of compounds (1969: 53–59). He recommends carrying out the analysis according to morphological, semantic and syntactic considerations, with several aspects becoming apparent on each of the three levels. For example, with respect to morphology, both the morphological form and the morphological structure have to be considered. The list of analytical levels was adopted, refined and added to by Kastovsky (1982: 168–215) and notably Lipka (1983, 1994: 4–6, 13 ff.).

The trend towards a continuous broadening of the perspectives on word-formation was thus already partially developed in structuralism. As I have already explained in section 1.3, this route should be consistently pursued further, because only such a *multi-level approach* (Lipka 1983) will allow us to understand and represent the tacit knowledge that native speakers of English apparently have about the word-forming potential conventionalized in their language as well as the communicative acceptability and appropriacy of the products of word-formation processes. Our starting point is the structural perspective predominant in structuralism and the theories that build on it, such as the generative approach.

5.3.1   Structural perspective

As outlined in sections 1.3. and 4.1, the structural perspective on word-formation focusses primarily on (established) complex lexemes themselves in an attempt to derive rules for, and restrictions on, the possible ways of forming new words. What interests us here in particular are **morphological form** and **morphological structure, the underlying sentence** and **semantic structure.**

Morphological form and structure

The first and most simple level of observation, which is equally relevant to all lexemes and patterns, is concerned with the **morphological form** of the morphemes or morpheme-like constituents involved. The morphological form of free morphemes is described by indicating which word classes they belong to; bound morphemes are marked by specifying their function in the complex lexeme. Morpheme-like components are identified as *bound roots, initial combining forms* (ICF) or *final combining forms* (FCF).

The analysis of morphological form is illustrated in Figure 5.4. using examples from the MUMC. The subsequent analysis of **morphological structure** is concerned with ascertaining the immediate constituents and with allocating the functional roles of modifier (Mod) and head (H). With two-part complex lexemes, this step in the analysis proceeds more or less automatically, since the second constituent generally functions as the head while the first is usually the modifier (cf. p. 90). This level becomes more important and more interesting when we are dealing with complex lexemes consisting of more than two parts which have to be split into hierarchically arranged pairs of immediate constituents, as it is usually assumed that immediate constituents are binary.

Fig. 5.4: Illustration of the analysis on the level of morphological form
(pfx = prefix, sfx = suffix, bd. r. = bound root)

greenhouse	*unable*	*democrat*	*special*
green + house	*un + able*	*demo + crat*	*speci + al*
Adj + N	pfx + Adj	ICF + FCF	bd. r. + sfx

The two lexemes *anti-establishment* and *disclaimer* in the corpus, for instance, basically have the same morphological form of prefix + verb + suffix. However, if we compare them from the point of view of their *modifier-head* structure, we discover differences in the structure of their immediate constituents.

Fig. 5.5: Illustration of the analysis on the level of morphological structure
(Mod = modifier, H = head)

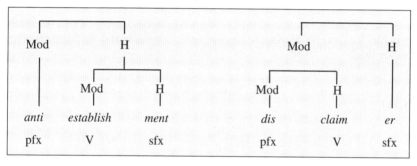

How can we establish and prove these differences (see also section 11.1)? In the case of *anti-establishment* the verb *establish* and the suffix *-ment* are the immediate constituents of the complex lexeme *establishment*, which is then the head modified by *anti-*. This structure can be determined unambiguously, since the verb **to anti-establish* does not exist and can therefore not be posited as the first constituent of a potential suffixation. The structure of *disclaimer*, however, is different. In this case only the prefix *dis-* and the verb *claim* can be plausibly labelled as immediate constituents, since the non-existent form **claimer* cannot be assumed to function as head.

Having said that, we must add that the morphological structure of many lexemes cannot be conclusively determined. For instance, in the case of the lexeme *re-establishment*, which can also be found in the corpus, both the verb *re-establish* and the noun *establishment* are institutionalized; therefore the morphological structure must remain open. In the case of the noun *disappointment* the semantic proximity of *disappointment* to the verb *disappoint* argues more in favour of the structure being analogous to that of *disclaim*, although from a purely morphological angle a prefixation of the modifier *dis-* to the head *appointment* cannot be ruled out. So-called *synthetic compounds* such as *watchmaker*, for instance, pose a specific problem in morphological structure analysis: they can neither be analyzed as compounds nor as *er*-suffixations, since the non-existent noun **maker* cannot serve as a potential head of a compound and the non-existent verb **to watchmake* does not qualify as a possible basis for suffixation (see p. 134 ff. for more details).

A space-saving alternative to the graphic display of morphological structure shown in Figure 5.5 is to use square brackets following the traditional notation of immediate-constituent analysis (or *IC-analysis*) in American structuralism. The structures shown in Figure 5.5 would then be rendered as *anti*[*establish-ment*] and [*dis-claim*]*er* respectively.

The underlying sentence

The concept of the underlying sentence in word-formation analysis moves our perspective from the morphological to the syntactic level. Here the concept that word-formations can be traced back to shortened sentences plays a role – an idea that has its roots in Marchand's syntagmatic approach and in the generative framework.[4]

The relevance of the underlying sentence for word-formation analysis can be illustrated using the two complex lexemes *day dreaming* and *song writing* from the MUMC:

(5.1) He proposes in 'Creative Writers and *Day Dreaming*' [...] that the artist and the neurotic are essentially similar ... (ICE-GB: W2a-002)

(5.2) A: I don't think that I could do it on my own, particularly
       B: Right. And it's singing and playing.
       A: Yeah but more the singing and actually more the *song writing*
       (ICE-GB: S1a-033)

Both lexemes manifest the word-formation pattern N + [V + ing]. They differ, however, with respect to their underlying sentences and, significantly, the syntactic functions which their consitituents have in these structures. The analyses are presented in Figure 5.6.

---

[4]   Marchand's concept of word-formation syntagmas being shortened sentences was inspired on the one hand by Saussure's and Bally's concept of the syntagma (cf. p. 89). On the other hand, in the second edition of his book (1969), the influence of early transformational grammar is noticeable (Chomsky 1957, 1965, Lees 1960) since nominalizations such as *meeting*, for example, are explicitly construed as transformations of complete sentences from the so-called deep structure into the surface structure (Lees 1960, Chomsky 1970).

Fig. 5.6:   Illustration of the analysis of the underlying sentence

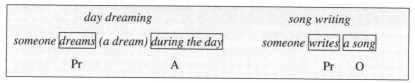

The underlying sentence behind the complex lexeme *day dreaming* consists of the constituents subject (*someone*), predicate (*dreams*), a non-obligatory object (*a dream*) and a temporal adverbial (*during the day*). In the complex lexeme, the predicate and part of the adverbial are explicitly expressed in the morphological form. *Song writing*, on the other hand, can be traced to a subject-predicate-object structure, and in this case the predicate and object are overtly realized in the complex lexeme.

The analysis of the underlying sentence proves particularly helpful when dealing with compounds and suffixations. It can be carried out and justified relatively unambiguously if the complex lexemes contain a verbal element, which usually marks the relation between the constituents and will also be posited in the underlying sentence. Where compounds do not contain a verbal element, for instance in N+N-compounds such as *wallpaper* and *police car*, a verb must always be introduced into the postulated underlying sentence. This can cause considerable difficulties, because the semantic relation remains underspecified by the morphological form. *Wallpaper*, for instance, could in principle be traced back to 'the paper is on the wall' or, equally plausibly, to 'the paper is designed to be on the wall'; *police car* could be expanded to 'the car belongs to the police', 'the car is driven by the police' or 'the car is designed to be used by the police'.

> **Further reading**: On word-formation in early transformational grammar: **Kastovsky (1982: 216–246), Bauer (1983: 140–201), Aronoff (2000)**. On the question of verbs in underlying sentences: **Kastovsky (1982: 198–209), Bauer (1983: 159–163), Hansen et al. (1990: 46–49)**.

Semantic structure

The problem mentioned above brings us to the analysis of the semantic structure of complex lexemes, which is based on the results of the analysis of the morphological form and structure as well as of the underlying sentence. This level is characterized by two steps: the identification of (a) the semantic relationships between the constituents and (b) additional semantic components that are not evident in the surface structure of the morphological form.

The semantic structure of a complex lexeme is usually described using a relative clause. *Day-dreamer*, for instance, would be paraphrased as 'someone who often dreams during the day', *wallpaper* as 'paper which is attached to the wall for ornamental purposes'. Naturally the same analytical problems occur here with non-verbal complex lexemes as in the underlying sentence analysis, since a verb has to be integrated into them. As an example of the systematic description of semantic relationships we shall take an extract from the semantic structures culled by Marchand from his data on the word-formation pattern V + N (1969: 73).

(5.3)

whetstone	'B denoting a material instrument designed for the action denoted by A'
bakehouse	'B denoting a place designed for the action denoted by A'
washday	'B denoting a point or period in time designed for the action denoted by A'
crybaby	'B denoting a person expected to perform the activity denoted by A'
drawbridge	'B denoting a thing designed to be the goal of the action denoted by A'

It is significant that Marchand only supplies such lists for complex lexemes with a verbal element; for patterns without a verbal element there is no comparable information, presumably because of the uncertainty of the semantic relationships.

As well as establishing the semantic relationship between the constituents, the semantic analysis must identify the semantic components resulting from lexicalization processes which do not appear in the morphological and syntactic analysis. In the two examples 'someone who often dreams during the day' for *day-dreamer* and 'paper which is attached to the wall for ornamental purposes' for *wallpaper* the relevant elements are *often* and *for ornamental purposes*. In structuralist approaches such semantic aspects are interpreted as so-called **semantic features** such as [HABITUAL] and [PURPOSE] (Lipka 1981: 128, Kastovsky 1982: 195–198). Since, apart from these two features, the only other recurrent one is [PROFESSIONAL], which is used to refer to nominalizations denoting professions such as *baker* or *reader* (in the sense of 'lecturer') (cf. Hansen et al. 1990: 38), the applicability of such features is restricted, in spite of their occurrence in a large number of complex lexemes. All other specific semantic features of word-formation products must be described quasi ad hoc depending on the lexeme in question. There is very little advice in the literature on how to identify them which goes beyond the established procedures of the semantic analysis of all words, including the simplexes. If we adopted a structuralist semantic theory, we would investigate these features by comparing lexemes that contrast with each other. On the basis of a cognitive-linguistic semantic approach, we would describe any additional semantic components as attributes. Ideally they should be elicited from informants by means of surveys (cf. Ungerer and Schmid 1998), although this is not normally practicable owing to the huge amount of effort required. It is therefore somewhat disillusioning that any semantic analysis of complex lexemes that goes beyond the morphological and syntactic aspects has been left largely to the intuition of individual linguists. The semantic description should in any case not be confused with the type of definition one would expect to find in a dictionary, which as a rule is not concerned with the formal components but only those pertaining to the content. In this respect, however, dictionary definitions can be an enormous help when it comes to determining additional semantic components.

5.3.2 The sociopragmatic perspective

The sociopragmatic perspective on language use is a further crucial source of help in semantic analysis. This means firstly that the communicative circumstances surrounding the use of a complex lexeme are taken into consideration, such as, for instance, the components of the communicative situation: speaker/writer and listener/reader, the situational and linguistic context, the medium (written or spoken), the text type (letter, leading article, detective story, science fiction novel), the type of interaction (job interview, panel discussion, party conversation), the role of speech in the situation (language game, meta-language) *inter alia*. Even knowledge of the cultural circumstances can play a role. Last but not least, a sociopragmatic analysis must also aim to give some indication of the degree of institutionalization of a complex lexeme, with the allocation to specific dialects, sociolects, registers (the language of sport, the language of advertising etc.) and languages for special purposes (legal language, medical language etc.) possibly being relevant factors.

While a consideration of all these factors may seem to form a natural part of linguistic description, it is definitely not a matter of course, since – as explained in section 1.3 – morphology and word-formation were dominated for a long time by structuralist and generative conceptions of language, which deliberately excluded pragmatic aspects from the study of language. However, early appeals for the integration of pragmatics into word-formation came from Downing (1977), Bauer (1979), Clark and Clark (1979) and Lipka (1981).

A central question to be asked from a pragmatic perspective concerns the **function** of the actual usage of a complex lexeme (Lipka 1983: 928; 1987; 2000: 7 ff.). As already mentioned (cf. p. 73), complex lexemes with a lexical function have to be distinguished from those with a syntactic function. While the purpose of lexemes with a lexical function is typically to name something, lexemes with a syntactic function are used for brevity. Products of the first type belong to the lexicon, while those of the second are part of the grammar (Hansen 1999: 85). Examples of complex lexemes with a syntactic function, e.g. *50-minute* and *American-supplied* from text (4.1), have already been discussed in the context of establishment (p. 73).

Furthermore, complex lexemes with a syntactic function often serve to refer back to something that has already been mentioned and have therefore been credited with the function of pronominalization (Kastovsky 1978: 362 ff., 1986: 595 ff., Lipka 1987: 63 ff.). They are therefore relevant not only in the traditional sentence-based grammar but also in a so-called *transphrastic*, i.e. text-based, treatment. As is illustrated by the use of *song writing* in example (5.2) (see p. 98), a secondary effect of these anaphoric reiterations is that they contribute to the coherence of the text.

Lexemes with a lexical naming function also serve the purpose of abbreviation in that that they condense information. A large amount of semantic content is encoded in relatively little linguistic material, which is particularly remarkable when complex lexemes are highly lexicalized. We can illustrate this using the already mentioned lexeme *boatpeople*, which expresses the complex meaning 'people who escape from bad conditions in their country in small boats' (LDOCE4) with only two morphemes. On the other hand, the products of word-formation, in particular unusual ad-hoc formations, can also be used in advertising or in newspaper headlines to attract the attention of the reader (Lipka 2000: 7).

In spoken language, which can draw information from the situational context, complex lexemes can also have a pointing function, which in a broader sense could be called **deictic**. To illustrate this, Downing (1977) refers to the example *apple juice seat*, an expression which was used in a specific situation to designate a place at a table at which a glass of apple juice had been set. Depending on the situation, even established lexemes can be used in deictic function with a meaning which differs from the lexicalized one. The compound *wine glass*, for example, which actually describes a glass of a particular type (made in a characteristic shape from relatively thin glass with a stem), can also be used when sitting at the table for a completely different type of glass that happens to contain wine (*can you pass me my wine glass?*). In the second case it serves a pointing function, since it refers to an object – marked *inter alia* by the possessive determiner *my* – that is present in that situation.

Coinings and other uses of complex lexemes can also be said to have interpersonal, social and expressive functions. For instance, the use of complex lexemes that are only institutionalized in parts of the speech community (specialist terminology or professional jargon) signals group membership and identity when used by insiders, but can also function as an exclusion mechanism against outsiders. Good illustrations include the many international abbreviations and acronyms in IT and telecommunications jargon such as *ISDN* (*integrated services digital network*), *DSL* (*digital subscriber line*) and *POP* (*post office protocol*), which cannot be deciphered by non-specialists. This does not just concern the question of whether one can utilize a certain complex lexeme appropriately or at least understand it, but it also manifests itself in striking clusters of particular word-formation types. Formal, academic and specialist texts with an abstract content, for instance, are typically characterized by an above average number of suffixations, particularly nominalizations. Speakers who adopt a style of this nature outside the appropriate text type can sound aloof and schoolmasterish. The non-morphemic processes of clipping and blending as well as many suffixations, e.g. those ending in *-ie* (*aerobie, archie, foodie, fundie, techie*; cf. Schneider 2003), on the other hand, have an expressive function.

5.3.3   The cognitive perspective

Our interest from the cognitive perspective – over and above what was said in section 5.2.5 – centres around questions about the cognitive process of concept-formation, the cognitive functions of word-formation and word-formation patterns, and the mechanisms for profiling concepts in complex lexemes. Since these questions are the subject of discussion in the chapters on individual word-formation patterns, we are only concerned here with laying the foundation for later implementations.

Concept-formation

The cognitive perspective has to provide information about concept-formation, i.e. about the degree of entrenchment reached by the concept underlying a complex lexeme. As this has already been addressed in chapter 4, I will restrict myself to the essentials at this point. The questions that have to be answered here are the following: Are the speakers of a language (still) aware of the semantic and formal relationship with the constituents or has the concept already been completely emancipated and become an autonomous element? Have elements been added to the conceptual structure which were not latent in the structures of the constituents? Can cognitive transfer processes such as metaphor and metonymy be observed superseding the connection between the new concept and the constituents (cf. Lipka 1994: 6–13)? Questions of this nature can be answered empirically at least to some extent using the method of attribute listing with informants (Ungerer and Schmid 1998) mentioned above (see p. 80).

Cognitive functions

A cognitive-linguistic approach must also investigate the cognitive functions of the various word-formation patterns. The term **cognitive function** highlights the notion that linguistic structures may be the result of, and have effects on, general cognitive processes such as categorization and concept-formation, perception, attention allocation, memory and problem solving. The background to this idea is the assumption advocated by cognitive linguistics that language structure and use basically follow the same underlying principles as these non-linguistic cognitive abilities. The investigation of such cognitive functions is particularly worthwhile for linguistic structures which are found in many languages or are even universal, because it is possible that structures are universal for the very reason that they serve basic cognitive functions. Evidence of the existence of certain cognitive functions must be adduced by systematic linguistic observation and interpretation and should, equally importantly, be supported by the quantitative evaluation of linguistic phenomena. It is therefore more convincing to ascribe cognitive functions to frequently occurring and thus presumably entrenched linguistic phenomena rather than to those which occur rarely, since their frequency is interpreted as a sign of their cognitive utility.

Potential cognitive functions of word-formation as such lie first and foremost in the field of concept-formation, but attention allocation also plays an important role, as will be shown below in the discussion of profiling. With regard to the individual patterns, the concept-combining patterns of compounding and blending should be kept separate from the concept-modifying pattern of prefixation. Suffixation, conversion and back-formation can be subsumed under the common function of conceptual re-categorization and re-profiling. Each of the chapters on morphemic word-formation patterns will include a section dealing with the specific cognitive functions that can be attributed to the patterns.

Profiling

The remaining issues to be investigated from the cognitive perspective can be summarized under the keyword **profiling**. In cognitive linguistics this term refers to the idea that the structures of linguistic constructions shed light on how speakers conceptualize a situation with respect to the prominence of the participants. One crucial indicator of this is the order of the constituents in a construction. It is clearly no coincidence that in sentences describing concrete human actions (e.g. *John cut the cake into pieces*), the position of the subject is typically occupied by the person or persons performing the action, since the energy that causes the action proceeds from them, so they play a prominent role. One can envisage these profiling processes as if they were linguistic spotlights directed at different actors on a stage or as if the camera were being used for close-ups and panning shots in a film.

The fundamental psychological principle behind profiling is the gestalt-psychological principle of **figure and ground** which is involved, for example, in perception when we look at an object or a person against some more or less nondescript background or listen to a solo instrument standing out as a figure from the background of the accompanying orchestra. In each case, the figure will attract our attention, while the ground is perceived less distinctly and consciously. Since, as we have seen, cognitive linguistics proceeds from the assumption that fundamental cognitive abilities such as perception and attention allocation also manifest themselves and are reflected in linguistic structures, its advocates have transferred the principle of figure and ground to the analysis of linguistic structures.

When applied to the special case of word-formation, we can distinguish three stages of profiling, which I will call **conceptual profiling**, **internal figure-ground profiling** and **concept-type profiling**.

Conceptual profiling: The idea behind this kind of profiling is that concepts are highlighted by the very fact that they are explicitly encoded by morphemes. The morphemes that constitute a complex morpheme are perceived as profiled figures, while the ground is provided by the mental image or representation of a situation or state of affairs, which the speaker has in mind and wants the hearer to activate. I will refer to this idea as a **scene** and define this term as a mental representation of a concrete situation (e.g. 'someone is cutting a cake into pieces') or an abstract state of affairs (e.g. 'environmental awareness is increasing'). In the literature, the terms *frame*, *schema* and *scenario* are often encountered to describe similar notions.

While each envisaged scene has its own specific protagonists, props and abstract components, linguistic descriptions have to abstract from individual scenes and work with generalizations. On a fairly high level of abstraction, scenes can be described by means of the so-called **semantic roles** of their components and the relationship between them. These include the following:

- AGENT: Who carries out an action?
- INSTRUMENT: By what means is an action carried out by an AGENT?
- EXPERIENCER: Who is engaged in a mental process?
- EXPERIENCED: What is the subject of a mental process?
- PATIENT: Who is affected by an action?
- OBJECT: Who or what is involved in some other way?
- LOCATION: Where does an event or an action take place?
- TIME: When does an event or an action take place?

These roles originally date back to Fillmore's case grammar (1968), which at that time was conceived as an approach to syntax. As has gradually transpired in Fillmore's later articles (1977, 1985), these roles are not of a syntactic nature, however, nor, strictly speaking, are they semantic, but cognitive (cf. Langacker 1991: 284 ff.). Like schemas (p. 94), they represent, as it were, extracts from human experiences, gained from observing what goes on in the world around us. In this respect semantic roles are at the same time the results of earlier cognitive processes and tools that help us both cognitively and linguistically to cope with new situations.

As already mentioned, scenes serve as ground in concept profiling. The noun *daydream*, for example, represents a figure in a daydreaming scene, which includes the semantic roles of EXPERIENCER (someone who daydreams), EXPERI-

ENCED (the dreams dreamt) and TIME (during the day). By virtue of the encoded component *day* and *dream* the noun profiles, i.e. highlights, the roles TIME (*day*) and EXPERIENCED (*dream*); the role of the EXPERIENCER, i.e. the daydreaming person, remains backgrounded, as it is not encoded on the morphological surface. The noun *daydreamer*, in contrast, profiles the role TIME (*day*) and EXPERIENCER (*dreamer*), while relegating the role EXPERIENCED to the background. That these roles are indeed profiled becomes particularly obvious when we consider other aspects of the daydream scene which could also be highlighted. For instance, the fact that the dreaming is done without being asleep and with open eyes is not profiled by the complex lexemes that are under consideration here, since they are not encoded. These aspects would be profiled in the potential, but uncommon complex lexemes *sleepless dreaming* and *open-eye dreaming*. The two competing lexemes *cell phone* (from *cellular phone*) and *mobile phone*, which are now typically used in the USA and Britain respectively, originally profiled different aspects of mobile telephoning. *Cell phone* puts the emphasis on the technical aspect that when transmitting mobile phone signals the areas receiving the signal are divided into sections called *cells* (OED, s.v. *cellular*), while *mobile phone* underlines the more practical aspect of the possibility of being able to move around freely while telephoning. A good German example of the profiling of a potentially available but usually not profiled component of a scene is the word *Blasharmonika* (lit. 'blow organ'), which my son coined on the spur of the moment when he was lost for the established word *Mundharmonika* ('mouth organ'). While *Mundharmonika* profiles the place of the instrument in the scene of mouth-organ playing, in the case of *Blasharmonika* the blowing component of the activity is highlighted, which is in principle just as plausible but is simply not institutionalized.

Internal figure-ground profiling: The second form of profiling concerns the order and arrangement of morphemes in a complex lexeme. As a forerunner of this profiling type can be found in the concept of *topicalization* in structuralist word-formation theory (Kastovsky 1982: 192), I will use this concept as a starting point for explaining internal figure-ground profiling.

Marchand already pointed out that the syntactically motivated distinction between *modifier* and *head* is superseded, or complemented, by a second perspective related to the communicative prominence of the constituents of complex lexemes (Marchand 1969: 32 ff.; cf. also Kastovsky 1982: 192, Lipka 2002: 105 ff.). The inspiration behind these considerations is again the structure of full sentences, though in this case it is not the syntactic structure, but the structure in terms of information distribution. Since the emergence of the so-called Prague School it has been well known that sentences normally lead from known or given information, the so-called *theme*, to new information, the *rheme*. The answer *He is cutting the cake into pieces* to the question *What's John doing?* takes up the given information (*John*) with the pronoun *he* and then adds the new information *is cutting the cake into pieces*. An analogous structure can be ascribed to word-formation syntagmas as well, with the head assuming the role of the 'given', or rather what is represented as given, information (theme), and the modifier the role of the rheme. The distribution within a complex lexeme is referred to as **topicalization**.

This insight can be transferred to the concept of profiling, but then it is the relative potential of the constituents to attract attention that is relevant rather than the relative status of the information content. The transfer to the cognitive perspective reflects the realization that attention allocation is not a genuinely linguistic phenomenon but a manifestation of a general cognitive principle which is also at work in other cognitive fields such as perception and memory. From this perspective the modifier is to be understood as the prominent figure and the head as the ground. While the head establishes the conceptual relationship to the underlying scene, the modifier highlights the figure for special attention. In the compound *daydream*, for example, the concept DAY is profiled to stand out from the ground of the expectations associated with the concept DREAM. What is portrayed by this compound as being really remarkable is that the 'dream' is dreamt in broad daylight. In *mobile phone* and *cell phone* the constituent *phone* functioning as head activates the scene of telephoning, while *mobile* and *cell* profile the aspects mentioned above. Essentially, then, conceptual profiling and internal figure-ground profiling are two zooming-in steps which direct attention by means of encoding: the morphemes encoded on the linguistic surface activate a scene and highlight certain components for attention (conceptual profiling); the arrangement of the encoded morphemes in terms of modifier and head gives particular prominence to one component while backgrounding the other.

The different cognitive prominence given to the two constituents is also reflected in the typical stress patterns of determinative compounds, which generally carry the main stress on the modifier (see pp. 121 and 133). As is well-known, a similar correlation between phonological and cognitive prominence can be detected in sentences where in the unmarked case the main stress coincides with the new information (cf. Quirk et al. 1985: 1361–1364).

Concept-type profiling: The third type of profiling is concerned with the nature of the concept that is expressed by the head and therefore also determines the whole complex lexeme. For reasons that will be explained below, the word class of the *head* is decisive in this.

In the framework known as **cognitive grammar**, word classes are understood to be the result of different profiling processes of cognitive units (Langacker 1987b). As an example, let us imagine a train pulling into the station. In linguistic encoding, this scene can be profiled in various ways. The verb *arrive* (*the train is arriving*) profiles the temporal extension of the event and the changes that occur from one moment to the next; one sees the train coming in one's mind's eye, as in a film. The suffixed noun *arrival* (*the train's arrival*), on the other hand, regards the event as *one* conceptual unit and profiles this, as Langacker (1987a: 248) says, as a **thing**. The event appears to be frozen as in a photo and as a result acquires a kind of atemporality more characteristic of objects than events, which always extend over a period of time.

According to Langacker, verbs suggest a time-related, sequential perception and conceptualization, and profile changes and relationships between elements. In the process of watching the train arrive we constantly scan the position of the train vis-à-vis, for example, the platform or people standing there. Accordingly, verbs typically encode action, event and process concepts, while nouns reflect the time-independent summary perspective on a scene and profile cognitive units as *things* or *regions*. In short, verbs typically profile scenes as dynamic action and event concepts, while nouns profile scenes as stative thing or 'region' concepts, which also include persons, animals and abstract ideas. These are the categories which I will refer to as **concept types**.

Now since, as we have seen, the word classes of complex lexemes are determined by the head constituent, it is also the head that determines the concept type of the whole complex lexeme. Concept-type profiling is naturally most noticeable in suffixation, where the suffix added determines, and thus changes, the word class. As will be shown in more detail in section 8.2, suffixes can, for instance, cause the re-profiling of (a) an event concept as an abstract concept (e.g. *starve – starvation* 'the act/state of starving/being starved'), (b) an event concept as an abstract modality concept (*detect – detectable* 's.th. that can/is likely to be detected') or (c) an object concept as a quantity concept (*tear – tearful* 's.th. that is full of tears/that causes many tears').

> **Further reading**: On cognitive grammar: **Langacker (2008)**. On word classes in cognitive grammar and profiling: **Langacker (1987b), Ungerer and Schmid (2006: 194–198)**.

5.3.4   Summary

The following checklist gives a summary of the questions and methods in word-formation analysis:

1. Structural perspective

- **Morphological form**: Which morphemes or morpheme-like constituents can the lexeme be broken down into and which morpheme types and word classes do they represent?
- **Morphological structure**: What is the modifier-head structure of the lexeme?
- **Underlying sentence**: Which sentence can the lexeme be traced back to and which of its constituents have found their way into the complex lexeme?

- **Semantic structure**: What is the semantic relationship between the constituents of the lexeme and how high is the degree of lexicalization? In other words, does the lexeme contain additional semantic components that are not derivable from the morphological and syntactic structures?

2. Sociopragmatic perspective
- **Context**: What are the communicative, sociolinguistic and cultural circumstances for the use of the lexeme?
- **Diffusion**: How widespread is the lexeme and how high is the degree of institutionalization?
- **Function**: Which functions does the lexeme fulfil in its actual use?

3. Cognitive perspective
- **Concept-formation**: How far have concept-formation and entrenchment progressed?
- **Cognitive functions**: Which cognitive functions does the lexeme or pattern fulfil?
- **Concept-profiling**: Which aspects of the underlying scene are profiled by the morphemes encoded in the complex lexeme?
- **Internal figure-ground profiling**: What is the configuration of the concepts and what is profiled as figure and ground respectively?
- **Concept-type profiling**: Which concept-type is profiled by the head of the lexeme?

6   Productivity

Not all the lexemes that can be analyzed structurally using the questions outlined in chapter 5 can serve as patterns for new formations, since word-formation patterns – just like words – can age and fall into disuse. Lexemes such as *growth*, *health*, *truth* and *warmth*, for example, without doubt reveal a pattern, but we know that no new lexemes have been formed according to this pattern for a long time. This pattern is therefore said to be no longer productive. In this chapter I will deal with questions concerning the relationship between productivity and word-formation patterns.

6.1   The productivity of word-formation patterns and elements

The following list shows all suffixations with the suffix *-ment* in the corpus of about 41,000 words, on which this book is based (see section 1.4):

(6.1)

accompaniment	*disappointment*	*pavement*
advancement	*displacement*	*re-establishment*
agreement	*embarrassment*	*replacement*
anti-establishment	*employment*	*resettlement*
appointment	*entailment*	*retirement*
assessment	*entertainment*	*retrenchment*
attachment	*equipment*	*settlement*
bereavement	*excitement*	*statement*
commencement	*government*	*treatment*
deployment	*impeachment*	*wish-fulfilment*
development	*investment*	
dinner engagement	*management*	

All these nouns sound more or less familiar and appear at first glance to be institutionalized, as can be confirmed by consulting the LDOCE4, an up-to-date learners' dictionary, in which all the lexemes in (6.1) can be found. It is not difficult to see that the lexemes in (6.1) have all been formed according to the same word-formation pattern V + *-ment* which, according to the argumentation at the end of the last chapter, leads one to the conclusion that competent speakers of English should be capable of creating new lexemes of the same type based on this model. This does not seem to be the case, however. In his analysis of a well-known dictionary of neologisms, the *Dictionary of New English* by Barnhart, Steinmetz and Barnhart (1973) published in the 1970s, Bauer (1983: 55) observed that during the relevant period only one fairly dubious new entry exists for this pattern, namely the lexeme *Englishment* (which does not even have a verb for a base). He concludes from this observation that the suffix *-ment* is either obsolete or at least dying out and hence no longer *productive*, meaning that the suffix *-ment* or rather the word-formation model V + *-ment* is no longer used systematically to form new words. Support for Bauer's claim can be found in more recent dictionaries of neologisms, e.g. the *Oxford Dictionary of New Words* (Knowles 1997), in which there is not a single lexeme formed according to this model.

In contrast to *-ment*, the suffix *-able* is rated as being highly productive by Bauer (1988: 60) in its function of deriving adjectives from transitive verbs. How can we verify this assertion? Firstly, by having another look at Knowles (1997), which does indeed register two adjectives in computer language, which were coined according to the word-formation model V + *-able* in the early 1990s: *bootable* ('of a computer: capable of being started up by loading its operating system into its working memory; of a disk: containing the software necessary to carry out this process') and *scrollable* ('relating to text or images on a computer screen which can be moved to bring other parts of them into view'). A second type of test again resorts to the material collected in up-to-date corpora, where one would expect to find new formations according to the model V + *-able* as opposed to V + *-ment*, if the V + *-able* model were in fact still productive today. But how can such 'new' formations be discovered and how can we prove that they really are new? A promising solution to this problem has been suggested by researchers who specialize in studying word-formation using corpora (e.g. Baayen and Lieber 1991, Plag 1999: 23–35, Plag et al. 1999, Schröder 2008). This approach is based on the assumption that even in large corpora new words are not documented several times but only occur once, for the very reason that they are not yet institutionalized. Such single occurrences are traditionally called *hapax legomena* (from the Greek 'spoken once'). However, not all instances of *hapax legomena* in a corpus have to be, or are, new words, since experience has shown that in large corpora about half of all types are only instantiated by one token. What we are generally dealing with here, then, is not new words but words that are rarely used. In order to establish whether a suspect *hapax legomenon* is in fact a new formation rather than a rarity, we must carry out a countercheck. There are three suitable sources to enable us to run this test, the first of which is a dictionary which is as comprehensive and up-to-date as possible, ideally the online version of the OED. If a case in point is contained in the corpus but not registered in the OED, then we can assume that it is a new, or at least a very recent, formation. Secondly, we could theoretically dispense with the dictionary test if the corpus used was so extensive that we could expect all the lexemes that are already institutionalized to occur several times in it. However, despite its considerable size of 100 million words, even the *British National Corpus* fails to fulfil this criterion, which means that the test using the OED still seems preferable. The third method is to make use of the well-established search engines on the internet in order to find out whether a hypothetical *hapax legomenon* has been used in this enormous electronic 'corpus' or not (Mühleisen 2010).

With regard to the suffix *-able*, despite the relatively small number of words in the MUMC, even this corpus contains two lexemes created in accordance with the model V + *-able*, which only occur once and are not documented in the LDOCE4 or in the OED.

(6.2) The censorious ego uses these narrative paths, based on association, to bestow acceptable formulation on the basically unknowable and *unformulable* latent dream thoughts. (ICE-GB: W2a-002 028)

(6.3) Frankenstein's monster is capable of behaviour that is autonomous and not always predictable or *imitatable* by the builder or by the experts on the design-standards committee of his professional association. (ICE-GB: W2a-035 074)

A Google search (on 24 September 2010) yielded 329 and 476 displayed (rather than estimated) hits for the searches *unformulable* and *imitatable* respectively, which means that the frequency of occurrence of these lexemes on the internet is relatively low. For comparison, the lexeme *unknowable* in (6.2) used by Chaucer in the 14th century (OED s.v. *unknowable*), which seems equally unusual, has an estimated hit quota on Google of about 794,000 websites. As regards the words *unformulable* and *imitatable* we are therefore at least dealing with very young formations according to the model V + *-able*. These findings illustrate that the combined application of corpora, the OED and the internet offers a seemingly adequate method for testing the present productivity of word-formation patterns and elements. Comparing the number of already institutionalized lexemes which are formed according to a particular model with the number of *hapax legomena* even allows assertions to be made about the extent of productivity and/or the comparison of productivity of competing patterns (Plag 1999: chs. 5–8, Bauer 2001: 143 ff.).

There is a limitation, however, that should always be kept in the back of one's mind. Since even very comprehensive dictionaries only want to register more or less institutionalized lexemes with a naming function, it is possible that complex lexemes that only occur once in a corpus are not registered in the OED for the simple reason that they predominantly have a syntactic or deictic function (see pp. 73 and 101). This is likely to be the case for those word-formation models whose products are mainly motivated syntactically rather than lexically. The currently fashionable model N + *-wise* (*jobwise*, *costwise*), for example, which has been investigated by Lenker (2002), is used above all in the formation of sentence adverbs, which have the function of placing the content of a sentence in a particular context or to illuminate it from a certain perspective. The frequency of *hapax legomena* observed by Lenker could be attributed to the fact that in each case lexemes formed according to this pattern serve context-dependent syntactic purposes and not the naming of a recurring circumstance.

Researchers have therefore tried to reduce the dependence on dictionaries. In one recent attempt to investigate the productivity of verbs prefixed by *over-*, *under-*, *up-* and *down-* (Schröder 2008, Schröder and Mühleisen 2010: 46–50), language users were asked to rate the acceptability of new words found by means of the corpus-cum-dictionary method to reveal the productivity of word-formation patterns. In addition, test participants were asked to produce words following the patterns which they believed to be new, and to provide plausible definitions of their meanings. This was done by means of online questionnaires run on the internet. In a second study on suffixations by *-ee* (cf. Mühleisen 2010, Schröder and Mühleisen 2010: 50–55), 1,000 potential candidates like *blamee* or *buchteree*, which were not found in dictionaries, were coined and then systematically queried on the internet. Of these 1,000 presumably new words, a staggering 748 were found on the Web with frequencies of occurrence ranging from 1 to more than 100. This method does not only contribute to investigating the degree of the current productivity of a given pattern but also supplies information on the typical properties of the words formed according to the pattern and the restrictions governing the formation of new words (cf. section 6.2).

What these studies also demonstrate is that from a sociopragmatic viewpoint the productivity of individual prefixation, suffixation and compounding patterns is, to a considerable degree, dependent on the medium and register. Plag et al. (1999) show, for example, that the suffixes *-able* and *-ish* are more productive in the spoken medium than the suffixes *-ness* and *-ize*, which for their part are more frequently used in coinings in writing. Baayen (1994) even plausibly maintains that texts can be classified on the basis of the productivity of specific derivational affixes. A second essential factor for the extent of the productivity of patterns is the type of everyday domain in which coinings arise. In this respect an analysis of the entries in Knowles (1997) offers illuminating information, since they are marked for the subject areas from which the new lexemes originate. While compounding is similarly productive in all subject areas, in the case of suffixation the field of computers stands out with an abundant use of the suffixes *-able*, *-ability* and *-er*, politics with *-ite*, *-ism* and *-ity* and mankind and society with *-er*, *-ing* and *-ism*. Particularly productive prefixes and combining forms are found in the areas of computers (*cyber-*, *inter-*, *super-*), the environment (*bio-*, *super-*), health and fitness (*pre-*, *semi-*, *super-*) and the natural sciences and technology (*bio-*, *chemo-*, *super-*, *trans-*). As expected, abbreviations and blends are found to be productive above all in the domains of the arts and music, as well as in pop-culture, computers, and lifestyle and leisure, whereas acronyms find the most fertile soil in the fields of computers, business, science and health.

The previous considerations have shown that productivity is not a dichotomous phenomenon (i.e. productive versus non-productive), but a scalar one (cf. Schröder and Mühleisen 2010). Productivity must be regarded as a continuum ranging from non-productive (or no longer so) to highly productive, with the upper end of the scale being undefinable. Theoretically, a maximum degree of productivity could be postulated for a pattern, if all of its conceivable realizations were at least potentially acceptable lexemes. This does not apply to any pattern, however, since they are all subject to so-called productivity limitations which prevent the coining of individual lexemes. We will deal with these restrictions in the next section, but firstly let me briefly explain the concept of the potential complex lexeme, something which has already been attempted many times.

6.2 Potential lexemes and restrictions on productivity

Potential or **possible complex lexemes** are lexemes that can be formed by regular application of a productive word-formation pattern. To illustrate this, let us invent the word *lexicologize* with the meaning 'to put in a lexicological perspective' (e.g. *he must always lexicologize everything*). In contrast to this formation, the deverbal adjectives **beable* and **resemblable* are of course *conceivable* lexemes, but not *potential* lexemes, since they break the 'rule' that the model V + *-able* is only applicable to verbs with a transitive base. (An interesting exception is *liveable*.)

The vast majority of established complex lexemes are derived from potential lexemes. Exceptions are idiosyncratic actual lexemes that were never potential lexemes as they do not follow word-formation patterns (e.g. *knowledg(e)able*; Plag 2003: 47) and coinings such as *Kodak* and *Teflon* (see p. 69) which neither originate from available morphological material nor utilize regular word-formation patterns; somewhat paradoxically, the latter are **actual words** without ever having been **potential words**. For this reason they are not regarded as a consequence of productivity, but of language **creativity** (cf. e.g. Farmer 1983: 63 ff., Lipka 2002: 108).

The set of potential complex lexemes in a language is limited by a series of factors described as **restrictions on productivity**. Cognitively speaking, this means that native speakers seem to have stored knowledge about degrees and potential limitations of the acceptability of new formations in the speech community. Three types of restrictions on productivity can be distinguished. These will be discussed next according to the following overview ranging from general to specific:

1. Pragmatic and cognitive restrictions on productivity

- existence of referents
- exclusion of the naming of the self-evident
- nameability

2. General structural restrictions on productivity

- blocking by synonym (including competition of word-formation patterns) and blocking by homonym
- etymological restrictions
- haplology

3. Word-formation model-specific restrictions on productivity

- phonological restrictions
- morphological restrictions
- semantic restrictions

6.2.1 Pragmatic and cognitive restrictions on productivity

Essentially, three types of pragmatic and cognitive restrictions on productivity are postulated in the relevant literature: firstly, it is claimed that a reasonable referent must exist in the real or a possible world for a formation to occur, making the coining of words such as *champagne warmer* or *carpet opener* highly improbable (cf. e.g. Kastovsky 1982: 159); secondly, the formation of complex lexemes is highly restricted when it comes to naming the self-evident (*eyed man*, *motorized car*); thirdly, complex lexemes are supposed to describe something nameable. According to Rose (quoted from Bauer 1983: 86) it is improbable, for example, that there would ever be the need for a denominal verb meaning 'grasp NOUN in the left hand and shake vigorously while standing on the right foot in a 2½ gallon galvanized pail of corn-meal mush'. In my opinion all three types of restriction are not very helpful, not so much because they appear trivial but because they are unsystematic and therefore only serve as ad-hoc explanations for gaps in otherwise productive word-formation patterns. Furthermore – as Kastovsky also notes (1982: 160) – with little imagination contexts can be constructed, for instance in science fiction novels or jokes, in which a need could arise for words that are excluded by these restrictions. Rather than this being an issue of genuine restrictions, it is more a matter of the basic principles that are normally adhered to by speakers of a language during word-formation.

6.2.2 General structural restrictions on productivity

The same is true for one of the two most important general structural restrictions, called **blocking**. This term refers to the phenomenon that potential complex lexemes are not created because actual lexemes (either simple or complex) exist which either denote the intended referent or have the same form conventionally associated with another meaning. The first case, blocking by a competing synonym, prevents, for example, formations such as *stealer (due to the existence of *thief*), **studier* (*student*) and **raper* (*rapist*; cf. Bauer 1988: 66). A special form of blocking by a synonym is the competition between two word-formation patterns, for example, between the suffixations *-ize* and *-ify*, discussed by Plag (1999: chs. 6 and 7). The second case, blocking by a competing homonym, can be illustrated in German by the word *Bauer* (derived from the verb *bauen* 'to build' and meaning 'someone who builds'), which is blocked by *Bauer* (the established word for 'farmer'), or in English by *liver* ('someone who lives') which is blocked by *liver* ('an organ of the body'). It is interesting that *Bauer* meaning 'builder' in German does occur in synthetic compounds such as *Häuslebauer* (lit. 'someone who builds (little) houses', lexicalized as 'low or middle income person having managed to buy or build a house, often by means of contributing their own manual labour', typically used in south-western dialects of German and/or to refer to people from that region).

The second general structural restriction to be broached here has a more systematic character. It concerns the possibilities for combining bases and affixes of Germanic and Romance, i.e. Latin or French, origin. A relatively up-to-date version of the underlying rule has been suggested by Plag (1999: 58): "Bases and affixes may combine only if their etymological features are compatible". This does not simply mean that Germanic and Romance elements cannot be linked, however. With regard to suffixes, according to Plag there are three different types: those derived from Latin, which are almost exclusively only juxtaposed with bases of Romance origin (*-ive*, adjective-forming *-al*, *-ity*, *-cy* and *-ize*); those that can be attached to both Germanic and Romance stems, which, with the exception of *-ment* and *-able*, are all of Germanic origin (e.g. *-ful*, *-less*, *-ness*); and finally a single Germanic suffix, *-en*, which only links to Germanic bases. Complex lexemes which, like suffixations of the second type, combine Germanic and Romance material – e.g. *readable* (Germ. + Lat.), *doubtless* (Lat. + Germ.) or *gentleman* (Fr. + Germ.) – are traditionally termed **hybrid combinations**.

Any further general structural restrictions on productivity tend to be rather theory-dependent (cf. Plag 1999: 45–61), so I will only mention one here: **haplology** or **consonance avoidance**, which means the avoidance of formations that would lead to the repetition of identical or very similar sound sequences. For example, it is very unusual for an adverb to be formed according to the model Adj. + *-ly* if the adjective already ends in *-ly*, such as *elderly*, *miserly* or *worldly* (Bauer 1983: 89). An exception is *surlily*. David Lodge plays with this productivity restriction in his novel *Therapy*:

> Gingerly I got to my feet. (Should that be 'gingerlyly'? No, I've just looked it up, adjective and adverb both have the same form.)

In German the result of consonance avoidance can be seen in words such as *Zauberin* (instead of **Zaubererin*).

6.2.3 Pattern-specific restrictions on productivity

In the area of phonology in particular, it is difficult to distinguish general restrictions on productivity from those that only relate to individual word-formation patterns. It is debatable, for example, whether forms such as *fishish or *bitchish are avoided because of the danger of consonance, or whether it is in the nature of the word-formation model N + -ish that the base may not end in /ʃ/ or /tʃ/ (exception: churchish). The observation that verbs ending in -en are not derived from bases that end in vowels (*dryen, *slowen; Kastovsky 1982: 161) is relatively clearly established as a pattern-specific restriction. Equally pattern-specific is the fact that the otherwise productive suffix -ful cannot be attached to nouns that end in a labiodental fricative: *loveful, *griefful, *leafful, in contrast to loveless, grief-less, leafless (Gussmann and Szymanek 2000: 433). Only verbs that are stressed on the last syllable allow suffixation with -al, cf. refuse – refusal, consider – *consideral (Bauer 1994: 3356).

A model-specific morphological restriction has been described inter alia by Aronoff (1976: 53 ff.), who showed that the adjective-forming suffix -al can only be attached to nouns ending in -ment, if -ment itself is not a suffix but part of a morpheme. This restriction explains why ornamental is allowed, whereas *employmental is unacceptable. An exception is the adjective developmental. Other cases of pattern-specific morphological restrictions affect the nominalizing pattern Adj. + -ity and the adjective-forming pattern N + -ful. The former is not applicable to bases that end in -ory (*satisfactority) and the latter does not function with derived nouns as the base (Kastovsky 1982: 161, Plag 1999: 42 and ch. 4). Exceptions exist for these restrictions as well, such as meaningful and truthful, which will no doubt confirm the impression the reader will by now have that very few productivity restrictions truly possess the characteristic of being incontrovertible rules.

Word-formation patterns can also be subject to semantic restrictions. The fact that adjectives ending in -able are only created from transitive verbs has already been stated. However, this is not entirely correct, since it is probably not the property of transitivity – traditionally seen as being syntactic in nature – that is the deciding factor, but a more fundamental, semantic quality of these verbs, whose precise description is pending (Plag 1999: 42). Semantic restrictions are not always unambiguously separable from pragmatic restrictions. The nature of the restriction that reversative prefixations using un- (as in undress, unfold or unscrew) only function with verb bases that designate a reversible process is indeed arguable. Deciding on whether *unswim and *unkill, for example, are unacceptable for semantic or pragmatic reasons depends ultimately on how we define the scope of these two perspectives (Rainer 2000: 881 f.).

A number of publications have addressed the problem of how to identify and formulate general restrictions concerning the ordering and combining of several affixes (Stein 2009). A case in point are the suffixes *-ion* and *-al*, which occur in that order in words like *sensational*, but in reverse order in *colonialization* (cf. Hay and Plag 2004). Factors that have been shown to play a role here include the phonological, morphological and semantic properties of the suffixes (and bases) as well as their etymology and frequency of occurrence. In addition, the degree to which a suffix has already merged with the base plays a role, which seems to reflect the fact that lexicalized suffixations are processed holistically (cf. Hay 2002, Plag and Baayen 2009). Zirkel (2010) investigates the combinability restrictions for sequences of prefixes and finds further evidence for such processing constraints.

6.3   Summary and sociopragmatic outlook

Two major aspects relating to productivity have been addressed in this chapter. The first concerned the methods that are available to investigate the current productivity of word-formation patterns. Here the identification of hapax legomena and very recent neologisms plays a crucial role. Corpus analyses supplemented by dictionary counterchecks, elicitation tasks and systematic investigations of the material available on the internet have proved useful.

With regard to productivity restrictions, we can conclude that the reasons for gaps in principally productive word-formation patterns have not been definitively clarified, despite decades of research. The fact that most restrictions on productivity have exceptions shows how flexible, and correspondingly elusive, English appears to be in this respect (cf. Mühleisen 2010).

This finding can be best explained from a sociopragmatic perspective: it is clearly not the case that speakers always adhere to the 'rules' of word-formation and productivity restrictions. Plank (1981: 181 ff.) and Clark (1981) have already pointed out, for instance, that blocking is frequently overridden when the speaker desperately tries to find the right word and in the speech of children (see also Plag 1999: 52, 2003: 65). The same can be observed in advertising and the press where restrictions on productivity are often breached in order to gain attention. Furthermore, the existence of idiosyncratic formations, such as the above-mentioned adjective *knowledgeable*, demonstrates that speakers sometimes ignore the 'rules' of word-formation. However, most irregular formations remain idiosyncratic in that they do not spread and are therefore also not established. It is ultimately not the individual speakers who always stick to the rules and restrictions, but the language community itself that acts in a collectively sanctioning manner. This also suggests that individual speakers do not really store their knowledge of morphology in their minds in the form of the rules that are so cherished in generative word-formation; instead they work with patterns as blueprints that are variable and permit exceptions for new formations (cf. p. 85 and 87).

Further reading: Baayen (1994), Baayen and Lieber (1991), Kastovsky (1986), Bauer (1994), (1998a: 414–420), (2001), Adams (2001: 146–153), Plag (2003: 44 ff.), Stein (2009), Mühleisen (2010), Raffelsiefen (2010).

7 Compounding

In this and subsequent chapters I will deal with each of the individual word-formation patterns in English in more detail. The present chapter on compounding takes typical cases of compounds and their characteristics as the starting point for describing the entire range of semantic and morphological structures (7.1). In section 7.2 the problems of borderline and transitional phenomena will be treated with reference to the demarcation between compounds and syntactic groups on the one hand (7.2.1) and other word-formation patterns on the other (7.2.2). Section 7.3 presents the results of a corpus study on the use of compounds in the MUMC from a structural and sociopragmatic perspective. Building on this, section 7.4 concentrates on the cognitive functions of compounding.

7.1 The morphological and semantic structures of compounds

7.1.1 Typical compounds

Typical compounds can be characterized from various linguistic perspectives based on the scheme by Olsen (2000: 898). Examples from the corpus are lexemes such as *barman, bedroom, building-block, dancehall, dustpan, fingertip, highlight, stronghold* and *timetable*.

---

1. Structural perspective
- Derivational morphology: typical compounds are composed of two constituents, each of which is either a free lexical morpheme (*barman*) or contains at least one free lexical morpheme (*building-block*).
- Inflectional morphology: the modifier cannot take an inflectional morpheme (**fingerstip*).
- Phonology: they are pronounced as an intonational unit with the main stress on the stressed syllable of the modifier and a secondary stress on the head (ˈbarˌman, ˈbuilding-ˌblock).
- Semantic structure: their modifier specifies the head ('a barman is a man who works in a bar', 'a building block is a block used for building'). Their meaning cannot be derived exclusively from the meaning of their constituents; i.e. they are semantically lexicalized (*barman* 'a man who serves drinks in a bar', *building-block* 'a piece or part of something'). Lexicalization, particularly the formal type, must not be so far advanced that the lex-

---

eme has lost its transparency with regard to form *and* content and is fully obscured (see p. 78).

2. Sociopragmatic perspective
- Typical compounds are institutionalized and have a naming function and not just a syntactic or a deictic function (as in *American-supplied*, see p. 73).

3. Cognitive perspective
- Typical compounds stand for an entrenched concept that is stored in the mental lexicon.

It is tempting to add the orthographic criterion of writing words together or with a hyphen. However, since writing the words separately is the rule in English in some patterns of compounding that otherwise produce prototypical compounds, e.g. [V + ing] + N (*nursing home*), this aspect will be disregarded for the time being (see section 7.2.1).

All typical compounds consist of nouns and/or adjectives. For reasons that will be discussed below (see p. 136), there are no typical verbal compounds in English in the sense of the criteria named above. The following morphological structures can be distinguished in typical compounds. Examples are taken from the MUMC and are given in the notation used there:

Nominal compounds:

- N + N: *backbone, barman, nutshell, pony tail, seat-belt, timetable, wallpaper*
- Adj + N: *greenhouse, high-chair, smalltalk, stronghold*
- [V + ing] + N: *dancing girl, building-block, dressing gown, racing car*
- V + N: *cease-fire, copyright, showroom, stopgap*
- N + [V + ing]: *credit rating*

Adjectival compounds:

- N + Adj: *accident prone, carefree*
- N + [V + ing]: *awe-inspiring, eye-catching, time consuming*
- Adj + [V + ing]: *good-looking, hard-drinking*[5]

---

[5] Strictly speaking, neither the pattern N + [V + ing] nor Adj + [V + ing] creates typical compounds, as in each case the second constituents are not established lexemes. We are therefore dealing with so-called *synthetic compounds*, which will be treated below as a borderline case with suffixation (see p. 134 ff.). As the second constituents are identical to the progressive form of the verbs ending in *-ing* and therefore look like established words, these patterns are classified as typical compounds.

Further patterns for the creation of typical adjectival compounds are N + [V + ed] and Adj + [V + ed], but all the examples in the MUMC have an atypical stress pattern and syntactic function, e.g. *paper-covered* and *American-supplied*.

As noted above, prototypical compounds are characterized with respect to their semantic structure by the fact that the modifier modifies or specifies the meaning of the head. The complete compound can accordingly be understood as a hyponym of the head. A *barman* is a type of *man* and a *greenhouse* a type of *house*. Compounds with this basic semantic structure are described as **determinative compounds** or **endocentric compounds**, although the two terms highlight different aspects. The term *determinative compound* emphasizes the type of relationship between the modifier and the head, while the notion of *endocentric compound* focuses on the fact that the head is decisive both semantically and grammatically for the whole compound, which is not the case with **exocentric compounds** such as *paperback* (see 7.2.2).

With regard to the specific semantic structures of the individual word-formation patterns that produce typical compounds, the range of semantic relationships between the elements is far too great to allow a detailed discussion even of only the most important types. We have already given a glimpse of the frequent types within the relatively restricted model V + N (*dancehall*) on page 100. It is the patterns without verbs, particularly N + N, that are known to have an extremely wide spectrum of semantic relationships. This touches on Jespersen's adage about this type: "The number of possible logical relations between the two elements is endless" (1942: 143). A number of linguists have construed this as a challenge and have researched into the internal semantic relationships of N+N-compounds, for example Adams (1973: 64 ff.) and in particular Warren (1978), who has developed the most comprehensive system of possible relationships based on an analysis of the data in the American 'Brown' corpus. Ryder (1994: ch. 2) gives a good overview of the state of research and reports on experiments aiming to bring to light the mental processes behind the interpretation of unknown N+N-compounds against the background of a cognitive-linguistic theory. Listed below are some of the semantic relationships within the pattern N + N using examples from the MUMC.

H denoting a person working in Mod	*barman, housewife*
H denoting a person belonging to group Mod	*policeman, police officer*
H denoting a container designed to contain/host/receive Mod	*art gallery, bedroom, courthouse, cupboard, dustpan, keyboard, notebook, picture book, timetable, waterbed, witness-stand*

H denoting a part of Mod	*backbone, bedhead, bed clothes, nutshell, pony tail, seat belt, weekend*
H denoting an object designed to be put at location Mod	*pocket money, wallpaper*
H denoting persons or objects located at Mod	*boatpeople, chairman, headline*
H denoting the source of Mod	*bullshit, candlelight, coal field*

The semantic relationships in abstract N+N-compounds such as *oil crisis* ('crisis caused by a shortage of oil', or 'crisis caused by rising prices of oil') and *will-power* ('power of a person's will') are vaguer and therefore more difficult to specify. In general it is apparent even in Warren's detailed classification that assigning individual N+N-compounds to groups of semantic relationships frequently seems arbitrary and is consequently open to criticism. Ad-hoc formations created according to the pattern N + N are also exceedingly ambiguous because they reveal very little information about their internal semantic structure due to the lack of a verb. On the other hand, as a rule the context clarifies what is meant (cf. Downing 1977, Adams 2001: 86–88, Ryder 1994: 196).

Examples such as *backbone, nutshell* and *pony tail* illustrate the fact that determinative compounds may contain metaphorical components or can be lexicalized with a literal and a metaphorical meaning. In such cases, of course, only the literal and not the figurative meaning shows the hyponymic relationship to the head. A few corpus entries in their respective contexts should serve to illustrate this here; an overview of the metaphorical compounds in the MUMC is given in section 7.3.

(7.1)   Under local anaesthetic, a small needle is inserted between two vertebrae in the lower part of the back and a small quantity of the fluid that surrounds the spinal chord (the nervous tissue contained inside the *backbone*) is drawn off. (ICE-GB: W2b-023)

(7.2)   Ernst Gelmer [...] sees this technology as used in education to be the *backbone* of capitalist society. (ICE-GB: W1a-012)

(7.3)   In a *nutshell*, it's probably uncomfortable. (ICE-GB: W1b-001)

(7.4)   You know, uhm, the little girl who had the striped T-shirt on and the long *pony tail* looked vaguely Latin American. (ICE-GB: S1a-058)

(7.5)   This letter is hand-written, in a style suited for the occasion, on expensive paper with a fine pen, and yet it's still probably *bullshit*!! (ICE-GB: W1b-008)

The compound *backbone* is equally lexicalized in the literal meaning *spine* (cf. 7.1) as in the figurative sense 'the most important part of something' (7.2). The lexeme *nutshell* is remarkable from a contrastive and a functional point of view. The formally equivalent compound in German *Nussschale* is lexicalized in its literal as well as its figurative meaning 'small boat or ship'. A figurative meaning which is also lexicalized exists in English, but it practically only occurs in the idiom *to put it in a nutshell* 'in short' or in the abbreviated form *in a nutshell*, as it appears in (7.3). *Pony tail* (7.4) is only considered to be institutionalized in its metaphorical meaning. Similarly in the case of *bullshit* (7.5) the potential literal meaning, which according to the OED never existed anyway, has been superseded by the figurative meaning 'nonsense' to such an extent that it is effectively blocked. The compound would only be used literally to refer to bulls' excrement for humorous effect.

Further reading on N+N-compounds: **Warren (1978), Ryder (1994)**.

7.1.2 Deviating semantic structure: exocentric and copulative compounds

The most fundamental divergence from the characteristics of typical compounds concerns their basic semantic structure. We can distinguish two types of compounds that do not exhibit the determinative relationship between the modifier and the head: exocentric compounds and copulative compounds.

Exocentric compounds

As already mentioned, **exocentric compounds** are characterized by the fact that they are semantically not subordinate to the head. A *paperback* is not a type of *back* nor is it a *paper*, but a book. As indicated by the term *exocentric*, the head of these compounds is not part of the compound itself. Frequently cited other examples of such compounds are *paleface*, *highbrow* ('intellectual'), *hunchback*, *redskin* ('Red Indian'), *egghead* ('intellectual'), *skinhead* ('gang member'), *redbreast* ('robin') and *greenback* ('dollar note'). As the examples demonstrate, exocentric compounds most frequently denote people by profiling salient characteristics which stand metonymically for the whole person. This type of word-formation is so old that there was already a technical term for it in Old Indic grammars of Sanskrit derived from an example: the word *bahuvrihi*, which literally means 'a lot of rice', denoting 'someone who has a lot of rice', i.e. 'a rich person'. This is the source of the term **bahuvrihi-compound**. Since the relationship between the profiled characteristics and the referent is very often that of 'having', i.e. a possessive relationship, the term **possessive compound** is also used in addition to the term *bahuvrihi compound*. Strictly speaking the terms *bahuvrihi compound* and *exocentric compound* are not synonymous, because apart from the typical bahuvrihi compounds there is another subcategory of exocentric compounds, including, e.g., the compound *pickpocket*. This type profiles the characteristic behaviour rather than a salient property of the referent. Both forms of exocentric compound can be explained on the basis of a metonymic relationship between the parts, characteristics or behaviour traits – which are explicitly expressed and therefore profiled – and the persons, or less commonly animals or objects referred to. (On the subject of metonymy see also p. 190 ff.).

An interesting example of a neologism in the form of a bahuvrihi compound is the use of the lexeme *heart-throb* in (7.6), which can be interpreted as a semantic ad-hoc formation. This complex lexeme is already lexicalized and institutionalized as a bahuvrihi compound with the meaning – according to the LDOCE5 – "a famous actor, singer etc who is very attractive to women" and according to Quirk et al. (1985: 1576) as "someone who causes the heart to throb in a person of the opposite sex, i.e. a sexually attractive person". However, the usage in the corpus suggests a different meaning, the gist of which is 'a text which, when read, makes the heart beat faster':

(7.6)   I spent a couple of nights in the underground at the height of the Blitz, and wrote what we called a *heart-throb* about the courage and cheerfulness universally displayed. (ICE-GB: W2f-014)

Copulative compounds

Old Indic grammar also had a term for the second compound type featuring a semantic structure that diverges from determinative compounds: **dvandva compound**. Compounds of this type, also called *copulative compounds*, are characterized by the fact that two concepts are linked together having a more or less equal status. The nouns *actor-director, actor-manager, fighter-bomber, study-bedroom*, the adjectives *bitter-sweet, deaf-mute, phonetic-semantic* and many combined nationality designations such as *Japanese-American* and *Swedish-Brazilian* are illustrations of this fairly infrequent type. In spite of their equal status the order of the two constituents is not completely irrelevant, at least from the point of view of the internal information structure, since for some compounds the second constituent is presented as given, while the first is remarkable. A *study-bedroom* is a bedroom with the distinctive feature that it is also used as a study. In addition, it should be mentioned that the established compounds of this type, e.g. *deaf-mute* and *bitter-sweet* are conventionalized in this particular order of the constituents, so that *mute-deaf* and *sweet-bitter* sound rather strange.

A good example from the MUMC is the three-part compound *owner occupier patient*, whose status as a compound in a given context is recognizable from the fact that only the final noun carries the plural marking:

(7.7)   This is, therefore, the most expensive form of institutional provision by the state and one in which *owner occupier patients* are not under any pressure to use their home equity assets to meet their health care costs. (ICE-GB: W2a-013)

Another tripartite dvandva compound with an abbreviated first element following the pattern of combining forms (see p. 129) is *tragi-comedy-farce* (ICE-GB: W1b-010). The only other potential example in the MUMC (cf. 7.8), *actor/journalist*, comes from the same text, a personal letter with conspicuous linguistic freshness and creativity. Whether this formation is a genuine dvandva compound is doubtful, because the author's spelling with a forward slash leaves one with the impression that she is not certain which profession the referent really has.

(7.8)　I've been asked out by this *actor/journalist* tonight that I went to see last week and I'm really not interested. (ICE-GB: W1b-010 064)

All three examples support Hansen et al.'s assertion (1990: 52) that copulative compounds following the pattern N + N are generally nonce words. A contemporary example from the magazine *Newsweek*, in which the former American general and candidate for the presidency, Wesley Clark, was described as a *soldier-scholar*, provides further corroboration.

Dvandva compounds also exhibit different intonation patterns from determinative compounds, which is a reflection of their peculiar semantic structure. Determinative compounds carry the main stress on the modifier primarily because the modifier contains the emphasized information. The semantic equality in dvandva compounds is signalized phonologically by the level stress of the two constituents or one main stress on the second element. In the case of *deaf-mute*, for instance, according to the LDOCE3 (but not LDOCE4!) both intonation patterns are possible, ˈdeaf-ˈmute and ˌdeaf-ˈmute, but not the pattern typical of determinative compounds ˈdeaf-ˌmute. As we shall see later, intonation can be an important criterion for the identification of compounds in general (see p. 133).

7.1.3　Special morphological structures: genitive compounds, particle compounds and neo-classical compounds

In addition to these semantic deviations from typical compounds there are also morphological deviations, which can be divided into three classes: genitive compounds, particle compounds and neo-classical compounds. Further compound-like processes, which share the characteristics of other word-formation patterns, are treated in section 7.2.

Genitive compounds

Genitive compounds (e.g. *driver's seat*) differ from typical compounds with respect to the morphological criterion, since the first constituent is inflected. Although there is a whole range of types in which the modifier occurs in the genitive, no examples of this pattern can be found in the MUMC. Commonly occurring examples include: *ladies' room, servant's quarter, driver's license* (predominantly AmE, in BrE *driving licence*), *beginner's luck, master's degree* (cf. Marchand 1969: 65–69). In grammars this use of the genitive is referred to as a *descriptive genitive* (e.g. in Quirk et al. 1985: 322, 327 ff.).

Particle compounds

Typical compounds are composed of lexical morphemes. Morphologically complex lexemes that are similar to compounds can also consist of grammatical morphemes, however. Conjunctions such as *however* and *although*, prepositions such as *into, throughout* and *without* and pronouns such as *anything* and *something*, which are members of closed grammatical word classes, are not normally accorded the status of compounds, since they have no lexical function. If prepositions or particles occur as the second constituent combined with lexical morphemes, then the situation is not so clear. Lexemes such as *breakdown, handout, setback* and *takeoff* for instance, are nouns, although their first parts are verbs and their second parts are particles. This shows that their morphological structure is more complex than their morphological form would suggest at first glance. Formations of this type are analyzed in the literature in various ways. Adams (1973: 124), for example, does not regard them as compounds but as nominalizations of phrasal verbs (*break down, hand out* etc.). Bauer and Huddleston (2002: 1646 ff.) pursue a different avenue in that they relax the rule that the right-hand constituent must always be the head of the compound, and then distinguish between noun-centred and verb-centred noun compounds. Lexemes such as *take-away* and *breakthrough* are accordingly analyzed as verb-centred noun compounds with a preposition as the second constituent (Bauer and Huddleston 2002: 1654 ff.). In order to explain the emergence of a noun from the morphological structure V + Prep, they have to take recourse to a process similar to conversion.[6]

Free grammatical morphemes can also occur as the first constituent in combinations with lexical morphemes and in so doing play a role in the formation of nominal, adjectival and verbal compounds. In this case, too, the most frequently encountered compounds are those with particles as the first constituent. The ICE-GB documents the following patterns:[7]

---

[6] "The process of forming the noun bears some resemblance to conversion – it differs from it, however, because the verb and preposition in clausal construction are separate words, so that the effect of combining them into a noun is to form a compound" (Bauer und Huddleston 2002: 1654).

[7] Apart from those already cited, a series of further patterns with particles also exists (cf. e.g. *upbringing, outbreak, bystander* in Hansen et al. 1990: 58). However, they produce formations with an ambiguous morphological structure that belong to the so-called synthetic compounds, which will be discussed further below (see p. 134).

Nominal:	Part + N: *afternoon, bypass, inmate, outhouse, overcoat, overtime, underground, underperformance*
Verbal:	Part (*out, over* or *under*) + V: *outrun, overcrowd, overlook, overcome, undergo, underlie, underline, undermine*
Adjectival:	Part + [V + ing]: *ongoing, outlying, overarching, overpowering*
	Part + [V + ed$_2$]: *inbuilt, underdeveloped*

Many of the verbal and adjectival **particle compounds** can be directly traced back to phrasal verbs. In contrast to their autonomous usage as particles or prepositions, where they have a locative meaning, particles usually appear in complex verbs with a figurative meaning (Kastovsky 1982: 180). Of particular note in this respect are *out, over* and *under* with the meanings 'surpassing' (*out*), 'excessive' (*over*) and 'too little' (*under*) respectively (cf. Quirk et al. 1985: 1542), which make them very similar semantically to prefixes indicating degree (see section 8.2.4). Verbs such as *overcrowd* are also closer phonologically to prefixations than to typical compounds, because they carry the main stress on the second constituent. In consequence, it is not surprising that many linguists – *inter alia* Quirk et al. (1985: 1542) and Schröder (2008) – categorize formations of this type as prefixations.

Further reading: Adams (2001: 71–77), Bauer and Huddleston (2002), Schröder (2008).

Neo-classical compounds

Lexemes such as *biography* and *biochemical, demographic* and *photographic* as well as *histological, technological* and *theological* present problems for anyone carrying out a morphological description of English. From a semantic point of view we can state that even people with no educational background of classical languages have no difficulty in ascribing at least vague meanings to the identifiable parts of many of these formations by comparing the meanings of morphologically similar lexemes. *Bio-* has something to do with life, *-graphy* and *-graphic* with drawing or writing, *hist-* with tissue, *techno-* with technology, *theo-* with God, and *-ology* or *-ologic(al)* are familiar as endings referring to scientific disciplines. It is fairly easy to interpret *biography*, for instance, vaguely but nevertheless appropriately as 'writing about life'.

As already explained in section 2.3 (see p. 41), morphological building blocks of this type are described as **combining forms**, which, following Bauer (1983: 213), can be divided into **initial combining forms** (ICFs) and **final combining forms** (FCFs) (see also Bauer and Huddleston 2002: 1661 ff.). Since, seen from a historic point of view, *combining forms* are free or bound roots from Latin or Greek that were borrowed and are still being used to form new lexemcs, the complex lexemes that comprise them are described as **neo-classical compounds** (cf. Adams 1973: 128–134, Bauer 1983: 213–216). There are other approaches, however, which extend the use of the term combining form to cover non-classical word building blocks that have been split off from existing words and used in the formation of other words, although they are not morphemes (Warren 1990). This process is referred to as **secretion**. Forms such as *-gate* in *Iraqgate* (by analogy with *Watergate*, to indicate scandals that are covered up), *-mare* in *nukemare* (from *nightmare*, to refer to the horror of a nuclear explosion) and *-speak* in *computerspeak* (in the style of George Orwell's coining *newspeak*, to refer to technical language) fall under this category. These elements are not regarded as being involved in the formation of compounds but are considered to be suffix-like elements.

The following neo-classical compounds can be found in the MUMC:

(7.9)   *archaeological, axoplasmic, biochemical, biography, daguerrotype, democrat, demographic, diameter, endoneurial, extra-extroverted, fibroblastic, histological, histologically, homogeneous, homogenizing, homosexual, melodramatic, microscopic, neuromuscular, perineurium, phagocytose, photographic, physiological, politico-military, pornographic, psychological, retrograde, technological, telephoned, telephoning, theological*

Even this small extract from the enormous inventory of this word-formation model illustrates various important aspects. We are immediately struck by the fact that most of the ICFs end with an <o>, rarely with a different vowel: *archae-, axo-, bio-, demo-, endo-, extro-, fibro-, homo-, neuro-* etc. are very typical examples. The reasons for this relatively uniform ending, which incidentally also led to the change in the combining form *-logy* to *-ology*, lie in the morphology of Ancient Greek (see OED, s.v. *-logy*). Furthermore, examples such as *fibroblastic* and *politico-military* show that ICFs can be created from free lexical morphemes (*fibre, political*), by adapting them to end in <o>. The lexeme *daguerrotype*, which refers to a type of photography named after its inventor, Jacques Daguerre, is evidence of the fact that even proper nouns can be turned into combining forms by adding an <o>. The adjective *politico-military* can be described as a neo-classical dvandva compound.

The small number of examples in (7.9) is sufficient to demonstrate the technical nature of many formations, which is also reflected in the large number of examples in the specialist texts of the corpus. While some of the lexemes are completely institutionalized in the common core of the English lexicon, e.g. *archaeological, biography, democrat, homogeneous, homosexual, melodramatic, microscopic, photographic, pornographic, psychological, technological* and *telephone*, the vast majority of neo-classical compounds is restricted in its distribution to specialist terminology.

Further reading on neo-classical compounds and combining forms: **Warren (1990), Bauer (1998a)**, Adams (2001: 110–120), **Bauer and Huddleston (2002: 1661–1666), Plag (2003: 155–159).**

7.2 Borderline phenomena and demarcation problems

It has already to some extent become obvious from the classes of compounds we have treated so far that the transition from relatively distinct representatives of this word-formation pattern to other types of formation is not clear-cut. The consequence of this for linguistic analysis and description is that difficulties in classification arise. The word-formation pattern of compounding is affected in particular by demarcation problems from two directions: firstly, when distinguishing between compounds on the one hand and syntactic groups and phraseological units on the other, and secondly, when defining the boundary to other word-formation models that superficially appear to produce similar formations. This section aims to provide help in making decisions about these two types of demarcation problem. At this point we must emphasize that these classification difficulties are not a symptom of the lack of available categories but the inevitable result of the fact that phenomena in living languages can rarely be compartmentalized into clearly definable and clearly distinguishable categories.

7.2.1 Demarcation from syntactic groups and phraseologisms

While the adjective *high* in *high jump* is a constituent of a compound, in the sentence *this was a high jump* it must be regarded as the premodifier of a noun phrase. The compound *high jump* is part of the English lexicon, while the nominal phrase *a high jump* is assembled during speech production using the resources of grammar. In the noun phrase, the adjective can be exchanged at any time for many others, e.g. *(that was) a low jump, a beautiful jump* etc.; in the case of the compound this is not possible. Compounds must therefore be distinguished from formally similar phrases, but the demarcation is anything but simple. The main reason for this is that some word-formation patterns are structurally identical to noun phrases, particularly the patterns Adj + N (*green house*), [V + ing] + N (*dancing girl*) and N + N (*credit card*), which produce typical compounds but formally also resemble noun phrases that are premodified by adjectives or nouns. Somewhat confusingly, in the literature *stock market* and *labour market*, for example, count as compounds, while *antique market, black market* and *world market* do not. As distinctions of this nature appear at first glance to be nothing less than random, we must clarify which criteria can be adduced to justify analytical decisions and whether they enable unequivocal classifications.

To begin with, the obvious criterion of orthography is highly unreliable, as we have already mentioned. Although writing words with a hyphen and writing them in one word can be regarded as visible indicators of more or less advanced establishment (Quirk et al. 1985: 1537, 1569), in practice English orthography is too inconsistent, even in patterns such as Adj + N and N + N, to be able to function as a decisive criterion for the status of compounds (Hansen et al. 1990: 51). Variations in spelling are documented even in the limited data of the MUMC, e.g. by the variants *girlfriend – girl-friend, screenplay – screen-play* and *wartime – wartime*. Nevertheless the spelling is not irrelevant, because even if it is not a necessary criterion, it is still often a sufficient criterion for 'compoundhood', since English formations that are consistently written as one word can be reliably classified as compounds. The converse argument, that combinations written separately are not compounds, is not true, of course.

From a cognitive perspective we can say that compounds represent new conceptual forms that are stored as integrated units in the mental lexicon, as opposed to syntactic groups, which are put together during on-going processing of individual concepts in actual language use as the need arises. While theoretically this criterion is without doubt the most important one, in practice it is exceedingly difficult to implement, not least because there are competing linguistic units that also consist of several words and are stored as gestalts, namely fixed expressions and phraseological units. These include not just classical idioms such as *to bite the dust* ('to die') and *to eat humble pie* ('to back down/give in'), which are almost certainly stored as units in the mental lexicon, but also phrasal verbs such as *to get up, to walk out* and many others.

Viewed from a semantic perspective, at least typical compounds are characterized by the fact that their meaning cannot be entirely derived from their constituents. Hence, typical compounds are lexicalized semantically. Unfortunately it is precisely this semantic **non-compositionality**, or **idiomaticity**, that is one of the characteristic and defining features of idioms (cf. Carter 1987: 58 ff., Gläser 1986: 54), which means that this criterion proves equally unsuitable for the demarcation of compounds and phraseological units. What the semantic criterion can be useful for, however, is the distinction between compounds and syntactic groups. The compound *dancing-girl* ('female dancer'), for example, can be distinguished from the parallel word group *a dancing girl* ('a girl who is dancing') by means of the additional attribute 'professional' (Hansen et al. 1990: 50).

A useful syntactic criterion for the demarcation between compounds and syntactic groups is the replacement test, i.e. replacing the head of the combination in question with *one* (Quirk et al. 1985: 1332). While the head of a syntactic group can be substituted by this pro-form (*she wants an oak table but I'd prefer a teak one*), this does not work with compounds. The sentence **that's not an oak tree but an elm one* is grammatically incorrect. In addition, the first constituents of syntactic groups are morphologically modifiable and can be substituted, in contrast to those of compounds. *A greener house* and *a very green house* can only be syntactic groups, not compounds with the meaning 'hothouse'.

In the case of *dancing girl* the phonological criterion can be applied, as it can in many other examples. Typical compounds have a **unit intonation** with the main stress on the first constituent and a weakened secondary stress on the second, reflecting the semantic and cognitive gestalt-formation, while the individual elements of syntactic groups maintain their full stress – with variations determined by the speech rhythm (Kastovsky 1982: 177). The compound ˈdancing-ˌgirl can be distinguished from the syntactic group ˈdancing ˈgirl by means of the characteristic stress distribution of typical compounds ˈ · ˌ · . However, the phonological criterion itself is not a panacea. We have already pointed out, for instance, that less typical compounds such as dvandva compounds carry **level stress** ˈ · ˈ · (e.g. ˈactor-ˈmanager, see p. 127). The same applies to many adjectival determinative compounds (e.g. ˈred-ˈhot; Hansen et al. 1990: 51) and even recognized N+N-compounds. Bauer (1998b: 70–72) shows that the intonation of N+N-compounds is by no means consistent among native speakers or in lexicographical practice for all debatable combinations.

According to Bauer, there is no observable convergence between the different criteria (Bauer 1998b: 78–81), which makes the analysis of N+N-compounds in particular even more difficult. In practice the demarcation of compounds from syntactic groups remains a challenge for research into word-formation, as will become apparent in the corpus study in section 7.3. On the other hand, the demarcation problems, especially insofar as they concern differences between different speakers, may just reflect the fact that some speakers have stored representations of 'whole' compounds readily available in their long-term memory, while this kind of lexical representation of the same compounds is less strong for others.

A special type of more or less clearly definable types of compounds in the borderline area to phrases are so-called **phrasal compounds** such as *ground-to-air* (*missile*) and *pen-and-paper* (*theories*). These formations are characterized by comprising entire or slightly shortened syntactic phrases. Further examples of this formation type from the MUMC are:

(7.8)   *dusk-to-dawn (curfew)*
one-to-one (system)
law and order (minister)
pen-and-paper (theories)
hundred-and-fifty pound (job)
not-necessarily-intuitive (transformations)
all-out (strike)
look-alike (sculpture)
free-and-easiness

From a sociopragmatic perspective, it can be stated that there is only a relatively limited number of institutionalized lexemes of this type. The most commonly used established formations are designations of relationships ending in *in-law* (*father-*

in-law, *daughter-in-law* etc.), names of plants such as *forget-me-not* and *love-in-the-mist*, certain coordinated constructions such as *bread-and-butter*, *pepper-and-salt*, *milk-and-water*, *deaf-and-dumb*, *rough-and-ready* and prepositional phrases such as *man-in-the-street*, *stock-in-trade* and the exocentric formation *good-for-nothing* (cf. Marchand 1969: 122 ff.). At the same time this must not obscure the fact that this type of lexical combination has become very popular, particularly recently, in spontaneous conversations, in the media particularly in newspapers, and is thus characterized by increasing productivity. It is precisely the possibility illustrated in (7.8) of using phrasal compounds as premodifiers in noun phrases that seems to be being increasingly exploited. The advantage of these formations for the registers mentioned are obvious, since they allow the encoding to be as semantically specific as possible in a highly succinct form optimally suited to the respective context. The nonce character of phrasal compounds can be put to use to strike a humorous or ironic note.

> **Further reading:** On the distinction between compounds and syntactic phrases:
> **Bauer (1998b), Bauer and Huddleston (2002: 144 ff.), Plag (2003: 137 ff., 159 ff.).**
> On stress assignment in compounds: **Plag (2006).**

7.2.2 The transition to other word-formation patterns: synthetic compounds and verbal compounds

Synthetic compounds

Synthetic compounds have been alluded to several times *inter alia* in connection with problems in determining the morphological structure of certain polymorphemic complex lexemes with several elements, which cannot be clearly analyzed as compounds or suffixations (see p. 98). Nouns with the morphological forms N + V + -*er*/-*ing*/Ø (*breadwinner*, *shareholding*, *bloodshed*) and adjectives of the type N/Adj + V + -*ing*/-*ed* (*time consuming*, *good-looking*, *sheep-shaped*, *handpicked*) are particularly affected by these problems. It should be stressed that this does not mean that these formations are in any way deviant or irregular; they simply do not lend themselves to descriptions in terms of frameworks which prefer to have binary divisions of constituents (cf. p. 96).

In order to illustrate the problems, let us investigate the morphological and semantic structure of the formations *hairdrier*, *breadwinner* and *horse breaker* from the MUMC. If we disregard the conversion of the adjective *dry* to the verb *to dry*, then all three lexemes can be segmented as exhibiting the same morphological form N + V + *er*. *Hairdrier* can be said to have the fundamental morphological structure of an N+N-compound with a complex head (N + [V + er]), i.e. *hair* + [*dry* + *er*]. The corresponding semantic structure can be paraphrased with the sentence 'a hairdrier is a drier that dries hair'. With regard to its morphological structure, *breadwinner* can be treated analogously to *hairdrier* (cf. *bread* + [*win* + *er*]), because the lexeme *winner* exists. However, the corresponding semantic structure, 'a breadwinner is a winner who wins bread', is not plausible, even if we substitute the metaphorical version of the relative clause 'who earns money for the family', since a *breadwinner* is, after all, clearly not a *winner* in the proper sense of this lexeme. In the case of *horse breaker*, the *hairdrier* type of analysis does not work on either of the two levels: *horse* + [*break* + *er*] and 'a horse breaker is a breaker who breaks horses' are equally odd for the simple reason that the potential noun **breaker* does not exist. Hence, analyzing the word here as a compound can definitely be rejected.

So what alternatives do we have at our disposal? From a semantic perspective suffixation presents itself as a second option. Just as *writer* can be paraphrased as 'someone who writes (professionally)' and *driver* as 'someone who drives (professionally)', the three complex examples could also be analyzed as 'someone who breaks horses', 'someone who wins bread' and 'an instrument that dries hair'. However, we run into difficulties with these paraphrases when it comes to suggesting a corresponding morphological structure, since we would have to postulate the structure [N + V] + *er*, i.e., for example, [*bread* + *win*] + *er*. This is problematic because a morphological structure of this type requires complex verbs to function as the base for the derivations, but these do not exist. **To hairdry*, **to breadwin* and **to horsebreak* are not valid verbs in English. We must therefore eliminate the analysis as a suffixation.

As long as nominalizations of the verbal constituents exist, as is the case in *drier*, the situation is not insuperable, since one can posit a compound with the structure N + [V + er]. *Breadwinner* is problematic, because when analyzing the word as a compound, the semantic and morphological levels produce incompatible results. This situation is referred to as a *bracketing paradox* between the semantic and the morphological analysis (Carstairs-McCarthy 2002: 80). Finally, the lexeme *horse breaker* simply cannot be assigned to either of these two categories, compounding and suffixation. It is for these cases that the special category of synthetic compounds is available. From a conceptual point of view (as opposed to the morphological and the semantic), there appears to be no doubt that synthetic compounds are processed in exactly the same way as formally comparable non-synthetic ones. It would not often occur to speakers of English that lexemes such as *law-breaker* and *watchmaker* cannot be divided into two valid lexemes, by analogy with *ship owner* and *bus driver*, because **breaker* and **maker* do not exist in their general vocabulary.[8] As we have already mentioned (see p. 122, Fn. 5), this holds true particularly for the adjectival compounds ending in *-ing* and *-ed* (*awe-inspiring*, *good-looking*, *hand-picked*), because these forms sound familiar owing to their possibilities for grammatical application, although they are not established lexemes.

---

[8] Of course, this by no means excludes the possible use of forms such as *breaker* and *maker* as a rhetoric means of attracting attention in specific registers such as the language of advertising or the media.

In short, the notion of *synthetic compound* is useful for the description of poly-morphemic formations following the patterns N + V + *er/ing/Ø* and N/Adj + V + *ing/ed* which resist both potential analyses, that as compounds (because the poten-tial head element is not an established lexeme) as well as that as suffixations (be-cause the potential complex verbal base is not either).

Further reading: Marchand (1969: 15 f.), Kastovsky (1982: 179), Hansen et al. (1990: 49), ten Hacken (2010).

Verbal compounds

One of the main causes of the difficulties encountered when analyzing synthetic compounds is that English has very few, if any, genuine verbal compounds. If compounds of the type **to horsebreak* and **to breadwin* did exist, then we would have no problem in analyzing the formations *horse breaker* and *breadwinner* as regular suffixations. In reality, however, apart from particle compounds derived from phrasal verbs such as *overlook, underline* (see p. 129), verbal compounds are genuinely rare. Marchand even goes so far as to state categorically that "verbal composition [= compounding] does not exist in present-day English" (1969: 100) and adds that verbal compounding did not exist in general in Old English or in Germanic. The phenomenon is in fact fairly rare in most of the other languages in the world, too (Gerdts 1998: 99). Marchand therefore characterizes verbal com-pounds (with the exception of the phrasal verb compounds) as **pseudo com-pounds**. Adams (1973: 108 f.) quotes examples from washing instructions for clothes such as *to hand wash, cold rinse, short spin* and *warm iron* as well as individual forms such as *to consumer-test* and *to chain-smoke*. She even pleads the case, with reference to Pennanen (1966), for recognizing verbal compounding as a new word-formation model. Nevertheless, in her later work Adams (2001: 100–109) leaves no room for doubt that the vast majority of verbs which on the surface look like verbal compounds did not come about by compounding but either by the conversion of nominal compounds or by the back-formation of nominal or adjectival – often synthetic – compounds (see sections 10 and 12.1).

The following examples of denominal derivations can be found in the MUMC: the conversions *to blackmail, to bankroll, to codename, to mastermind* and *to press-gang* (which has already been mentioned in chapter 4), and the back-formations *to ghost-write* (from *ghost-writer*) and *to sunbathe* (from *sunbathing*). Further estab-lished lexemes are *to baby-sit, to gatecrash, to tape-record, to handcuff, to wise-crack, to brainwash, to sightsee* and *to air-condition* (cf. Adams 1973: 107 ff., Hansen et al. 1990: 137).

7.3 Corpus study II: compounds

In this section the use of compounds will be described using data from the MUMC. As a rule only compounds consisting of two free morphemes will be considered. Compounds with more than two free morphemes will be treated in section 12.2 on multi-constituent compounds.

Owing to the borderline phenomena and in particular the problems of demarcation from syntactic phrases, it will be worth our while to pursue a two-track approach. On the one hand, all combinations of lexemes can be taken into account that are composed morphologically like established compounds, irrespective of their function in context, their intonation pattern, their degree of establishment, lexicalization and entrenchment, and their function and conceptual status. On the other hand, it seems sensible to restrict the analysis to typical compounds in the sense described in section 7.1.1, in order to be able to assess their usage in the corpus separately. The two-track approach also promises insights into the applicability and significance of the criteria for differentiating compounds and syntactic groups as discussed in 7.2.1. Since the characteristics of typical compounds mentioned in 7.1.1 are rather theoretical, they must first be put into practice. This is achieved by only taking into account compounds that are recorded in the OALD5 (Crowther 1995), as well as being listed as having the main stress on the left constituent, as is typical of determinative compounds. The idea behind this procedure – which is, of course, open to criticism – is to limit ourselves to typical compounds, since compounds only have entries in desktop or learners' dictionaries if they are lexicalized and thus not semantically derivable from their constituent parts (Adams 2001: 14), and/or have the typical compound intonation pattern, and/or are considered by lexicographers to be widely established. (Furthermore, the frequency of use can play a role.)

The larger dataset including all compounds and combinations similar to compounds also contains – in addition to the typical compounds –

- combinations that have a predominantly syntactic or deictic function and were only constructed for a specific context, which means that they cannot be entrenched as proper concepts nor can they be recorded in dictionaries;

- combinations that are fully established and largely self-explanatory and, presumably for this reason, are not entries in the OALD5 (e.g. *city centre, computer programme, pay rise*);

- combinations which, maybe somewhat counterintuitively, according to OALD5 carry the main stress on the second constituent, as is typical of phrases (*ground floor, head teacher, home town, interest rate, world war*);

- combinations of a technical nature that therefore have no place in a general dictionary for learners (e.g. *axon death, cell body, effector site, end-organ*).

137

For the sake of terminological simplicity, all questionable combinations will be referred to as *compounds* in the following, irrespective of their theoretical status.

7.3.1 Structural perspective

The morphological patterns of compounds documented in the MUMC are listed in Table 7.1. The table is divided into typical and other types of compounds; it illustrates all patterns by randomly chosen types and tokens and states the observed frequencies in each case. As the table shows, nominal compounds are used far more frequently than adjectival ones: there are 528 uses of noun compounds as against 42 of adjectival ones. We can therefore state that in this corpus compounding is portrayed as a basically noun-forming process. Although this is only a small sample, I consider it unlikely that this trend would fundamentally alter if the amount of data were larger.

Tab. 7.1: Frequency of types of compounds in the MUMC (selected examples)

pattern	typical compounds		all compound-like items	
	tokens	*types*	*tokens*	*types*
nouns				
N + N	118	76	405	309
	air raid, beauty parlour, bedhead, boatpeople, breast stroke, coursework, land mine, prayer rug, role model, speedboat, water bed		*air transport, bed frame, bus service, childhood games, curtain fabric, fringe show, link belt, muscle atrophy, tax form*	
Adj + N	18	12	71	50
	blackmail, Foreign Office, greenhouse, high level, highchair, large-scale, long-stay, nervous system, right-hand, small-talk, stronghold		*antique market, Catholic Church, civil war, high treason, Paediatric Unit, sulphuric acid, Supreme Commander*	
[V + ing] + N	10	6	34	23
	building-block, dressing gown, housing association, learning difficulties, nursing home, racing car		*bridging inference, farming implements, housing authorities, investigating magistrates*	
V + N	6	4	6	4
	cease-fire, copyright, showroom, stopgap			

N + [V + ing]	1	1	12	12
	credit rating		*consumer spending, street fighting, theorem-proving*	
adjectives				
N + [V + ing]	3	3	5	5
	awe-inspiring, eye-catching, time-consuming		*girl-bedding, information-carrying*	
Adj + [V + ing]	2	2	4	4
	good-looking, hard-drinking		*dumpy-looking, ever-shrinking*	
N + Adj	2	2	2	2
	accident-prone, carefree			
N + [V + ed]	0	0	19	19
			government-appointed, hand-picked, institution based	
Adv + [V + ed]	0	0	6	6
			closely-guarded, oddly-poised, sharply-defined, well-equipped	
Adj + [V + ed]	0	0	6	6
			American-supplied, dark-haired, long-forgotten, white-rendered	

In accordance with expectations, the pattern N + N is by far the commonest. The only other patterns worth mentioning as regards numbers of occurrences are the two nominal compounds Adj + N (*greenhouse*) and [V + ing] + N (*building-block*). However, even for these three patterns, only between a quarter and a third of the examples are recorded in the OALD5 with the intonation pattern typical of compounding. This means that the vast majority of the material collected consists of combinations which do not count as typical, institutionalized compounds for the various reasons given above, although quantitatively, alongside technical combinations, the formations with a context-dependent syntactic function account for the largest share. As the examples and statistics show, formations with a syntactic function are particularly frequent for the patterns N + [V + ing] (*model-making*), Adv + [V + ed] (*oddly-poised*), N + [V + ed] (*government-appointed*) and Adj + [V + ed] (*American-supplied*), the reason being their close resemblance to the grammatically generated forms ending in *-ing* and to the participial forms ending in *-ed*. On the other hand, we can see that all the examples of the patterns V + N (*ceasefire*) and N + Adj (*accident prone*) are typical compounds. No syntactically motivated formations according to these patterns were found in the data investigated, which could indicate that their productivity has ceased or is dwindling.

With regard to the semantic structures of the compounds in the MUMC, we have already mentioned that *paperback* and *heart-throb* are the only two examples of bahuvrihi compounds. Compounds with metaphorical components are more frequent. Here we must distinguish between those that (can) carry a figurative meaning as a whole and those where only one constituent is metaphorical. A summary comprising both types is given in Table 7.2:

Tab. 7.2: Metaphorical compounds in the MUMC

compound	metaphorical constituents(s)	metaphorical meaning (adapted from OALD5)
backbone	whole compound	'the most important part of a system, an organization etc.'
blackmail	whole compound	'the crime of demanding money from a person by threatening to tell sb else a secret about them'
bullshit	whole compound	'nonsense'
cold war	whole compound	'a very unfriendly situation between two countries who are not actually fighting each other, usually used about the situation between the US and the Soviet Union after the Second World War'
honeymoon	whole compound	'a holiday/vacation taken by a couple who have just got married'
stopgap	whole compound	'something that you use or do for a short time while you are looking for something better'
time bomb	whole compound	'a situation that is likely to cause serious problems in the future'
bridging inference	Mod	'inference that fills a gap between two pieces of information'
headmaster	Mod	'a teacher who is in charge of a school, especially a private school'
headteacher	Mod	'a teacher who is in charge of a school'

heartland	Mod	'the central part of a country or area'
pony-tail	Mod	'a bunch of hair tied at the back of the head so that it hangs like a horse's tail'
small-talk	Mod	'polite conversation about ordinary or unimportant subjects, especially at social occasions'
bedhead	H	'the part of the bed which is at the end, behind the person sleeping in it'
night owl	H	'a person who enjoys staying up late at night'

The metaphorical motivation for most of these compounds should be clear. It is immediately manifest that the constituent *head* in *headmaster* and *headteacher* stands for the part of an organization with the control and the responsibility. *Blackmail* comes from an old meaning of the word *mail*, 'rent, tribute' (OED), so that viewed historically, only the modifier is actually being used metaphorically. The OED describes the origin of the word *honeymoon* somewhat ironically by comparing a romantic relationship with the phases of the moon "which is no sooner full than it begins to wane". Samuel Johnson, on the other hand, interpreted the constituent *moon* literally, referring to a *honeymoon* as being the first "honey-sweet" month after the wedding.

7.3.2 Sociopragmatic perspective

Of particular interest from a sociopragmatic perspective, alongside the degree of establishment and the function (about which a considerable amount has already been said), is the distribution of compounds in the MUMC's five registers. Table 7.3 presents an evaluation of this, showing a comprehensive survey of all compounds plus the distribution of the most frequent type, the N+N-compounds, separately.

Tab. 7.3: Frequency of compounds in the MUMC according to register

	conversation	letters	fiction	reportage	academic
typical compounds					
all patterns	16.88 %	13.13 %	28.75 %	25.00 %	16.25 %
N + N	16.95 %	16.10 %	33.05 %	27.12 %	6.78 %
all compound-like combinations					
all patterns	9.84 %	11.78 %	14.59 %	34.62 %	29.17 %
N + N	10.37 %	11.85 %	15.31 %	31.11 %	31.36 %

The table shows that the frequency of use of compounds in the various registers varies considerably. Basically they occur less often in conversations and personal letters than in more formal and abstract registers. The precise distribution depends on whether we restrict ourselves to typical compounds or take all the combinations in question into account. In the latter case we see a division into two types of register. The proportion of typical compounds is higher in the less formal registers of conversation, letters and fiction, compared to the totals for all combinations, while the opposite is the case in press and specialized texts.

If we look at this in detail, the specialized texts make a relatively small contribution to the occurrence of typical compounds; but if we count all compound-like combinations, a far greater proportion is found in this register, particularly the type N + N . The reason for this is that compounding is in principle an important pattern for specialized texts, but these technical compounds are not counted as typical compounds following the procedure introduced above, as they are not sufficiently institutionalized. Conversely, narrative texts in the fiction category make the greatest contribution to established compounds, but a comparatively small contribution to other types. The syntactically motivated compounds, which are also used for abbreviation, are used more often in press texts and in academic texts than in other registers.

7.4 The cognitive functions of compounds

Compounds consist of at least two free lexical morphemes or lexemes. If we proceed on the plausible assumption that lexemes stand for relatively autonomous conceptual units, then we can derive from this the most important cognitive function of the word-formation pattern of compounding: the concept-linking function. A compound such as *barman*, for instance, links the concepts MAN and BAR, so that a new concept arises with the content 'a man who serves drinks in a bar' (LDOCE4). While the idea of concept-linking strikes us as being almost trivial, the effect that a new concept is created is highly significant. Unless we are dealing with a syntactically motivated formation, the new lexeme produced by the link stands for an autonomous concept that does not simply represent the combination of its parts in its conceptual structure. Compounds are not simply lexicalized; their entrenchment as new concepts seems to be their ultimate *raison d'être* (cf. Ungerer 2002: 557 ff.). In contrast to syntactic groups, compounds are morphological and conceptual units that are stored as wholes in the mental lexicon and retrieved and used wholesale as it were in speech processing. Interestingly, as long ago as 1937 Koziol (1937: 46 ff.) states that the hallmark of compounds is their psychological unity. This criterion was rigorously swept under the carpet not least by Marchand (1969: 20) because of the difficulties involved in its implementation, but it is currently beginning to regain respect in the course of the cognitive fashion in linguistics (cf. Schmid 2008).

Compounds serve to condense information not only due to their uniting two or more concepts in one lexeme, but also because of their additional semantic specifications. The aspect of serving, for instance, is not included in either *man* or *bar*. A large amount of specific information is encoded with relatively little morphological material. As we have already mentioned in 5.3.3, the effect of information condensation can be equally exploited by compounds with a syntactic function and those with a lexical function. However, it is characteristic of compounds with a syntactic function that they only stand for a temporary idea that is dependent on context, not stored in the mental lexicon for future use and therefore not a concept in a strict sense. The large number of compounds in the MUMC which are not fully established in the general vocabulary, at least according to the operationalization using the OALD5, indicates that speakers consider these disposable concepts to be extraordinarily useful.

The profiling function of compounds is in a sense an inevitable corollary of the compression of information. Since a small amount of morphological material encodes a large amount of information, compounds entail a selective emphasis (*profiling*) of individual aspects of the conceptualized scene: the barman filling glasses and mixing drinks but not preparing meals; his standing behind the bar rather than in front of it; and that he is usually responsible for taking payment for drinks consumed at the bar – all these aspects of the scene are potentially available but backgrounded by the compound *barman*.

In this connection our finding from the corpus study that compounds with the structure N + N are by far the most frequently used is significant. In these nouns the semantic relationship between the two constituents is not profiled, i.e. remains unspecified, because of the lack of a verbal element. When we encounter N+N-compounds for the first time, we deduce the semantic relationship by taking into account the context, our experience gained from our previous exposure to familiar compounds and considerations concerning the relevance of the two constituents to each other and the context (cf. Ryder 1994, Schmid 2010). The high frequency of occurrence of this pattern, particularly in non-established compounds, is evidence that this poor specification is not a deficit but rather an advantage. The conceptual openness of the N+N-pattern is obviously a good compromise between information condensation on the one hand, and specific encoding on the other. Any potential vagueness or ambiguity is accepted in view of the low effort involved in production.

7.5 Summary

I will start this summary by making an inventory of the array of forms and meanings from a structural perspective. With regard to their internal semantic structure there are three basic types of compound: determinative, possessive (bahuvrihi) and copulative (dvandva) compounds.

- **Determinative compounds** have a true modifier-head structure, i.e. the first constituent specifies the second, and the compound is a hyponym of the head, as long as there is no figurative meaning involved.
- **Possessive** or **bahuvrihi compounds** mostly refer to people, less often to objects or plants, by profiling striking or typical characteristics representatively. The relationship between the characteristics and the referent is interpreted as being metonymical.
- **Copulative compounds** connect two lexemes on the same level. In principle their constituents ought to be interchangeable, but they are frequently institutionalized in a specific order.

As for the morphological structures of compounds, the first thing to point out is that true verbal compounds, with the exception of phrasal compounds (e.g. *underline*), are exceedingly rare. Most lexemes that appear on the surface to be verbal compounds are formed by conversion or back-formation from adjectival or nominal compounds (e.g. *to baby-sit*).

The most important patterns of nominal compounds are (listed in order of their frequency of occurrence):

- N + N (*barman*)
- Adj + N (*high-chair*)
- [V + ing] + N (*building-block*)
- V + N (*copyright*)
- N + [V + ing] (*street fighting*)

The most frequent adjectival patterns are:

- N + [V + ing] (*eye-catching*)
- Adj + [V + ing] (*good-looking*)
- N + [V + ed] (*earmarked*)
- Adj + [V + ed] (*dark-haired*)

A number of these patterns – notably N + V + *er/ing* and N/Adj + V + *ing/ed* – form synthetic compounds that have to be categorized as being on the borderline between typical compounds and suffixations, since their morphological structures cannot be segmented either as compounds or as suffixations. Bahuvrihi compounds are generally formed using the patterns Adj + N (*redskin*) and N + N (*egghead*), and dvandva compounds using the patterns N + N (*actor-manager*) and Adj + Adj (*bitter-sweet*).

The following categories are treated as special forms of compounding or borderline phenomena with neighbouring word-formation patterns:

> - nominal, adjectival and verbal compounds with particles as the first component which strictly speaking are grammatical and not lexical morphemes (*afternoon, overlook, inbuilt*).
> - neo-classical compounds consisting of one or two combining forms, which are therefore not composed of free morphemes, but morpheme-like components (*archeological, biochemical*).
> - phrasal compounds consisting of free lexical morphemes, but frequently also comprising grammatical morphemes (*dusk-to-dawn curfew*).

Phonological aspects of compounding were considered in connection with the distinction between determinative and copulative compounds, and the demarcation of compounds from syntactic groups and phraseological units. Typical determinative compounds are pronounced as an intonation unit with a main stress on the modifier and a secondary stress on the head ($^{|}dust$ $_{|}pan$, $^{|}racing$ $_{|}car$). However, the corpus study shows that barely one third of the compounds in the MUMC follow this pattern. Copulative compounds generally exhibit level stress ($^{|}bitter$-$^{|}sweet$), and syntactic groups and phraseological units carry equal main stress on all lexical constituents (*a* $^{|}black$ $^{|}board$ 'board that is black' vs. $^{|}black_{|}board$, 'blackboard used for teaching').

From a cognitive perspective, the functions of concept-linking, concept-formation, information condensation and profiling can be attributed to compounding. Typical compounds stand out because they are entrenched as independent concepts and are stored as such in the mental lexicon.

The sociopragmatic point of view reveals that there are preferences for certain patterns in various registers, e.g. phrasal compounds in press texts and technical N+N-compounds in academic writing. In general, the more informal registers of spontaneous conversation, personal letters and fictional texts are characterized by containing a larger proportion of typical and established compounds than any other compound-like elements.

Further reading: On compounding: **Olsen (2000), Lieber (2009), Lieber and Štekauer (2009).** On demarcation problems between compounding and derivation: **ten Hacken (2000).** On creative compounding: **Benczes (2006).** On compounding from a cognitive-linguistic perspective: **Heyvaert (2009).** On the processing and representation of compounds: **Libben and Jarema (2006).**

8   Prefixation

8.1   Typical prefixations, variations and transition phenomena

8.1.1   Typical prefixations

Typical prefixations are combinations of free lexical morphemes (bases) with preceding bound lexical morphemes (prefixes) which form paradigms in the sense that they operate on definable types of bases. As with compounds, prefixes typically modify the bases. In all typical prefixations the word class of the head also determines the word class of the complex lexeme. Prefixations are in general, therefore, word-class maintaining word-formation processes. (For exceptions to this rule see section 8.1.3).

The stress pattern of prefixations can vary according to the phonetic and syntactic environment and the speech rhythm, and can even depend on the individual prefix. In typical prefixations such as *unbelievable*, as a rule a double stress is observed, with the primary stress falling on the stressed syllable of the base and the prefix carrying the secondary stress (*ˌunbeˈlievable*). Deviations from this trend will be discussed below under each prefix.

From a semantic perspective we can distinguish three types of prefixes (Marchand 1969: 134, Hansen et al. 1990: 67) by comparison with free lexemes expressing similar meanings to prefixes:

1. Prefixes with an adjectival role occur with nominal bases and are comparable in semantic content to premodifying adjectives in nominal phrases; *ex-minister*, for example, corresponds to *former minister*.

2. Prefixes with an adverbial role occur with adjectival or verbal bases; cf. *rebuild* 'build again' or *unable* 'not able'.

3. Prefixes can correspond semantically to prepositions with a locative or temporal meaning; cf. *extracellular* 'outside the cell' and *pre-existing* 'existing before a certain time'.

The third type of prefix frequently participates in forming untypical, synthetic and pseudo-prefixations, which will be discussed in detail in the next section.

In contrast to compounds, for which a medium degree of lexicalization is required for typical representatives, typical prefixations are weakly lexicalized, since semantic and formal – in particular phonological – lexicalization processes lead more quickly to the loss of transparency. From an historical perspective we should mention that formations that are formally still analyzable but are already clearly lexicalized were frequently borrowed as complex lexemes from Latin or French. We will refer to degrees of lexicalization again in the description of individual prefixation patterns in sections 8.1.3 and 8.2, which will provide surveys of class-changing and class-maintaining prefixes respectively.

8.1.2   Synthetic prefixations and pseudo-prefixations

By analogy to compounding, we can isolate two classes of untypical prefixations that are striking with respect to their morphological structure.

Synthetic prefixations are characterized by the fact that they are not immediately analyzable morphologically as prefixations, since their bases are not existing English lexemes. For the same reason their analysis in terms of suffixation can also be rejected, with the result that a satisfactory binary morphological analysis is not possible. The adjective *undoubted* and the derived adverb *undoubtedly*, for example, cannot be traced back as prefixations to the base **doubted* nor as suffixations to the base **to undoubt*. As in the case of synthetic compounds, a potential lexeme must be postulated here – but not an actually existing one – as an element taking part in the formation. Since it would be more plausible to analyze *undoubted* as being a prefixation meaning 'not doubted', this argues clearly for treating it as a special form of prefixation – to say nothing of the fact that for reasons of semantic restrictions the verb **to undoubt* cannot even be regarded as a potential English lexeme in the sense of the discussion in section 6.2.3, since the verb *to doubt*, being a non-conclusive verb, is not suitable as the base for the verb-forming prefix *un-*.

So-called **pseudo-prefixations** have to be distinguished from synthetic prefixations. As an example we can take the deonymic (i.e. derived from a name) adjective *post-Freudian* in the noun phrase *the post-Freudian reader* (ICE-GB: W2a-002). From a purely morphological viewpoint there is no reason to reject the segmentation *post + [Freud + ian]*, since the adjective *Freudian* exists. What is problematical, however, is the fact that this morphological analysis cannot be reconciled with the semantic analysis, since the prefix, which has a temporal prepositional function, does not relate to the whole base *Freudian*, but only to the noun *Freud*. *Post-Freudian* means 'existing after Freud' and not 'after Freudian'. As with synthetic compounds we consequently find here an incompatibility between the most plausible semantic and morphological analyses. Formations of this type, which occur in a series of formal variants, will be treated subsequently as prefixations, since if one weighs up the various aspects they fit this pattern best. In the discussion of individual prefixes in the next section and in 8.2, the synthetic and pseudo-prefixations will be pointed out in each case.

8.1.3   Class-changing prefixes

There is a small number of prefixes which have the effect of changing the word class of the base: *a-* (*asleep*), *be-* (*beloved*), *en-* (*encourage*), and certain patterns of *de-* (*declassified*), *dis-* (*displace*) and *un-* (*unsaddle*). How these prefixes and their class-changing effects are dealt with depends on the framework subscribed to. Quirk et al. refer to the prefixes *a-*, *be-* and *en-* as 'conversion prefixes' (1985: 1546), pointing out that they resemble suffixes insofar as they cause a change in word class. Adams (2001: 22 ff.), without any further justification, treats the prefixes *de-*, *dis-* and Germanic *un-* together with denominal verbs that are formed with suffixes such as *-ize*, *-ify* and *-ate*. Bauer (1983) distinguishes simply between 'class-changing' and 'class-maintaining prefixes', but does not comment further on the fundamental functional difference. In contrast Marchand (1969: 134 ff.) and Hansen et al. (1990: 70) direct their attention to the change in word class and argue that this is not triggered by the prefix but by a zero morpheme. The following models of prefixes that change word classes are documented in the MUMC:

a- (/ə/): This prefix, which originates from an Old English preposition, must be distinguished from the homographic, but not homophonic, prefix *a-* (/eɪ/ or /æ/) as in *amoral*. It forms adjectives and adverbs from frequently occurring nominal or verbal bases and adverbs from adjectival bases. Examples of the first type are *ahead, alight, alike, alive, ashamed, aside, asleep, awake*. Examples of the second type are *aloud* and *around*. According to Bauer the prefix was still productive to a limited extent at the beginning of the 1980s (1983: 217).

be-: This prefix forms verbs from verbal, adjectival or nominal bases. The small number of examples in the MUMC are *beloved, bespectacled* and *bestow*, the last example being analyzable although lexicalized to a high degree. Both of the other examples illustrate the most common type of formation with *be-*, viz. denominal adjectives ending in *-ed*. Many verbs of this model occur only in this participial form. According to Quirk et al. (1985: 1546), both institutionalized and new formations derived from this only marginally productive model have a derogatory or ironical undertone.

de-*, *dis- and ***un-*** (with a privative or ablative meaning): These three prefixes occur with several functions and do not change the word class in all usages. We will therefore encounter them again in section 8.2. The uses of these three prefixes which involve a change in word class and are relevant here can be easily isolated semantically, since they express either a privative or an ablative meaning, the *privative* meaning being "to remove the base noun's referent from something", and the *ablative* "to remove an entity from the base noun's referent" (Adams 2001: 23). Examples of privative verbs in the MUMC are *descale, deform, discourage* ('to remove N from something'); the only ablative verb is to *displace* ('to remove something from N'). In addition, the privative synthetic prefixation *dis-*

hearten ('to take away someone's heart/courage') is documented. Formations of this type with *un-* are not found in the MUMC; Adams lists as examples *uncork*, *unmask*, *unburden* (privative) and *uncage*, *unearth*, *unhinge* (ablative). The above-mentioned verb *to descale* is interesting in that the non-prefixed form of the verb, *to scale* (a fish), which is derived by conversion from the noun, also has a privative meaning.

en-: This prefix forms verbs from verbal, adjectival and nominal bases. It occurs in the formal variants *en-* and *em-* (preceding bases with an initial bilabial, i.e. /b/ or /p/; see p. 153 on the allomorphy of *in-* for more details on formal variation). Denominal examples in the MUMC are: *embed* and *engorge* with the locative meaning 'put something in N', and *empower*, *encourage* and *entitled* meaning 'provide someone or something with N'. Deadjectival examples with the meaning 'make something Adj.' are *enable* and *enlarge*. *Enclose* is the only deverbal example with an intensifying meaning. With regard to *engorge*, we should note that it was already a prefixation when it was borrowed. It is however more transparent than the lexemes *embrace* and *enchanted*, which were also borrowed as prefixations and are segmentable but more or less obscured.

8.1.4 Prefixes and related elements

As one might expect, it is not possible to provide a watertight definition of the category PREFIX. Fuzzy boundaries and corresponding demarcation problems occur above all when describing the particles in phrasal compounds and initial combining forms (ICFs) in neo-classical compounds. Although the particles *out*, *over* and *under* fulfil semantic or grammatical functions in compounds that are very similar to those of prefixes, the morphological autonomy of these elements as free morphemes is ultimately decisive for classifying the resulting formations as compounds.

Differentiating between certain initial combining forms and prefixes can be more difficult, because both are by definition bound elements. The large number of divergent classifications to be found in the literature show how blurred the line is between these two categories. The form *hyper-*, for instance, is classified by Bauer (1983: 215) as a combining form, because it can occur together with final combining forms (cf. *hypertrophy*); *super-*, on the other hand, despite its synonymy with *hyper-*, should be regarded as a prefix according to Bauer because it does not appear with final combining forms, but only with free lexical morphemes. On the other hand, Hansen et al. (1990) list both *hyper-* and *super-* as prefixes, although they treat combining forms and what they call *prefixoids* such as *mini-* in a special category defined as formations with prefix-like word-formation elements (1990: 86 ff.). Conversely, Bauer classifies combining forms as prefixes.

What are the criteria that can help to determine the status of unclear cases? Distributional considerations with regard to the **freedom** and **combinability** of questionable elements, as suggested by Bauer for *super-* and *hyper-*, are certainly particularly important, because they are comparatively objective. This means that we have to check in how many other formations a certain element can occur and what the status of the remaining constituents in these formations is. In the case of the form *para-*, for example, the main argument for treating it as a combining form is that it occurs not only with free morphemes, such as *paramilitary*, found in the MUMC, but also with final combining forms, as in *paragraph*. We must also take into account that the demands on prefixes with respect to their productivity, applicability and ability to form paradigms with comparable bases are higher than those on combining forms, which function less predictably and a less rule-governed way when forming lexemes. As a consequence, the notion of *potential lexemes* as described in section 6.2 above makes much more sense with respect to prefixes than to combining forms. Semantic criteria, however, such as the specificity of meaning and complexity of the underlying concept, as well as historical criteria, such as the grammatical status of an element in the source language, are comparatively unreliable.

Ultimately, all these criteria do not permit a final decision, since what we are dealing with here are indeed borderline phenomena. It should be added that postulating a special intermediate category such as *semi prefix* or *prefixoid* as suggested by Hansen et al. (1990: 86) only refines the classificatory problems rather than solving them. Significantly, in the second edition of the best known textbook on German word-formation by Fleischer and Barz (1995) the intermediate category *affixoid*, proposed in the first edition, has also been abandoned and replaced by an exact description of the core area and periphery covered by the category *affix* (Fleischer and Barz 1995: 27–29).

8.2 Corpus study III: overview of prefixation patterns

Now that we have tackled the most important problems we can turn to describing the data in the MUMC to provide a survey of the main patterns of prefixation. To accomplish this, certain patterns will be taken as an opportunity to address basic aspects such as the allomorphy of prefixes, the significance of stress and the degree of lexicalization of prefixations. Apart from that, remarks about the various patterns will be limited to just the essentials. More particulars can be found in the detailed descriptions given by Marchand (1969: ch. III) and Hansen et al. (1990: ch. 2.3.3), from whom I have also taken over the information on semantic types of prefixation on which the following is based.

Of the approx. 41,000 words in the MUMC there are only 291 tokens and 231 types of prefixation. The number of lexemes which occur only once is relatively high, which is not surprising considering the very limited scope of the corpus. On average a prefixation occurs in this corpus every 125 words.

What is more interesting from a sociopragmatic perspective than the frequency of prefixations as a whole is their distribution over the five registers. This is shown in Table 8.1, with the sum total of all tokens and types serving as a reference:

Tab. 8.1:   Distribution of prefixations over the registers of the MUMC

	conversation	letters	fiction	reportage	academic
tokens	4.81 %	9.28 %	19.24 %	23.37 %	43.30 %
types	6.06 %	10.39 %	23.81 %	21.65 %	38.10 %

The table indicates a clear correlation between the formality of the register and the degree of abstractness of content on the one hand, and the frequency of occurrence of prefixations on the other. In spite of the fact that the five parts of the corpus are comparable in length (each containing some 8,000 words), the frequency of prefixations in personal letters is double that found in conversation – the difference being in the dimension of the medium and the form but not the content – and fiction texts contain twice as many as letters. By far the highest proportion of prefixations is found in the most formal and the most abstract variety of text, academic writing, where on average one in sixty words is a prefixation. This confirms the opinion of many authors that the products of certain prefixation models are used particularly frequently in specialist terminology (cf. e.g. Adams 2001: 41).

The following discussion of the corpus findings has been arranged onomasiologically according to the most important semantic groups of prefixes. This shows the semantic and functional similarities to a better advantage than using alphabetical order. Unless stated otherwise, examples of prefixations that occur as bases of derivations (e.g. *interactive* from *interact*), will be cited in the non-extended form (if such a form exists and we are therefore not dealing with a synthetic prefixation).

8.2.1 Negative, reversative and privative prefixes

The prefixes *dis-*, *de-*, *in-* and *un-* denote different variants of negation (**negative**) or reversal (**reversative**) of what is expressed by the base or the **privative** meaning of removal already outlined above.

 The prefix *de-* generates the aforementioned privative and ablative verbs and the reversative deverbal verbs that are relevant here. The only examples of this type are the two nominalizations *depolarisation* and *denervation* (the first of

which could be equally plausibly analyzed as a suffixation of the prefixed verb *depolarise*).

dis-: The prefix *dis-* also occurs in the uses referred to above as well as in adjectives, nouns and verbs with a negative or reversative meaning.

Examples with a negative meaning ('not Adj', 'lack/absence of N', 'not V'):

adjectives:	*disabled, disquieting, dissatisfied*
verbs:	*dislike*
nouns:	*disadvantage, disuse*

Examples with a reversative meaning ('reverse the action of V/N')

verbs:	*disappear, disclaim, discover, disguise*
nouns:	*disorganisation*

Another segmentable but highly lexicalized lexeme that follows this pattern is *disappoint*. *Discover* and *disappear* are also lexicalized, but are more transparent semantically than *disappoint*. All three were either borrowed in a prefixed form or their prefixation was modelled on a French word. Since the stress on the prefix *dis-* is inconsistent even in the case of less lexicalized formations and depends on the number and prominence of the following syllables, it can only be used to a limited extent to determine the degree of lexicalization (compared to *re-*, see p. 156).

in-: This prefix negates adjectives and nouns. Examples in the MUMC are all adjectives, deadjectival nominalizations or adverbs. Due to its many formal variants it is ideal for illustrating the allomorphy of prefixes.

Examples: *illegal, impassive, impatient, impersonal, implausible, impossible, inactive, inadequate, inappropriate, incomplete, incorrect, independent, indirect, indiscriminate, indistinguishable, inessential, infinite, infirm, inflexible, informal, irrational, irresponsible, irreversible*

As the examples show, the prefix *in-* is realized in the formal variants *il-* (*illegal*), *im-* (*impatient*), *in-* (*inactive*) and *ir-* (*irreversible*). The choice of allomorph depends on the initial sound of the base: *il-* occurs before /l/, *im-* before the bilabials /b/ and /p/, and *ir-* before /r/. This consonance is called **regressive assimilation**, since the final phoneme of the prefix is adapted to the first phoneme of the base. The model for this phenomenon were loan words from Latin and French, which were borrowed in an already assimilated form (Hansen et al. 1990: 71).

non-: This prefix, which also produces nonce words, expresses a contradiction, i.e. it does not describe the end of a gradable scale like *in-* and *un-* (cf. *rather impatient, very impatient*), but a binary contrast (**rather non-violent*, **very non-*

violent). It can be combined with nouns, adjectives and adverbs and is sometimes written with a hyphen.

Examples: *non-algorithmic, non-violent*

The noun *nonsense* was also originally formed according to this model. Its spelling without a hyphen, the primary stress falling on the (former) prefix and the reduction of the vowel of the (former) base are all evidence of its high degree of lexicalization (cf. OALD5: /ˈnɒnsns/, s.v. *nonsense*).

Un- is by far the most frequently used prefix in the MUMC, accounting for 80 tokens and 53 types distributed across all five registers. It is also highly productive. In contrast to *in-, un-* has only one formal realization, the reason being that it is of Germanic origin and therefore has no assimilated precursor in Romance languages.

The ablative and privative applications of this prefix have already been discussed alongside *de-* and *dis-* (see p. 152). In addition, there are adjectives and nouns with a negative meaning and verbs with a reversative meaning. The only two examples of nouns are *unreality* and *unrest*, all other nouns being deverbal or deadjectival nominalizations. There are also only two examples of reversative verbs, namely *undo* and *unscramble*.

Adjectival examples: *unable, unacceptable, unaided, unappreciative, uncanny, uncertain, unchanged, uncomfortable, uncommon, uncompromising, unconscious, unconventional, undecided, undeserved, undisturbed, undoubtedly, unduly, undusted, unedifying, uneven, unfavourable, unforgiving, unformulable, unfortunate, unhappy, uninsulated, uninterested, unjust, unknowable, unknown, unlikely, unmade, unnecessary, unprecedented, unreasonable, unruly, unsafe, unsigned, unstable, unsubstantial, unsuspected, untidy, untroubled, unusual, unwarranted, unwashed, unwelcome*

A number of examples are synthetic prefixations: *unchanged, undecided, undoubtedly, unformulable, unknowable, unknown, unmade.*

A further prefix of this type that is not documented in the MUMC is the Latin prefix *a-* (/eɪ/ or /æ/) as in *amoral, asymmetric* and *asexual.*

8.2.2 Locative prefixes

Two examples of word-class changing prefixations with a **locative** meaning have already been mentioned, viz. *embed* and *engorge*. Prefixes with a locative or spatial meaning that preserve the word class are *co-, extra-, inter-, intra-, sub-* and *trans-*. Prefixes of this type generally have meanings comparable with those of locative prepositions.

co-: Quirk et al. (1985: 1542) do not classify this prefix as locative, but as indicating degree with the meaning 'joint(ly)', 'on equal footing'. Since its basic meaning can often be accurately paraphrased using the locative concepts 'joint' or simply 'together', we shall treat it as a locative prefix here. It can be attached to nouns, verbs and adjectives.

Examples: *co-accused, coexist, co-operate, co-ordinate, co-write*

The verbs *co-operate* and *co-ordinate* were borrowed as already prefixed forms from Latin and are semantically clearly more lexicalized than the other examples. Phonologically they also behave differently from the other examples in that the prefix does not carry a secondary stress, cf. ˌco'write vs. co'ordinate.

extra-: The meaning of this prefix is 'outside' or 'beyond'. It occurs frequently in denominal adjectives, with the prefix relating semantically to the nominal base. The only segmentable example of this pattern in the MUMC is the pseudo-prefixed adjective *extra-cellular* 'located outside the cell'. The highly lexicalized adjective *extraordinary*, which was already in existence in Latin and French, is also documented. The second vowel of the prefix has either already coalesced with the initial phoneme of the base or been lost entirely /ɪkˈstrɔːdənərɪ/.

inter-: This prefix meaning 'between', 'among', or 'reciprocally' is still productive and forms nouns, adjectives and verbs. Apart from expressing a locative meaning it can also have a temporal one.

Examples: *interact, interchange, interface, international, interview*

Nouns with bases of one syllable carry the primary stress on the prefix, cf. 'interchange, 'interface and 'interview.

intra-: The only example of this comparatively rare prefix in the MUMC is the pseudo-prefixation *intracellular* 'located inside the cell'.

sub-: Like *intra-* the prefix *sub-* is prevalent in specialist terminology, in particular scholarly texts. Its basic meaning being 'below', it often expresses a relationship of subordination.

Examples: *subdivide, sub-editor, subordinate, subsequent*

Cognate forms of *subordinate* and *subsequent* were already in existence in Latin and French.

trans-: This prefix meaning 'across' occurs mainly in denominal adjectives and verbs, cf. *transatlantic, trans-Siberian; transplant, transship* (Quirk et al. 1985: 1544). The MUMC contains the highly lexicalized borrowed lexeme *transport*, which in its nominal use is stressed on the prefix as in Latin. On the other hand the second documented lexeme, *transform*, being a verb, carries the stress on the base, although it too is borrowed.

8.2.3 Temporal prefixes

Temporal prefixes express a point or period in time relative to a sequence of events. They include elements such as *ex-*, *post-*, *pre-* and *re-*, which are all of Latin origin like the locative prefixes, as well as the Germanic prefix *fore-*.

ex-: This prefix means 'former' and occurs with nouns referring to people or roles. There are two lexemes in the MUMC, *ex-Minister* and *ex-Nazis* both of which can be found in the newspaper reports.

fore-: This prefix can also have a locative meaning. The only example in the MUMC is the noun *forepleasure*, a hybrid formation in which a Germanic prefix is combined with a French loan word.

post-: This prefix meaning 'after' produces adjectives and nouns that often occur syntactically as premodifiers in nominal phrases. Both forms can be regarded as pseudo-prefixations.

Examples: *post-Freudian (readers), postinjury (peripheral innervation density), post-war (traumas), post-1948*

pre-: The semantic opposite of *post-*, *pre-*, is superior to *post-* as regards its applicability. Meaning 'before', it is productive in nouns and adjectives and to a lesser extent in verbs. The only examples in the MUMC are the verb *pre-exist* and the noun *pre-war*, which is used in a premodifying function.

re-: This is a fairly frequent prefix, appearing in semantically transparent formations (e.g. *rebuild, reconnect*) as well as in constructions that are only indicative of the pattern morphologically but are semantically obscured (e.g. *recover, repair*). It mainly occurs in verbs of the accomplishment type to express the repetition of an action, though occasionally it is found in nouns.

The borderline between fully analyzable and more or less obscured formations of this model is fuzzy. In addition to the meaning, the spelling, stress and vowel quality of the prefix are indicators of the degree of lexicalization. Lexemes written with a hyphen, carrying a secondary stress on the prefix and retaining a long, nonreduced vowel /iː/ clearly belong to the analyzable category (*re-educate, re-establish, re-train*). With reference to the spelling, it is striking that the hyphen is particularly often used with bases beginning with an <e>, irrespective of the degree of lexicalization. At the other end of the scale we have semantically demotivated formations with no secondary stress and the vowel /e/ in the prefix, e.g. *recommend* and *represent*. Verbs without secondary stress having the vowel /ɪ/ or /i/ in the prefix – depending on the IPA variant used – are slightly less lexicalized. Examples of this type are *recover, remove, repair, research, resolve, restore, return* and *review*, most of which – like *recommend* and *represent* – were borrowed with their prefixes already in place. *Reappear, react, relax, remind, renew* and *replace* are verbs that can be more or less decomposed semantically but also feature the reduced vowel /ɪ/ in the prefix.

It is interesting to note that the existence of lexicalized verbs does not block prefixations of the same verb; analyzable prefixations are marked by their stress and often also by their spelling, which are signs of their nonlexicalized meaning (cf. *recover* /rɪˈkʌvə/ 'get better' vs. *re-cover* /ˌriː ˈkʌvə/ 'cover again', *recall* /rɪˈkɒl/ 'remember' vs. *re-call* /ˌriː ˈkɒl/ 'call back, again', *represent* /ˌreprɪˈzent/ 'speak for' vs. *re-present* /ˌriː prɪˈzent/ 'present again'. Of all the occurrences of prefixations in the corpus only the following are analyzable:

Examples: *reappear, rebuild, re-train, recombine, reconnect, re-educate, re-establish, re-explore, re-extend, refinance, reincarnate, reinnervate, renarrate, reopen, repackage, repost, reproduce, resettlement, restructure, reunite*

8.2.4 Prefixes denoting degree

The only clear cases in the MUMC of prefixes denoting **degree** are *mini-* 'little' and *ultra-* 'extreme, beyond'. *Mini-* occurs in the interesting lexeme *mini-sub*, a clipping of *mini-submarine*, while *ultra-* is documented in the two adjectives *ultra-right* and *ultrastructural*, the last example being a suffixation of the noun *ultrastructure*, which was lexicalized via the analyzable paraphrase 'beyond the structure' to the current meaning 'pertaining to biological material that is visible only under greater magnification than can be obtained with optical microscopy' (OED, s.v. *ultrastructure*).

Further prefixes of this semantic type which are not recorded in the MUMC are *arch-* and *super-*. Insofar as we want to treat them as prefixes, the three elements *out*, *over* and *under* meaning 'surpassing', 'excessive' and 'too little' respectively, also belong in this category (cf. p. 129). Examples with these meanings are *over-crowding, over-obviously* and *underperformance*. Combining forms such as *mega-* and *nano-* ('on a molecular scale', cf. *nanostructure, nanocrystal, nanotechnology*) seem to be in the process of becoming productive prefixes of this type (cf. Knowles 1997, s.v. *mega-, nano-*).

8.2.5 Number prefixes

The prefixes *bi-* 'two', *mono-* 'one', *multi-* and *poly-*, both meaning 'many', *semi-* 'half' and *tri-* 'three' express **numerical concepts**. They occur chiefly in nouns – also as pseudo-prefixations – and in denominal adjectives in scholarly texts.

Examples:

bi-: bidirectional, bicycle
mono-: monosyllabic

multi-: *multi-layered, multi-tribal*
poly-: *polytechnic*
semi-: *semi-detached, semi-official*
tri-: *trilaminar* 'consisting of three thin sheets'

Bicycle is phonologically lexicalized (cf. the stress on the prefix /ˈbaɪsɪkᵊl/). The nouns *polytechnic* and *semi-detached* are abbreviations of *polytechnic institution* (OED, s.v. *polytechnic* 2) and *semi-detached house*.

Further prefixes of this type are: *di-* 'two', *demi-* 'half' and *uni-* 'one'.

8.2.6 Prefixes denoting attitude

Clear cases of prefixes that express **attitudes** and **opinions** are the antonymous *anti-* 'against' and *pro-* 'for' or 'on the side of'. The other two recorded prefixes of this type, *mis-* and *mal-*, are treated by Quirk et al. (1985: 1541) together with *pseudo-* (*pseudo-intellectual*) as pejorative prefixes. The distinction is justified in that *anti-* and *pro-* denote an attitude with respect to the base (cf. *anti-communist* 'being against communism'), while *mis-* and *mal-* convey the stance of the speaker (*mislead* 'lead wrongly'). For the sake of brevity they are nevertheless subsumed in the category of *attitude-denoting* prefixes.

anti- and *pro-* occur most frequently in adjectival pseudo-prefixations and in nouns; *mis-* and *mal-* prefix verbs and nouns.

Examples:

anti-: *Antarctic, anti-climax, anti-communist, anti-establishment, anti-Syrian*
pro-: *pro-Communist, pro-Israeli, pro-Palestinian, pro-Syrian*
mal-: *malnutrition*
mis-: *mislead, mistrust, misunderstand*

Antarctic and *anti-climax* are not typical examples of the meaning 'against'; a better paraphrase is 'opposed to', the meaning in *Antarctic* being actually more spatial than attitudinal. The word *mistake*, which is both a noun and a verb, is practically unsegmentable and obscure, from both a phonological point of view (since there is no secondary stress on the prefix and the vowel in the prefix can be reduced to /ə/) and a semantic one (since it means 'do the wrong thing' and not 'take wrongly').

Further prefixes denoting attitude include: *contra-* (*contradistinction, contra-factual*) and *counter-* (*counterattack, counter-revolution*).

8.2.7 Summary

Before we can draw any conclusions from the empirical observations with respect to the cognitive functions of prefixation, it will be worthwhile briefly summarizing the most important findings.

The vast majority of the prefixes we have discussed are of Latin or Greek origin. Only the class-changing prefixes *a-*, *be-*, *en-*, and the reversatives *un-* (*unscramble*) and *fore-* are of Germanic origin. The adjectival and nominal negative *un-* (*uncertain*) shares a common Indo-European root with the Ancient Greek *a-* or *an-*, Latin *in-* and German *un-*, which is why it has the character of a native prefix. The origin of this prefix is relevant in several respects even for a synchronic description, for instance in order to explain why the phonetic assimilation of *in-* also appears in the spelling whereas with *un-* it does not. It also has a bearing on the evaluation of the formation pattern of prefixation on the pragmatic level of usage, because there is a connection between the dominance of prefixes of a classical origin and the formality and abstractness of text types and registers. Although some prefixes of classical origin can occur with Germanic bases (e.g. *pre-*, *post-*, *re-*, *un-*), when viewed purely statistically, prefixations are far more frequently Latinisms than native Germanic words and are therefore found more often in formal contexts and texts with an abstract content. Many of the formations discussed here clearly belong in the register of scholarly texts, for instance those with locative prefixes and number prefixes; others are typical of newspaper reports (e.g. *anti-*, *pre-*, *pro-*, *post-*). Above all, the negative prefixations beginning with *un-* and highly lexicalized formations with various prefixes (e.g. *de-*, *dis-*, *pro-* and *re-*) occur extremely frequently in the everyday common core of the English lexicon. They were borrowed in an already prefixed form and are only analyzable in English morphologically, being phonologically adapted and semantically demotivated. Strictly speaking, one could argue that they should not be included in a description of English word-formation. On the other hand, native speakers are acutely aware of their segmentability, and this has been the reason why they were discussed here after all. In terms of quantity, the most frequently occurring semantic types of prefixation patterns are negative adjectives prefixed by *un-*, followed by adjectives prefixed by *in-* and verbs with temporal *re-*. All other semantic types are represented in the corpus in relatively small numbers. There is in general a quantitative preponderance of adjectival formations. Concrete nouns, both animate and in particular inanimate, occur far less often as prefixations than abstract ones. Prefixed verbs exist with reversative (*de-*, *dis-*), locative (*co-*, *inter-*, *sub-*, *trans-*) and temporal meanings (*re-*), but they are far less common than adjectives and nouns. The bases of prefixed verbs are almost exclusively durative and conclusive verbs of the accomplishment type (Quirk et al. 1985: 208), i.e. verbs that refer to processes leading to an end-point (cf. Adams 2001: 43). One exception are stative verbs with the negative prefix *dis-* (e.g. *disbelieve, disagree*).

8.3 Cognitive functions of prefixation

In section 6.1 the fundamental cognitive function of concept-linking with the long-term objective of creating a new, independent concept was attributed to compounding. From a structural and lexical perspective this process can be described as lexicalization. While prefixations can also be lexicalized, it is unlikely that their formation principally serves this purpose, because the most typical prefixations are the ones that are not lexicalized. Which cognitive function then (see p. 103) is behind the existence of prefixations? And what specific use do speakers and – figuratively speaking – the 'English language' make of the existence of this word-formation pattern?

One basic function of prefixation shared by all formal and semantic variants can be deduced from the patterns described in the previous section and their frequency of occurrence: the profiling of a contrast or, in other words, the concept 'different from X'. This concept is based on the fundamental cognitive ability of comparison, i.e. the ability to perceive and recognize differences and contrasts (cf. Langacker 1987a: 101 ff.). That comparison and the perception of contrasts are indeed central aspects of our cognitive system can be seen most clearly perhaps in the conscious and unconscious allocation of attention, which is another basic cognitive ability. Even babies direct their attention involuntarily to changes of states, i.e. situations and activities that are 'different' from before, such as talking after a period of quiet, movement after inactivity and touch after lack of bodily contact. Situations that are 'different' from what occurred before or different from what we would have expected arouse our attention more easily than stable or highly predictable situations. What I am claiming here is that the function of prefixations is **to encode contrasts** by lexical, rather than grammatical, means.

The strongest evidence for this idea can be found in the negative prefixes, which are significantly the most frequent category in the corpus investigated. The basic meaning of the two most common prefixes *un-* and *in-* is simply 'not X', and this covers not just binary contrasts (*even – uneven number*), but also scalar ones (*happy – unhappy*), which are, however, more appropriately paraphrased as 'other than X' (Mettinger 1994: 21 ff.). The third most common prefixation type in the corpus, temporal *re-*, can equally plausibly be interpreted in terms of a contrast. The important point here is that, as we have mentioned, the verbal bases are almost exclusively verbs of the accomplishment type. By definition, part of the meaning of these verbs is the expectation that the action being described is or has been brought to an end (cf. e.g. *build, connect, open, unite*). It is this very expectation that contradicts the meaning 'again' expressed by the prefix *re-*. If something has been completed, why does it have to be done again? *Rebuild, reconnect, reopen* and *reunite* could therefore be paraphrased as 'in contrast to what might be expected, someone builds/connects etc. again'. A comparable expectational stance can also be postulated for the reversative verbal prefixes *de-* (*depolarize*) and *dis-*

(*disappear*) – 'although something is/has already (been) polarized/appeared, the process is reversed'.

The remaining prefixes that do not explicitly express an opposition or a contrast can be assigned to one of four basic conceptual categories: SPACE (locative prefixes), TIME (temporal prefixes), QUANTITY (prefixes denoting degree and number prefixes) and ATTITUDE. Significantly, these categories are cognitively so important that they are all encoded by closed classes and grammatical categories – SPACE by prepositions and the system of deixis, TIME also by prepositions and the category TENSE, QUANTITY by the number system (singular, plural) and ATTITUDE by the modal verbs. Keeping this in mind, we can make a case for the concept 'different' being involved in these four categories as well. In the case of locative and temporal prefixes the bases serve as a reference point for spatial or temporal specifications. *Pre-war* is equivalent to 'not during or after but before the war', *sub-editor* 'not editor but operating at a lower level', *extra-cellular* 'not inside but outside the cell'. The impression that we are dealing here with contrasts as well is reinforced by the semantic opposition between the individual prefixes: *extra-* vs. *intra-*, *intra-* vs. *inter-*, *sub-* vs. *super-*, *pre-* vs. *post-*. This type of opposition is also essentially responsible for producing contrast in prefixes denoting attitude. *Pro-Palestinian* has its opposite in *anti-Palestinian*, and in the other two prefixes of this type *contra-* and *counter-* the contrastive factor is semantically inherent. Lastly, prefixes indicating degree such as *ultra-*, *sub-* and s*uper-* have the meaning 'more than' and 'less than', which also already incorporates the comparison and contrast with a norm which is not specified but is implied by the speaker. *Ultra-right*, for instance, means 'excessively right from my point of view'.

Other significant observations supporting the claim that the principal function of prefixations is to profile contrasts are pattern-specific gaps in productivity and the frequencies of occurrences mentioned above. It has already been pointed out that prefixed verbs occur almost exclusively with verbs of the accomplishment type. The very reason why prefixations cannot be formed with stative verbs (**unlive*, **unsit*) or nonconclusive durative verbs (**unsleep*, **unrain*, **unplay*) is that they do not have any 'natural' contrasts. For the same reason nouns that describe concrete objects are not suitable as bases for prefixations, since they do not have any obvious opposites. It is not by chance that the vast majority of antonyms (*good – bad, high – low, poor – rich* etc.) and other types of simplex opposites comes from the word class of adjectives – which, as we have established, also seem to be the most productive type of prefixation. Adjectives typically have a one-dimensional conceptual structure, which is ideally suited to setting up contrasts. This is not true of concrete nouns, whose conceptual structures are more complex. Hence we find it easy to answer the question 'What is the opposite of *big*?', while we have difficulties dealing with 'What is the opposite of *tree*?'. *Rich* immediately calls up *poor*, but *money* has no comparable counterpart. The same applies to nouns denoting people, which significantly also seldom occur as bases in prefixations. Insofar as contrasts immediately spring to mind, for instance in the case of gender-specific lexemes, the antonyms are already institutionalized as simplexes (cf. *man – woman, boy – girl, father – mother*) or, interestingly, are encoded by means of suffixation (vgl. *waiter – waitress, actor – actress*). This means that the contrast here leads to the conceptual re-profiling as a different type of concept (cf. section 9.4 on the cognitive functions of suffixation).

Finally, the typical phonological structure of prefixations can be invoked as an argument for the contrast theory of prefixation. It has been mentioned several times that highly lexicalized lexemes that have lost the status of prefixations, or have never had it in English (because they were borrowed), can be distinguished by the loss or the absence of secondary stress on the prefix. The reason why the secondary stress is not or no longer necessary in lexicalized formations is that as lexicalization progresses, the contrast profiled by the prefix is also lost. Pairs of the type *recover* /rɪˈkʌvə/ 'get better' vs. *re-cover* /ˌriː ˈkʌvə/ 'cover again' clearly demonstrate that the secondary stress in the nonlexicalized prefixation alludes to the contrast.

What is the cognitive advantage of prefixation if – as we have noted – the same contrast can be expressed by means of an adjectival, adverbial or prepositional phrase? In what ways are *pre-war* and *before the war, unhappy* and *not happy, re-educate* and *educate again* and *ex-minister* and *former minister* different from one another? First of all, the potential syntactic simplification and condensation undoubtedly plays a role, particularly in cases such as *pre-war*, which frequently functions as a modifier (cf. *the pre-war years* vs. *the years before the war*). However, this is not the crucial point. What is more important is the fact that a state of affairs is moulded into a concept, an idea is entrenched and can be stored in the mental lexicon. *The pre-war years* is more than merely *the years before the war*: The expression does not just refer to the period of time itself, but says something specific about these years in the sense of 'those years before the war, we all know what they were like'. *Unhappy* is not simply *not happy*, which strictly speaking could mean 'neither happy nor sad', but 'the opposite of *happy*'. While syntactic groups have to be assembled anew during processing and interpreted according to their structure, prefixations need only to be recalled from the mental lexicon where they are stored. Prefixations therefore imply a gentle 'You know what I mean and what the two of us (and the speech community as a whole) associate with it'. Compared to compounds, prefixations may typically be less lexicalized, but they are institutionalized as words and entrenched as concepts in exactly the same way. Unlike superficially synonymous syntactic constructions, they have their own conceptual substance and plasticity and can conjure up a huge number of associations (see p. 81 on entrenchment and concept-formation).

Further reading: On the prefix *un-*: **Mettinger (1994), Plag (2003: 30 ff.), Hay (2007)**.

9 Suffixation

When viewed from a purely formal, morphological perspective, suffixation – or
suffix derivation – is the mirror image of prefixation. A bound lexical morpheme
is attached to the end of a base consisting of at least one free lexical morpheme, as
for example in *enjoy-able*, *weak-ness*, *slow-ly*. The suffix determines the word
class of the whole derivation and thus functions as head in spite of the fact that it
is a bound morpheme. Since the suffix brings about a change of word class in the
vast majority of suffixations, this transposition is regarded as the key function of
the word-formation pattern of suffixation from a structural grammatical point of
view.

9.1 Typical suffixations and transitional phenomena

9.1.1 Typical suffixations

Typical suffixations are distinguished by the fact that the base survives the suffixation process without undergoing any changes to its phonological or morphological form. Typical suffixes such as *-able* and *-er* are highly productive and
form paradigms, i.e. they can be attached to a large number of bases that are
grammatically and semantically similar. The degree of lexicalization of typical
suffixations is probably lower than that of prefixations.

The following deviations from or variations of prototypical cases of suffixation
can be observed: morphological and/or phonological changes in the base occur
(see section 9.1.2); instead of free morphemes bound elements can function as
bases (9.1.3); and finally, the status of the added elements as suffixes can be questionable with regard to the criterion that suffixes should be applicable to a range of
bases and form paradigms (9.1.4).

9.1.2 Stem allomorphy and morphophonological variation

In a considerable number of suffixations in English the base does not remain
unchanged but emerges in a phonologically and/or morphologically altered form.
The term **allomorph** offers itself as a suitable name for this phenomenon, since we
have already come across it in inflectional morphology as referring to formal
variants (see section 2.4). Bases such as *irony*, which change their intonation
pattern and their vowel quality in suffixations (cf. *ironical*), are consequently
described as **stem allomorphs**. Thus the stem morpheme {irony} is realized in the

two variants /ˈaɪərənɪ/ (in *irony*) and /aɪˈrɒnɪ/ (in *ironical*). As we have already mentioned in section 3.1.2, the interface between morphology and phonology, which deals with such phenomena, is called **morphophonemics** or **mor(pho)- phonology**. Stem allomorphs are therefore also referred to as morphonological **alternants**. The aim of this section is to discuss the most important types of mor- phonological variation.

(9.1) is a list of examples from the corpus illustrating the smallest change in the base, namely the assimilation of the final consonant of the base with the initial sound of the suffix:

(9.1)   *commit*   →   *commission*
        exclude   →   *exclusive*
        express   →   *expression*
        relate   →   *relation*
        use   →   *usual*

Most instances involve the assimilation of final plosives (/p, t, k, b, d, g/), often leading to palatalization to /ʃ/ or /ʒ/. The catalyst for such sound changes is the initial /i/ or /j/ of suffixes such as *-ion*, *-ive* and *-ial*.

In many cases the assimilation is accompanied by a change in the vowel of the stressed syllable:

(9.2)   *decide* (/dɪˈsaɪd/)   →   *decision* (/dɪˈsɪʒən/)
        divide (/dɪˈvaɪd/)   →   *division* (/dɪˈvɪʒən/)
        please (/pliːz/)   →   *pleasure* (/ˈpleʒə/)
        describe (/dɪˈskraɪb/)   →   *description* (/dɪˈskrɪpʃən/)

As the examples in (9.2) indicate, the long vowel in the base usually becomes shortened. The diphthongs in *decide*, *divide* and *describe* become monophthongs in the derived forms, and the long vowel /iː/ in *please* is shortened to /e/ in *pleas- ure*. These changes are caused by the extra syllable of the suffix changing the prosodic structure of the word. In *appear* (/əˈpɪə/) → *apparent* (/əˈpærənt/) a vowel change takes place without assimilation.

The most frequent morphonological alternation pattern is probably the combina- tion of a shift of stress within the base with a qualitative and quantitative change in the vowels.

(9.3)   *adore* (/əˈdɔː/)   →   *adoration* (/ædəˈreɪʃn/)
        combine (/kəmˈbaɪn/)   →   *combination* (/kɒmbɪˈneɪʃn/)
        economy (/ɪˈkɒnəmi/)   →   *economic* (/ekəˈnɒmɪk/)
        Italy (/ˈɪtəli/)   →   *Italian* (/ɪˈtælɪan/)
        major (/ˈmeɪdʒə/)   →   *majority* (/məˈdʒɒrɪti/)
        mobile (/ˈməʊbaɪl/)   →   *mobility* (/məʊˈbɪlɪti/)

Whether suffixations are affected by such changes or not depends in the first place on historical factors and, in addition, on the individual suffixes (cf. Quirk et al. 1985: 1590 ff.). Words of Germanic origin and early borrowings from French do not change their stress pattern even when a suffix is added. In later borrowings, however, and in derivations from bases of a Latin or Greek origin, the stress shifts depending on the suffix. Adjectives ending in *-ic* and *-ian*, for example, are always stressed on the syllable before the suffix, i.e. the penultimate syllable (cf. *economic*, *Italian*); the same applies to nouns with the suffixes *-ion* (*combination*) and *-ity* (*mobility*). These changes in stress patterns are also responsible for the changes in the vowels, since they cause syllables to become stressed which were previously unstressed and vice versa. In the case of *major – majority*, for example, the weak vowel /ə/ in the second syllable becomes the full vowel /ɒ/. A complementary case is the pair *economy – economical*, in which the full vowel /ɒ/ in the second syllable of *economy* is reduced to /ə/ in *economical*, because the main stress is shifted to the next syllable.

While the shift of stress and its accompanying sound changes are still productive and regular today, other morphological changes are only relevant and explicable historically. The discrepancy between the base and the derivation can often be traced to the fact that historically no derivation took place in English, since both lexemes were borrowed independently of each other from Latin or French, as was the case with the already cited example *appear – apparent*. In a number of cases this is quite striking, for instance when the potential base and its derivation differ markedly from one another (e.g. *deceive – deception, receive – reception*) or when extra sounds are inserted, as in *compete – competition, crime – criminal* and *imply – implication*. Interestingly, according to the OED this historical explanation also applies to *economy – economical* and many other lexemes which can nevertheless be analyzed synchronically as derivations without any problems.

9.1.3 Derivational correlation and suffixations with bound roots

Certain problems in the analysis created by word pairs such as *intricate – intricacy* and *aggressive – aggression* and paradigms such as *special – specific – specify* and *distal – distant – distance* also have historical causes. All these cases have in common that despite the obvious participation of frequently occurring derivational suffixes such as *-ate, -ous, -ity* and *-ify*, they cannot be easily segmented morphologically, because the deletion of the supposed suffixes does not leave us with free but bound elements, cf. *intric-, aggress-, spec-/specif-* and *dist-*.

There are various ways of dealing with this problem. Firstly, it is possible to adhere strictly to the definition of suffixation, which would mean not segmenting lexemes of this type any further because the supposed root is bound, and thus interpreting the lexemes as monomorphematic. However, this runs counter to the strong feeling that a meaning equivalent to that of free lexical morphemes can indeed be assigned to the potential base.

Three other approaches argue the case for segmentation into base plus suffix: The first, which lends itself above all to systematic pairs of suffixes such as *-ate* and *-acy* or *-ive* and *-ion*, assumes a so-called **correlative derivation** and is based on an historical argument. Such correlations originated from pairs of loan words; forms were created in English in analogy to these borrowed pairs, which served as models, even if just one part of a potential pair was actually borrowed. According to Hansen et al. (1990) for instance, the adjective *cautious* was derived from the previously borrowed noun *caution* by analogy with *ambition – ambitious*. The implicit prerequisite for this type of explanation is that a loan word undergoes a process called **truncation**, in the course of which parts of an existing lexeme are split off as genuine or supposed suffixes, and are replaced by other suffixes. Truncation also plays a decisive role in the second model (Aronoff 1976: 87 ff.), in which the lexemes in question are accounted for by means of a combination of truncation and stem (or root) allomorphy. The third possibility is to work with the idea of a **bound root**, a morphological unit which has already been introduced in section 2. This makes sense particularly for potential bases that are highly productive. In this approach the semantic segmentability is given priority over the demands on the autonomy of the base. As we have already pointed out (cf. p. 40), bound roots may only be posited if a meaning can be assigned to them which is recognizable in all its uses, if they produce paradigms, and if the remaining element can be clearly identified as an existing suffix.

9.1.4 Suffixes and related elements

There are blurred boundaries between suffixes and similar elements in various directions. Typical suffixes must be able to be attached to all the representatives of a grammatically and semantically definable group of lexemes and ideally be productive or at least have been productive over a long period of time with an identifiable meaning. Furthermore they should, of course, also unquestionably be bound morphemes.

With regard to this criterion of being bound, transitional phenomena are often postulated when it comes to distinguishing between suffixations and compounds. It has been argued, for instance, that compounds ending in *-man* (*policeman*, *postman*, *salesman*) are increasingly taking on the characteristics of suffixations, since the element *-man* meaning 'person' and having the weakened pronunciation of *-man* as /mən/ is very similar to an affix (Hansen et al. 1990: 65 ff., Ungerer 2002: 558–560). Elements such as *-dom*, *-hood* and *-ful* prove that this reasoning is by no means implausible, since they are treated today without doubt as suffixes, although they also arose from independent lexemes by means of shortening and reduction of the vowels. Further free forms that seem to be adopting suffix-like features are *-like* (in the corpus *waif-like*, elsewhere e.g. *childlike, fish-like*), *-wise* (*workwise, moneywise*) and *-type* (*California-type barbecues, questionnaire-type of work-sheet*, cf. Dalton-Puffer and Plag 2000, Lenker 2002).

A second transitional area is found between typical suffixes and final combining forms in examples such as *-ology*, *-crat* and *-graph*, as well as in the area of the suffix-like elements resulting from secretion, both of which have already been mentioned (see p. 94, 130). Table (9.4) shows examples of the latter type of forms taken from Warren's article (1990: 129) and provides their source lexemes:

(9.4)	'suffix'	derived form	source
	-(a)holic	*workaholic, spendaholic*	*alcoholic*
	-athon	*bikeathon, swimathon*	*marathon*
	-erati	*glitterati, slopperati*	*?literati*
	-gate	*Yuppiegate, Iraqgate*	*Watergate*
	-boom	*vegeboom*	*baby boom*
	-speak	*computerspeak, econospeak*	*newspeak*

The hallmark of the process of secretion is that important aspects of the meaning of the original word are projected into the separated elements, which then gain productivity as they are used in new coinings. In my opinion these forms should not be treated as suffixes in the strict sense of the word because their meaning is generally much more specific than that of typical suffixes. Moreover, with regard to their grammatical and cognitive functions they bear very little resemblance to typical suffixes and can only form paradigms to a limited extent. The intention of being original and linguistically creative is clearly perceptible in all coinings of this type.

9.2 Corpus study IV: overview of types and models of suffixation

Viewed from a purely quantitative point of view, suffixation is a far more significant word-formation pattern than prefixation. There are about ten times as many examples of suffixations than there are prefixations in the MUMC, and the number of suffixed lexemes (qua types) is also greater than that of the prefixed ones. A detailed treatment of all the patterns of suffixation is not possible here due to lack of space. It is also not absolutely necessary insofar as publications such as Marchand (1969: ch. IV), Urdang (1982), Hansen et al. (1990: chs. 2.3.4) and more compactly Kastovsky (1985: 223–227), Quirk et al. (1985: App. I.31), Adams (2001: ch. 4), Bauer and Huddleston (2002: 1666 ff.) and Plag (2003: 86 ff.) offer overviews of the field of suffixation and detailed information on the individual suffixes. Of course, suffixes also feature prominently in Stein's (2007) dictionary of English affixes. Compared to the rather neglected area of prefixation, there is also a large number of individual studies on the meaning, usage and productivity of various suffixes, the most important of which will be cited in the references at the end of this chapter.

The sources mentioned above are very similar in that they all approach the field from a semasiological perspective. This means they list individual suffixes and comment on their meanings and uses. In contrast to this approach, the following sections will be structured using a combination of a grammatical and an onomasiological perspective. As usual the suffixes will be specified according to the word class of the derived form (e.g. noun-forming suffix) and of their bases by means of adjectives with the prefix *de-*. **Deverbal noun-forming suffixes,** for instance, create nouns from verbs (e.g. *agreement, baker*); **deadjectival verb-forming suffixes** have adjectives as a base and form verbs (e.g. *legalize, weaken*).

9.2.1 Noun-forming suffixes: reification

Noun-forming suffixes can be attached to verbal, adjectival and nominal bases, the latter – denominal noun-forming suffixations – being quantitatively by far the least significant. The most frequent types are deverbal nominalizations, followed by deadjectival ones, of which there are, however, only about a third as many in the corpus.

From a cognitive-semantic perspective and on a high level of generalization, the effect of noun-forming suffixes can be described as **reification** (i.e. 'turning into an object', from Latin *res* 'thing' + *-ify* + *-ation*). Nominal concepts, which seem to have the notional status of 'things' (see p. 108) even when they are abstract, are created from verbs and adjectives that typically express event, action or process concepts on the one hand, or quality concepts on the other. While verbs such as *confirm* and *meet*, for instance, profile actions as processes which take place over time, the derived nominalizations *confirmation* and *meeting* suggest the existence of a 'thing' which appears conceptually like a concrete object: stable in time, spatially bounded and to a certain degree tangible. This effect of reification is particularly striking in the not infrequent cases where the nominalization of an action is actually lexicalized with the meaning of a concrete object 'product of V-ing' as, for example, in *declaration* and *invitation*. Both of these nouns can refer to concrete products of writing via metonymy from the speech act of declaring or of inviting to the carrier medium of the speech act. Nominalizations of such speech act verbs and also of many other action verbs are notoriously ambiguous (cf. Bauer 1983: 185–187, Schmid 2000: 149–151). Typical meanings range from 'action of V-ing' through 'individual instance of V-ing', 'result of V-ing' to 'concrete product of V-ing', with the degree of reification of the action increasing significantly.

Deverbal noun-forming suffixes

On a more fine-grained level of description, the effects of deverbal noun-forming suffixes can be divided into four semantic categories which profile central aspects of actions:

- profiling of the actions as such as things ('action-reifying' suffixes): *-(a)(t)ion, -ment, -ence/-ance, -ing, -al, -age, -ure*. (The term *action* is used here to subsume both actions in a narrow sense, which are carried by wilfully acting agents, and non-agentive processes and events.)
- profiling of the persons involved in the action ('personizing' suffixes): *-er, -or, -ent, -ant, -ee*.
- profiling of the instruments used by agents ('instrumentizing' suffixes): *-er, -or, -ent, -ant*.
- profiling of the place where actions are carried out ('localizing' suffixes): *-age, -ery*.

The rationale behind this description of noun-forming suffixes was explained in section 5.3.3 (see p. 105 f.), where it was claimed that complex lexemes profile parts of larger scenes in certain ways. For example, both *baker* and *bakery* activate the scene of someone baking in a bakery, but *baker* reifies the action by profiling the agent involved in the event, while *bakery* profiles the location.

The most frequent **action-reifying suffixes** are shown in Table 9.1 with examples from the MUMC, their *token*-frequency and information on their productivity.

Tab. 9.1:   Action-reifying suffixes

suffix	selected examples from the MUMC	tokens	productivity
-(a)(t)ion	*decision, imagination, impression, operation, projection, restriction, transformation*	452	productive, esp. with verbs ending in *-ize*, *-ify*, *-ate*
-ment	*achievement, assessment, development, equipment, impeachment, settlement*	101	no longer productive
-ence/ -ance	*acceptance, appearance, difference, existence, confidence, insistence, resistance*	97	productive
-ing	*beginning, blessing, building, meeting, painting, warning*	78	productive

-al	approval, arrival, betrayal, burial, denial, proposal, trial, withdrawal	27	productive
-age	blockage, coverage, marriage, package, shrinkage	17	productive
-ure	failure, mixture, pleasure, pressure, seizure	13	not productive

On the face of it, it may seem patently absurd to ascribe a reifying effect to these suffixations, which are well known to be **abstract nominalizations**. However, we must regard reification as a process which produces thing-like concepts in the sense that they can be worked with cognitively like object concepts, that is they seem to represent bounded, countable, in a way even tangible entities. If we understand the notion of reification along these lines, then the term *abstract action reification* turns out to be no longer paradoxical.

As has already been indicated, many of these nominalizations cover a broad semantic range which is not arbitrary but exhibits an inner coherence based on metonymic relationships. This is shown in Figure 9.1 with typical examples expressing the illustrated meaning in each case.

Fig. 9.1:   Selected semantic variants of action-reifying suffixations

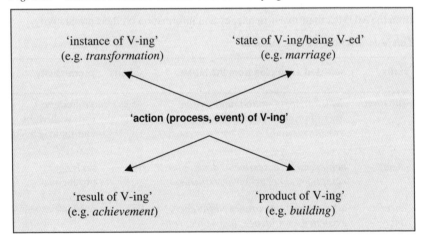

The meaning 'action (process, event) of V-ing' given in the centre of Figure 9.1 should be regarded as a neutral or superordinate form of reification as described above, which has more specific variants, including reference to specific instances of actions (cf. *transformation* 'instance of transforming'). Further possibilities for the reification of actions result in the meanings 'state of V-ing/being V-ed' (*marriage* 'state of being married'), the already mentioned 'result of V-ing' (*achievement* 'result of achieving') and 'product of V-ing' (*building* 'product of building'). The 'product' meaning can be described as metonymic transfer based on the everyday experience that actions usually pursue a goal that often lies in creating an object or in bringing about a state of affairs. The ideal bases for nominalizations of this type are verbs of the accomplishment type, i.e. conclusive verbs implying an end point (Quirk et al. 1985: 208).

The difference between the reification of states or processes per se as opposed to references to individual instances is reflected grammatically by the fact that nouns of the abstract type are not countable and only occur in the singular (cf. example 9.5), while those of the non-abstract type occur as countable nouns with articles and numerals and in the plural (9.6).

(9.5)   Rains have failed for four years and, says the United Nations, 1.9m people are on the brink of *starvation* in the nine provinces where … (ICE-GB: W2c 002-073)

(9.6)   At the same time, the NCC will send its *recommendations* for 14 to 16-year-olds to McGregor … (ICE-GB: W2c 002-014)

Personizing suffixes profile perhaps the most prominent aspect of actions, namely the people involved in them (cf. Table 9.2).

Tab. 9.2:   Personizing and instrumentizing suffixes

suffix	selected examples from the MUMC	tokens	productivity
-er, -or	*buyer, dealer, killer, leader, writer, teacher* *boiler, duster, computer, wrapper*	123	very productive
-ent, -ant	*combatant, inhabitant, student* (*coolant, disinfectant*)	17	productive mainly in technical registers
-ee	*amputee, trustee, refugee* (base: noun)	7	productive

It is not by chance that by far the most frequent personizing suffixes relate to the most striking role of the deliberate instigator of actions, the *agent*, which is profiled by means of the forms *-er*, *-or* and the less frequent *-ent* and *-ant*. This is the type described traditionally as **nomina agentis** or **agent nominalizations**. The examples *boiler* (which could also be analyzed as denoting a container), *duster*, *computer*, *coolant* and *disinfectant* show that, besides personizing, instrumentizing can also be produced by these suffixes, which is not surprising in view of the close cognitive connection between agents and the instruments they use. This can also be regarded as a case of metonymic transfer, i.e. as a personification of the instruments.

Far less frequent is the profiling of people who are involved in actions carried out by somebody else or are affected by them (e.g. in the role of *patient*), by means of the suffix *-ee*. The suffix *-ee* usually carries the meaning 'person who is/has been V-ed' (e.g *interviewee*), less common 'person who V-s' (as in *refugee* 'someone who takes refuge'), although it is crucial that the affected person does not control the action himself but acts reluctantly and reactively (Barker 1995: 11 ff.). As shown in a detailed empirical study by Mühleisen (2010), the suffix *-ee* is a particularly good example of the semantic variability and heterogeneity of word-formation patterns.

Localizing suffixes are of comparatively marginal significance. They profile places, buildings and institutions that serve specific purposes and are structured specifically for these purposes. The main types are *-age* (*storage*) and *-ery* (cf. *bakery*, *brewery*, *refinery*), but the MUMC does not include any examples of them. From a cognitive perspective action concepts are transferred to domain concepts (Ungerer 2002: 544).

Deadjectival noun-forming suffixes

As one would expect, the function of deadjectival noun-forming suffixes is to reify qualities. Apart from the more frequent suffixes of this type collated in Table 9.3, the MUMC also contains *-ency* as a correlative derivation of *-ent* (*emergency*, *currency*, *urgency*) and *-dom* (*freedom*, *wisdom*), *-hood* (*likelihood*) and *-acy* (*supremacy*).

Tab. 9.3: Suffixes that reify qualities

suffix	selected examples from the MUMC	tokens	productivity
-ity	*ability, complexity, feasibility, hostility, reality, relativity, responsibility, validity*	143	productive, esp. with Adj. ending in *-able*
-ness	*awareness, bitterness, darkness, greyness, kindness, madness, slowness, weariness*	34	productive
-th	*depth, length, strength, truth, warmth*	28	not productive

Most uses of these suffixes – unless they have been lexicalized to a high degree like *currency* for instance – can be satisfactorily paraphrased as having the general meaning 'quality/state of being Adj' (e.g. *ability*: 'state of being able').

The personalizing of qualities can be observed in deadjectival nominalizations ending in *-er* such as *commoner, foreigner* and *stranger*, and in *-ster* as in *youngster*.

Denominal noun-forming suffixes

Denominal noun-forming suffixations, while not being very significant quantitatively, are conceptually interesting in that reification can hardly be said to be operative here because there is no change of word class. Since traditionally a change of word class is considered to be the *raison d'être* of suffixation, we have to resort to the hypothesis that there is a change of word subclass from concrete to abstract or from animate to inanimate nouns. In fact the profiling as an abstract or a person concept is the most important semantic effect of denominal noun-forming suffixations. Suffixes of this type are listed in Tables 9.4 and 9.5:

Tab. 9.4: Denominal noun-forming suffixes profiling abstract concepts

suffix	selected examples from the MUMC	tokens	productivity
-ship	*censorship, companionship, dictatorship, friendship, leadership, relationship*	30	low degree of productivity
-ism	*criticism, feminism, optimism, pessimism, symbolism, terrorism*	22	productive

Tab. 9.5: Denominal noun-forming suffixes profiling person concepts

suffix	selected examples from the MUMC	tokens	productivity
-ist	*archaeologist, economist, journalist, Marxist, naturalist, receptionist, theorist*	37	productive
-er	*banker, farmer, gardener, honeymooner, lawyer, prisoner*	25	productive
-ian, -an	*American, Christian, historian, Italian, Palestinian, mathematician, politician*	21	productive
-ie, -y	*Aussie, Aunty, groupie, nightie*	8	productive
-ese	*Chinese, Lebanese, Portuguese*	3	productive

The suffix *-ship* forms lexemes that can be paraphrased either as 'state of being N' (e.g. *companionship, dictatorship*) or as 'collective of Ns' (*leadership*) (Hansen et al. 1990: 110 ff.). Lexemes formed with the suffix *-ism*, which are semantically less specific (often meaning 'connected with/based on'), correlate to a certain extent with those ending in *-ist* or are derived from bound roots (see section 9.1.3). According to Knowles (1997: 162 ff.), both *-ism* and *-ist* have become increasingly popular since the 1980s in the wake of the political correctness movement, and what is remarkable is their combination with native bases (cf. for example the more or less serious formations *bodyism, beardism, peopleism*).

The most common meaning for denominal suffixations ending in *-er* is 'person who works at' (*banker, farmer, gardener*), but, as the examples *prisoner* ('person being held in prison') and *honeymooner* ('person currently on a honeymoon') show, other meanings are possible. The forms *-an/-ian* and *-ese* compete for the person profiling of designations for countries, while *-y* and *-ie* can be distinguished by whether they indicate familiarity (*Aunty*), or have ironical undertones (*Aussie*). Dictionaries of neologisms reveal that this suffix has recently been quite fashionable, cf. *aerobie, archie, foodie, fundie, techie* in Knowles (1997). Conversely suffixes such as *-ette* and *-ess*, which form feminine counterparts to masculine or gender-neutral lexemes (cf. *sailorette, usherette, godess, waitress, stewardess*), have almost ceased to be productive, if we disregard more or less sexist or humorous formations such as the suffixation of a shortened base *proette* ('female professional golfer', Adams 2001: 56).

Apart from these suffixes there are individual cases of localizing and temporalizing ones ending in *-age, -ery* and *-hood*, e.g. *orphanage* ('place where orphans live'), *perfumery* ('place where perfume is made or sold') and *childhood* ('period when a child').

9.2.2 Adjective-forming suffixes: modalizing and relationizing

Given that adjectives typically profile quality concepts, on the maximum level of abstraction the attribution of qualities could be postulated as the main semantic effect of adjective-forming suffixations. Not much is gained by this, however, because this description only reflects the typical semantic function of adjectives in grammar. Nevertheless it is important to bear in mind that adjectives are not completely independent concepts, but express specifications of the characteristics of object concepts in an attributive (*the green house*) or predicative position (*the house is green*). The reason why it is impossible to generalize about this type of suffixation is that the profiling of qualities turns out in completely different ways, depending on whether the underlying base is a verbal action concept or a nominal object concept. When the base is a verb, the derived adjective expresses action-related characteristics of the modified nouns: e.g. what one can do with the referents of the nouns (*enjoyable moments*); what the referent is doing possibly or probably (*explosive material*); what one can achieve by it (*preventive social work*). If the underlying concept is a noun, however, then the derived adjective expresses a relationship between the modified noun and either a thing (e.g. *poison* in *Is that sort of descaler not poisonous?*), an idea (*theology* in *theological people*) or a social domain (*culture* in *cultural significance*, or *economy* in *economic environment*). These two variants of adjective-forming suffixations are therefore treated under the headings *modalizing* and *relationizing*.

Deverbal adjective-forming suffixes: modalizing

The three deverbal adjective-forming suffixes documented in the MUMC are collated in Table 9.6.

Tab. 9.6: Modalizing deverbal adjective-forming suffixes

suffix	selected examples from the MUMC	tokens	productivity
-ive	*attractive, creative, explosive, interactive, progressive, preventive, supportive*	85	productive
-able	*adorable, comfortable, detectable, enjoyable, predictable, remarkable, suitable*	73	productive
-ant, *-ent*	*dependent, different, pleasant, significant, sufficient, violent*	54	not productive

Both the productive suffixes *-ive* and *-able* express meanings that can be interpreted as specific forms of modalization. In other words, like the modal verb *can*, which can often be used to paraphrase these suffixes, they profile possibilities, probabilities and inclinations. The uses of *-able* and *-ible* – these being orthographic variants of the same suffix – can be defined with the semantic complex 'can be V-ed' or 'is likely to be V-ed' (e.g. *detectable, enjoyable*), and 'is worthy of being V-ed' (*adorable*) (Hansen et al. 1990: 111 ff.). The suffix *-ive* also encodes probabilities, but in contrast to *-able* it expresses the active perspective 'tending to V' (cf. *attractive, creative* etc.) and not the passive 'likely to be V-ed'.

Denominal adjective-forming suffixes: relationizing

The fairly general expression *relationizing* has been deliberately chosen in order to have at our disposal an umbrella term subsuming different types of interrelationships. The most general form of relationizing can be described using paraphrases such as 'connected with N', 'of the nature of N', 'having qualities associated with N' and 'having the properties of N'. Relationships with specific domains or fields are established (cf. Ungerer's term *adjectival domain concepts*, 2002: 550). Many lexemes of this type lend themselves to the evaluative establishment of relationships, i.e. appraising or critical expressions (e.g. *cynical, marvellous, ridiculous*). Individual aspects may be more or less applicable depending on the suffix, base and context, and of course further semantic specifications are added as a result of lexicalization. If we disregard these differences – which have been described in the reference books already mentioned – and look for common ground, the following suffixes can be assigned to this semantic complex:

Tab. 9.7: Denominal adjective-forming suffixes of the type 'connected with N'

suffix	selected examples from the MUMC	tokens	productivity
-al, -ial, -ical, -ual	*anatomical, colonial, financial, mathematical, sentimental, sexual, spiritual, traditional, technological*	341	productive, esp. with bases ending in *-ation*
-ic	*academic, algorithmic, artistic, bureaucratic, dramatic, scientific, symbolic*	92	productive
-ary	*domiciliary, elementary, necessary, parliamentary, revolutionary*	32	low degree of productivity
-ous	*monstrous, nervous, ominous, religious, synonymous*	32	productive
-ist	*capitalist, feminist, imagist, symbolist*	15	productive, esp. correlated with -ism
-ian, -an	*Darwinian, Freudian, Hamiltonian, Wallerian, Christian*	14	productive, esp. with proper names
-ar, -ular	*fascicular, intracellular, linear, muscular*	6	productive in technical registers

As the examples suggest, all these suffixes occur principally with non-native bases and are productive. There is a series of parallel forms ending in *-al* or *-ical*, some of which exhibit semantic differences, e.g. *economic problem* ('relating to the economy') vs. *economical car* ('not wasteful, frugal') and *historic building* ('famous in history, significant') vs. *historical research* ('concerned with events of the past') (cf. Quirk et al. 1985: 1554). Adjectival formations with the suffix *-an/ -ian* are identical to their respective nouns and can only be distinguished from them in context. In addition to the **deonymic** adjectives, i.e. those derived from proper names, there are designations for geographic and linguistic affiliations such as *African, American, Angolan, Italian, Palestinian, Russian* and *Syrian*, which also run parallel to nouns. In the function of expressing such concepts, *-an* competes with the suffixes *-ish* (*British, English*) and *-ese* (*Japanese, Lebanese, Vietnamese*). The form *-ish* in this meaning should not be confused with its use as a deadjectival suffix as in *youngish* or *greyish*. The suffix *-ern* is used to refer to directions (*Northern, Western* etc.).

A more specific form of establishing relationships concerns the expression of quantities, e.g. 'full of N' and 'without N'. Apart from the obvious suffix *-ful*, and its antonym *-less*, we should also mention *-ous* and *-y*.

Tab. 9.8: Quantifying denominal adjective-forming suffixes

suffix	selected examples from the MUMC	tokens	productivity
-y	*bloody, crowdy, crinkly, hilly, hungry, lucky, sunny, witty*	46	productive
-ful	*awful, beautiful, cheerful, graceful, powerful, tearful, wonderful*	42	productive
-ous	*dangerous, glamorous, gracious, humorous, poisonous*	10	low degree of productivity
-less	*colourless, fearless, harmless, helpless, rudderless, ruthless*	16	productive

Further denominal adjective-forming suffixes that occur less often are *-ed* ('characterized by N', e.g. *aged, dark-haired*), *-en* ('made of N', e.g. *woollen*) and *-ate* ('characterized by N', 'having N', e.g. *fortunate*).

9.2.3 Verb-forming suffixes: dynamizing

Compared to the variety and productivity of nominal and adjectival suffixation patterns, the field of verbal suffixations is much more limited. Basically there are only four important suffixes, namely the native Germanic *-en*, which is no longer productive, and the Romance suffixes *-ate*, *-ify* and *-ize* (or *-ise*). As Table 9.9 shows, the number of examples in the MUMC is fairly small. With the exception of the suffix *-en*, which is no longer productive anyway, all the verb suffixes occur mainly in technical texts and are only really frequent and productive in such contexts. Around three quarters of the examples in the MUMC come from academic texts. According to Quirk et al. (1985: 1557), formations outside this register, in particular those ending in *-ify*, are often facetious or pejorative (*speechify, dandify*). The bases of non-Germanic verb suffixes are borrowed adjectives and nouns that are frequently neo-classical forms. The number of verbs ending in *-ate* is in principle relatively high, but most of these forms (cf. e.g. *communicate, differentiate, dominate, intimidate, predominate*) are adapted borrowings from Latin or back-formations of nouns ending in *-ation* (Hansen et al. 1990: 121).

Tab. 9.9: Verb-forming suffixes

suffix	selected examples from the MUMC	tokens	productivity
-ize, -ise	*criticise, emphasize, idealize, italicize, materialize, poeticize, realize, summarize, trivialize*	25	productive, esp. in technical registers
-ify	*clarify, classify, glorify, intensify, justify, mummify, signify*	21	productive, esp. in technical registers
-en	*broaden, fasten, harden, soften, stiffen, straighten, weaken, widen*	19	no longer productive
-ate	*formulate, motivate, myelinate*	8	productive in technical registers

From a semantic point of view, the semantic complex 'make s.th. Adj or more Adj' (*weaken, trivialize*), 'make N of s.th.' (*symbolize, mummify*) and 'convert s.th. into N' (*italicize, summarize*) (Hansen et al. 1990: 121 ff.) is clearly dominant. The claim by Quirk et al. (1985: 1557) that suffixed verbs are generally transitive is called into question by the intransitive verbs *materialize* and *myelinize* in the MUMC. Nevertheless it is true that practically all suffixed verbs are dynamic, agentive, and moreover mostly causative, i.e. they refer to a deliberately performed action that causes an effect. The most important conceptual function of verb suffixations is thus 'dynamizing', i.e. the profiling of nominal or adjectival bases as dynamic events or actions.

9.2.4 Adverb-forming suffixes

By far the most prevalent pattern of adverb-forming suffixations is the deadjectival derivation with *-ly* (*calm – calmly, personal – personally* etc.), which is so productive and grammatically determined to such an extent that some linguists do not regard it as a derivative pattern of word-formation, but as a case of inflection. Hansen et al. (1990), for instance, do not mention this model in their overview of English word-formation. However, there can be no doubt that adding *-ly* to an adjective brings about a change in word class. Since it fulfils this most important criterion for derivative word-formation processes, we shall include this pattern, which with 502 examples is the most common single suffixation model in the MUMC.

Nevertheless it has to be admitted that there is only a very slim semantic basis for this pattern, as the meanings of adverbs ending in *-ly* are substantially dependent on their grammatical function, above all on whether the adverb modifies the whole sentence (as in 9.7), the verb phrase (9.8) or an adjective phrase (9.9).

(9.7)   *Normally*, a theory and its methods are considered as one entity, but this is likely to be unjust to other subjects besides AI ... (ICE-GB: W2a-035)

(9.8)   Like fallen leaves that the wind sweeps to and fro, we are *indiscriminately* swayed by our unsubstantial and frivolous emotions. (ICE-GB: W1b-001)

(9.9)   No doubt you're working *extremely* hard. (ICE-GB: W1b-001)

While the sentence adverb *normally* in (9.7) could be most easily rephrased as 'under normal circumstances' or 'from a normal point of view', the adverb *indiscriminately* in (9.8), functioning as an *adjunct*, manifests the typical adverbial meaning 'in an Adj (*indiscriminate*) manner' and the adverb of degree *extremely* in (9.9) has the commensurate meaning 'to an Adj (*extreme*) degree'. Consequently, it is not possible to make any further general statements about the semantics of adverbs ending in *-ly*, which supports the position that this adverb-forming suffix must be placed at the borderline to inflectional morphology. Some of the most common adverbs ending in *-ly*, many of which have been lexicalized to a high degree, are *actually, basically, certainly, completely, easily, especially, finally, hardly, merely, nearly, normally, obviously, probably, really, slightly, suddenly, totally* and *usually*.

Apart from *-ly*, the only other suffixes to mention in the adverb-forming group are *-wards* and *-wise*. Adverbs ending in *-wise* are derived from nouns (*clockwise, jobwise, moneywise*), while those ending in *-wards* can be derived from nouns (*homewards*) or from adverbs (*eastwards*) or prepositions (*onwards, towards*). Although Lenker (2002) shows that formations ending in *-wise* are apparently in fashion currently as sentence adverbials, we have to point out that neither of the two suffixes (except for a few common lexicalized formations such as *afterwards* and *otherwise*) occurs frequently or is very productive.

9.3   Quantitative summary

9.3.1   Structural perspective: distribution of corpus data according to word class

Figure 9.2 collates all suffixes that occur five or more times in the MUMC. The figure indicates the direction of derivation of the suffixes by arrows pointing from the word class of the base to that of the derived form. The thickness of the arrows reflects the observed frequency of examples of each type. The arrows clearly indicate which word classes function as 'donors' (i.e. bases) and which as 'receivers' (i.e. derivations).

Fig. 9.2:   Overview of the most frequent patterns of suffixation according to word classes

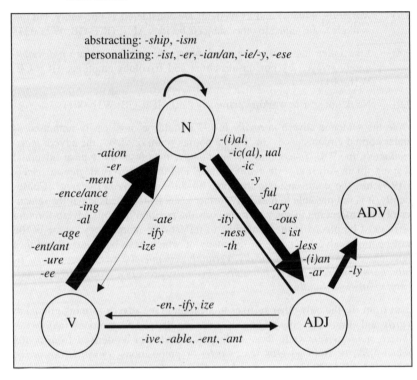

If we disregard the borderline case of adverbial suffixation by means of *-ly*, suffixation – seen from a grammatical angle – predominantly produces nouns and adjectives. Verbs mainly serve as bases for noun-forming suffixations, hardly ever appearing as suffixations in their own right; adjective-forming suffixations are mostly derived from nominal bases.

The following suffixes stand out as being the most common ones:

noun-forming:	*-(a)(t)ion* (452 examples in the MUMC)
	-ity (143)
	-er (123)
	-ment (101)
	-ance/-ence (97)
adjective-forming:	*-al/-ial/-ical/-ual* (341)
	-ic (92)

From an etymological point of view it is remarkable that with the exception of *-er*, the origin of which has not been fully clarified (cf. OED, s.v. *-er*, Marchand 1969: 273, Kastovsky 1985: 224, 239 ff.), all these frequent suffixes are of non-Germanic origin. Moreover, again with the exception of *-er*, they all only combine with borrowed bases or were borrowed in an already suffixed form.

All in all we can state that the word-formation pattern of suffixation – providing we neglect the deadjectival adverbs ending in *-ly* – mainly affects the Romance domain of the English lexicon, which tends to come to the fore in the more formal style-levels and more abstract registers.

9.3.2 The sociopragmatic perspective: distribution of corpus data according to register

The frequency distribution of suffixations over the five registers of the MUMC reinforces the impression given in the previous section insofar as the formal and abstract registers of academic writing contribute the highest percentage of the occurrences for all word classes. This is substantiated by the figures in Table 9.10:

Tab. 9.10: Relative distribution of suffixations in the five registers of the MUMC

suffixes	conversation	letters	fiction	reportage	academic
noun-forming	4 %	9 %	14 %	29 %	44 %
adjective-forming	8 %	10 %	16 %	21 %	44 %
verb-forming	3 %	10 %	10 %	17 %	58 %
adverb-forming	21 %	19 %	23 %	11 %	26 %

The contribution of the individual registers is reasonably balanced only in the case of adverb-forming suffixes. As for the other three word classes, the table demonstrates clearly that the need to use suffixed lexemes is relatively small in the more informal conditions of spontaneous conversation and personal letters. As the formality and the degree of abstraction of the texts increase, the number of suffix derivations also rises drastically, with the relative proportion of verbal suffixations being highest in academic texts. No less than 46 of the 54 examples ending in *-ate*, *-ify* and *-ize* come from the academic texts, and they are all of Latin or (occasionally) Greek origin. This adds weight to the impression that verbal suffixations have a particularly 'scholarly' slant.

9.4 Cognitive functions of suffixation

Basing our conclusion on the discussion above, we can claim that the fundamental cognitive functions of suffixation are re-conceptualization and re-profiling (cf. Ungerer 2007). This has, of course, not been overlooked by other researchers.

Kastovsky (1986: 595), for example, already attributed a re-categorization function to nominalization, although what he had in mind were mainly grammatical, rather than conceptual, categories. The observations by Heyvaert (2003: 51, 94 ff.), on the other hand, are explicitly couched in cognitive-linguistic terms. The idea is that established concepts are re-profiled in the form of different concept types by means of suffixation. Noun-forming suffixes, for instance, can cause action concepts to be re-profiled as abstract concepts. From the conceptual, 'scenic' potential of events, actions or processes consisting of agents, affected persons or objects and actions that take place in space and time, persons, objects and even locations can be profiled in a new 'thing-like' conceptual form yielding a reifying effect. Concepts of people, objects and abstract ideas can be turned into relational concepts by means of adjective-forming suffixes. Concepts of events, actions or processes can be transformed, again by adjective-forming suffixes, into linguistic encoders of modality concepts such as POSSIBILITY, PROBABILITY, INCLINATION and FEASIBILITY. The fundamental cognitive potential of suffixation therefore lies in changing the conceptualizing and profiling types of conceptual units.

If I take into account the frequency distribution according to word classes and register discussed in section 9.3, an even more pointed assessment of the cognitive functions of suffixation is possible, since the processes of abstract reification caused by -ation, -ment, -ence/-ance and -ity, the personizing accomplished by -er and the relationizing produced by -al, -ical, -ial, -ual and -ic have proved to be quantitatively predominant, at least in the data of the MUMC. The evidence of word class changes indicates that suffixation is a cognitive process of reification (in the broadest sense as described on p. 168) and establishing relationships. The transfer of object concepts to action concepts is only marginally relevant here, while – as I will show in chapter 10 – featuring prominently in conversion. It cannot be coincidence that the vast majority of suffixations are of an abstract nature, which also ties in well with the distribution of the registers. In a nutshell and neglecting personizing suffixes, we could say that suffixation is not particularly relevant for conceptualizing concrete daily experiences but is at home in the world of abstract ideas and relationships. Needless to say this world plays an important role in academic texts, whose writers accordingly make enthusiastic use of the results of suffixation processes and continue to produce new formations moulded on this pattern.

Further reading: On diminutive suffixes such as *-ie, -ette, -let, -ling*: **Schneider (2003)**. On *-ize*: **Plag (1997)**. On *-ify, -ize* and *-ate*: **Plag (1999)**. On deverbal *-er*: **Ryder (1999), Panther and Thornburg (2001), Heyvaerts (2003: 99–176)**. On *-ee*: **Bauer (1983: 243 ff.), Barker (1995), Mühleisen (2010)**. On *-ic* and *-ical*: **Gries (2001)**. On *-wise*: **Lenker (2002)**. On the borderline status of *-wise, like* and *-ful* **Dalton-Puffer and Plag (2000)**. On *-tion*: **Szawerna (2007)**. On nominalizations: **Lees (1966), Chomsky (1970), Heyvaert (2003)**. On synonymous suffixes (like *-ity* and *-ness*): **Raffelsiefen (2010)**. Useful resources when investigating suffixes are the reverse index dictionaries of **Lehnert (1971)** and **Muthmann (1999)**.

10 Conversion

We will now leave the field of typical morphemic word-formation processes and turn our attention to a linguistically seemingly unproblematic phenomenon: lexical items that are established in several word classes, such as *love*, *fish* and *land*, each of which occurs as a noun and a verb, and *calm*, *empty* and *dry*, which can all function as adjectives and verbs. Straightforward and simple as this phenomenon may seem, accounting for it in a theoretically sound way is by no means an easy matter. In fact, there is not even agreement as to whether this phenomenon is to be regarded as a word-formation pattern in the first place, because there is nothing to observe at the formal morphological level that resembles the typical patterns of compounding, prefixation and suffixation. Insofar as parallels to these processes exist, they relate to comparable underlying sentences and semantic structures, but not to morphological forms and structures.

Amongst the researchers who accept this phenomenon as a word-formation process there is an additional debate as to how it should be understood theoretically. The two most prominent schools of thought work with the concepts of **conversion** and **zero-derivation** (or **derivation by means of a zero morpheme**). In order to avoid a premature commitment to one of these positions, in this chapter I will initially describe the linguistic facts from a synchronic and a diachronic viewpoint (10.1), steering clear of theoretical issues as far as possible. Subsequently, various ways of modelling these facts will be discussed (10.2). After that we will turn to the question of how the direction of derivation from base to derived element can be determined in those models that view multiple word-class membership as the result of derivation processes (10.3). In the concluding section (10.4) we shall attempt to clarify the essence of conversion from the cognitive perspective of word-formation as introduced in this book.

10.1 The linguistic phenomenon

10.1.1 The synchronic view

This chapter is concerned essentially with lexical items that are not only able to occur functionally in different word classes depending on the context, but do this so regularly that they can be regarded as members of more than one word class. Basically, there are two options for conceptualizing this situation. On the one hand, if we adhere to the view that lexemes are marked for word-class membership, then we have to say that morphologically identical forms are established as members of different word classes and thus essentially represent homonymic lexemes. This view would be supported by the fact that they have at least slightly different meanings in each word class and are therefore recorded in most dictionaries with separate entries for each one. On the other hand, if we emphasize the overall semantic similarity and the shared conceptual basis, and at the same time neglect the importance of grammatical properties, we can claim to be dealing with grammatical variants of one polysemous lexeme.

One of the most extreme examples of this phenomenon is the form *round*, which occurs in no fewer than five word classes; as an adjective (10.1), a verb (10.2), a preposition (10.3), an adverb (10.4) and a noun (10.5):

(10.1) And in fact theirs has got a *round* head on it. (ICE-GB: S1b-073)

(10.2) That's why this is to smooth them and *round* them off. (ICE-GB: S1b-043)

(10.3) There's an interesting band *round* the walls. (ICE-GB: S2a-059)

(10.4) Now if you come *round* here we have the Indian room… (ICE-GB: S2a-059)

(10.5) A mass rally at Brent Magistrates Court is planned for January 10 when the next *round* of summoned offenders face the court. (ICE-GB: S2c-009)

The form *down* is similarly multi-functional. Although there are very few forms that are characterized by such a high degree of versatility, the proportion of items in the English lexicon belonging to more than one word class should not be underestimated. In the MUMC no fewer than a quarter of the approximately 41,000 tokens are examples of forms that can either potentially occur in more than one word class or comprise such elements. Even a quick look into one of the most common desktop dictionaries such as the LDOCE or the OALD confirms that an astonishingly high proportion of the lemmas have entries for two or more word classes.

The following combinations of word classes occur most frequently:

N, V	*aim, attack, bank, block, blow, call, control, fence, fool, love, man, move, pass, result, spell*
Adj, V	*alert, blind, dirty, empty, idle, mature, narrow, open, quiet, slim, sober, tense, thin, warm*
N, Adj	*adult, black, chemical, dark, final, intellectual, narrative*
N, Adj, V, (Adv)	*back, calm, clean, clear, close, cool, near, pale, uniform, wrong*

While similar polyfunctional forms can be found in other languages, it is not an exaggeration to maintain that the extent of this phenomenon is unusually high in English. The reasons for this exceptional position lie in the history of the language.

10.1.2 The diachronic view

It is very important to realize that the present situation has arisen historically from a number of different sources. The main factors are the decline in inflections described in section 3.2 – keeping in mind the reservations of Marchand (1969: 363 f.) and Kastovsky (2005: 46) – and the rich history of borrowing in English. Due to the fact that most inflectional endings have fallen out of use, the formal merging of nouns, verbs and adjectives has been promoted; and in the wake of enthusiastic borrowing, above all from Latin and French, many lexemes have been adopted into English as members of different word classes. The historical origins of the merging of present-day word classes can be reconstructed in detail by referring to the evidence in the OED in the form of first attestations of the use of words and their dates:

Firstly, lexemes whose stems had the same form in Old English, but whose usage at that time was marked as different by means of inflectional morphemes, have now become formally unified due to the erosion of these morphemes. A good example of this type is the word-form *love*, which exists today as both a noun and a verb. Both forms can be traced back to the Old English root *luf-*, which at that time did not occur in isolated form, but only in inflected word-forms of the noun *lufu* or the verb *lufian*. The Old English words *andswaru* (N) and *andswarian* (V), precursors of Modern English *answer* (N + V), behave in an analogous way. The loss of inflectional morphemes in late Old English and Middle English meant that word-class differences were no longer marked, and noun and verb became formally identical even in their respective citation forms (i.e. in the singular common case of nouns and the base form of verbs).

Secondly, both forms were borrowed from French or Latin and were already formally more or less identical, or soon became so due to the inflectional decline in English. The form *camp*, for example, has two sources in French, where the noun *camp* and the verb *camper* already existed. In the OED, the first entries in English are dated 1528 for the noun and 1543 for the verb. In the etymological information on the verb, the OED accordingly names the French verb *camper* as well as the English noun *camp*, thus avoiding committing itself. This may be a reasonable decision, since determining the origin of first attestations so close to each other in time will often be impossible.

Thirdly, one of the two forms was derived from another form over the course of English history. This is particularly plausible if a rather long period of time elapsed between the two first attestations, which is the case with the form *hand*, for example. The lexeme already existed as a noun in Old English and in other early stages of Germanic languages, such as Old Frisian, Old Norse and Old High German. The first known use in English dates from the year 825, i.e from one of the earliest written sources. The verb, on the other hand, is first attested in 1610, used by Shakespeare in his play *The Tempest*. Of course, not only its later appearance but also the complex meaning of the verb 'to hand, manipulate with the hand, hand over' suggests that the verb is derived from the noun.

A good example of the fourth possibility is the form *hate*, which in Old English occurred in two clearly different forms, the verb *hatian* and the noun *hete*. According to the OED, the merging of the two forms resulted from an assimilation of the nominal form to the verb that took place in Middle English, with the related Old Norse noun *hatr* possibly also having had an influence. A similar process resulted in the present-day form *work*, an amalgamation of the Old English forms *wyrcan* (V) and *weorc* (N). In this case the phonetic development shows an assimilation of the verb to the noun.

It is not always easy for the OED to distinguish between these two types of origin, since apart from the dates of the first attestations there is frequently no indication of the historical development. Accordingly, the OED often suggests several possibilities and brings additional factors into play, such as the above-mentioned interference of Scandinavian words. From a synchronic point of view, we can say that for today's speakers the various historical causes of the phenomenon remain a mystery. The present-day English pairs *love* (N) and *love* (V), *answer* (N) and *answer* (V), *hand* (N) and *hand* (V), *camp* (N) and *camp* (V), *hate* (N) and *hate* (V), and *work* (N) and *work* (V) all appear at first sight to be very similar. Linguists who work purely synchronically are basically in the same situation. With this in mind I will now turn my attention to theoretical attempts to model multiple word-class membership from a synchronic perspective. In this endeavour I shall use the term *conversion* as a neutral designation.

10.2 Theoretical approaches

10.2.1 Grammatical indeterminacy and complex word classes

A fairly extreme attempt at dealing with this problematic phenomenon involves the assumption that in English stems, i.e. free lexical morphemes, do not belong to specific word classes at all, but are grammatically undetermined in the mental lexicon. Grammatical functions which can be interpreted as membership of a word class arise as a result of words being embedded in syntactic structures. This approach was adopted by the well-known American linguist Benjamin Whorf, who researched extensively into native American languages in which the word classes are less distinct than in Indo-European languages. A similar suggestion was also put forward by Farell (2001).

In the American structuralism of the 1940s and '50s, in contrast, the precise and, above all, objective definition of word classes was an important goal (cf. Fries 1952: 65 ff.). While multiple word class membership did not fit in naturally with these aspirations, Charles Hockett (1969: 225 ff.) took the bull by the horns and permitted complex word classes such as *noun-adjective* (NA), *noun-verb* (NV), *adjective-verb* (AV) and even *noun-adjective-verb* (NAV) in addition to the traditional classes of nouns, adjectives and verbs. These classes took into account the most important types of multiple word-class membership mentioned on p. 184, but at the same time they complicated the system of grammatical rules.

All these approaches have in common that they conceptualize multiple word-class membership as a state rather than a process or the result of a process. Accordingly, the question as to which of the two or more grammatical functions is more fundamental and which secondary, i.e. derived, does not arise.

10.2.2 Functional transposition and conversion

The concept of modelling multiple word classes as a process is much more common than these static approaches. According to this approach, words belong to one basic word class, with membership of one or several others being the result of some kind of more or less regular mechanism. This concept is described using terms such as **functional change, functional shift, transposition** and **conversion**, which has already been mentioned (cf. Marchand 1969: 360, Pennanen 1970: 17 ff., Štekauer 1996: 23 ff. and Bauer and Valera 2005b for overviews of the application of these terms). The commonly accepted idea is that a lexeme changes from one word class to another without formal marking while at the same time remaining in the original word class. This always implies a directionality of the process from a source word class to one (or more) target word classes – which, as we have seen in chapter 9, is also characteristic of suffixation. This functional similarity to suffixation thus suggests this phenomenon should be treated as a derivational process in word-formation, although there are no formal indications of a derivation, at least on the morphological level.

The term **conversion** dates back to Sweet's grammar (1900: 38 ff.), which describes the noun *walk* in *he took a walk* and *three different walks of life* as a "converted noun" and the process of its development as "conversion". According to Sweet, a lexeme is fully converted when it accepts all the formal characteristics of the new word class – in the case of the noun *walk*, for instance, the use with the article *the* and in the plural (1900: 39). Examples such as *the poor, the British* and *at his best* (Don, Trommelen and Zonneveld 2000: 944) which, according to Sweet only show **partial conversion**, should be treated separately because the words only occur in isolated formal and functional realizations of the new word class. *The poor*, for example, cannot occur with an inflectional marker for plural as would be expected if it was a fully-fledged noun (cf. **the poors*). Being theoretically at least a relatively neutral and unrestricted term, *conversion* is also used by many other linguists, e.g. Kruisinga (1932), Biese (1941), Bauer (1983: 226 ff.) and Quirk et al. (1985: 1558 ff.). While Marchand accepts the term *conversion* for cases of partial conversion, he interprets complete conversion as so-called *zero-derivation* (see 10.2.3 below).

The most important models and types of conversion are summarized in Table 10.1 following Quirk et al.'s description (1985: 1560 ff.; see also Schönefeld 2005: 158 f.):

Tab. 10.1: Main types of conversion according to Quirk et al. (1985: 1560 ff.)

deverbal nouns	
'state', 'state of mind'	*desire, dismay, doubt, love, smell, taste, want*
'event/activity'	*attempt, fall, hit, laugh, release, search, swim*
'object of V'	*answer* ('that which answers'), *bet, catch, find*
'subject of V'	*bore* ('s.o./s.th. who/that bores'), *cheat, coach*
'instrument of V'	*cover* ('s.th. with which to cover things'), *paper*
'manner of V-ing'	*walk* ('manner of walking'), *throw*
'place of V'	*divide, retreat, rise, turn*
denominal verbs	
'to put in/on N'	*bottle, corner, catalogue, floor, garage*
'to give/provide with N'	*butter (bread), coat, commission, grease, oil*
'to deprive of N'	*core, peel, skin*
'to … with N'	*brake, elbow, fiddle, hand, finger, glue*
'to be/act as N with respect to'	*chaperone, father, nurse, parrot, pilot*
'to make/change … into N'	*cash, cripple, group*
'to send/go by N'	*mail, ship, telegraph; bicycle, boat, canoe*
deadjectival verbs	
'to make (more) Adj' (trans. V)	*calm, dirty, dry, humble, lower*
'to become Adj' (intrans. V)	*dry, empty, narrow, weary (of), yellow*

Quantitatively, the formation of verbs predominates over that of nouns in conversion (cf. Don, Trommelen and Zonneveld 2000: 949).

10.2.3 Zero-derivation

The idea of the word-class change being triggered by a formally unmarked morpheme, the so-called **zero morpheme**, existed before Marchand. Jespersen (1942: 85) stated that the term "suffix zero" was in fashion at his time and that one should not talk about *converted verbs* but "verbs formed from sbs [= substantives] with a suffix zero". Zero elements were and still are popular in post-Saussurean French structuralism, American structuralism and of course in generative grammars as place holders for functional slots which can be filled by elements with morphological substance (cf. Pennanen 1970: 25 ff. for a good overview). In spite of this long-standing tradition, it is fair to say that Marchand and his students Kastovsky and Lipka as well as Hansen are to be regarded as the most significant proponents of the zero-derivation approach. It has to be stressed that zero morphemes – along with all other zero elements – are purely theoretical constructs, whose psychological reality is uncertain.

How is the postulation of this theoretical construct justified? The decisive aspect is the analogy to suffixation, to which we have already alluded. Hence Marchand (1969: 359) claims that the parallels between the overtly marked deadjectival verb suffixations in (10.6) and the formally unmarked word-class changes in (10.7) are so apparent that they justify the postulation of a zero morpheme.

(10.6)	Adj	+ suffix	V	meaning
	legal	*-ize*	*legalize*	'make legal'
	national	*-ize*	*nationalize*	'make national'
	sterile	*-ize*	*sterilize*	'make sterile'

(10.7)	Adj	+ suffix	V	meaning
	clean	-Ø	*clean*	'make clean'
	dirty	-Ø	*dirty*	'make dirty'
	tidy	-Ø	*tidy*	'make tidy'

The examples show that it is not only the grammatical parallels with word-class change but also the semantic analogy between the suffixations and the zero-derivations that are decisive. Marchand (1969: 360) explicitly states that the zero morpheme must only be postulated if a visible formal marker with the same function exists.

Like other suffixes, the zero morpheme functions as the head within a modifier-head relationship and therefore determines the word class. Using this assumption, Marchand succeeds, on the one hand, in integrating conversions into English word-formation without overriding the basic principle of the structure of word-formations. On the other hand, the notion that a formally unmarked morpheme, i.e. a morpheme that does not even have morphological substance, assumes the important role of determining the word class, is not very convincing. A further problem is that the zero morpheme must be able to effect a whole range of different word-class changes and semantic variations: verbs from nouns and adjectives, nouns from verbs etc., and within each of these types it causes various semantic changes, as outlined in Table 10.1. Either the zero morpheme has the exceedingly general function 'changes word class' or we have to assume the existence of several homonymous zero morphemes with different functions.

10.2.4   Metonymy

The approaches we have discussed up till now all proceed semasiologically. By contrast, endeavouring to understand conversion as a form of metonymy requires an onomasiological perspective. In this respect there are parallels with the explicitly onomasiological approach of Štekauer (1996), in which each separate conversion is interpreted as an individual **conceptual re-categorization**. According to Štekauer, and of course highly reminiscent of our account of suffixation, the noun *experiment*, for instance, denotes a process via conceptual re-categorization as an action concept; *feature* is a quality concept which is also re-categorized as an action concept, while *insert* is an action concept which is re-categorized as a substance concept (Štekauer 1996: 46 ff.).

Whereas Štekauer suggests a complex multi-level model in order to explain the mechanism of re-categorization (1996: 47 ff.), Dirven (1999) attempts to trace it back to conceptual metonymies of event schemas for the limited but strongly represented group of verbs converted from nouns. He understands metonymy as a strategy of the speaker to relate to an intended referent by means of a reference point shared with the listener. This can be illustrated by a standard example such as *The steak and kidney pie wants to pay*, where the noun phrase refers to the guest who has ordered and eaten this meal. More generally, metonymy can be understood as a relationship of "one element standing for another" within a scene. This relationship prevails not only in the *steak-and-kidney-pie* example, where the meal stands for the customer, but also in the bahuvrihi compounds of word-formation, where a prominent attribute is often profiled as representing the whole person, e.g. *paleface, hunchback, redskin* (see p. 126).

Dirven (1999: 277) points out that in conversions some components of scenes stand metonymically for other components of the same scenes, these scenes – Dirven uses the term *schema* – being delimitable by the semantic roles the verb is required to fill. The scene underlying the verb *clean*, for instance, demands as semantic roles AGENT, the cleaned OBJECT, possibly an INSTRUMENT, the MANNER of the action and the OUTCOME (see also p. 105). According to Dirven, the adjective *clean* characterizes the conceptually prominent role OUTCOME in this scene (X makes Y clean with Z), and this is transferred by metonymy during conversion to the verb, which then comes to stand for the entire process (see also Schönefeld 2005).

It depends on the type of scene which components of scenes are eligible as the source and which as the target of the metonymy. Dirven distinguishes three types that are brought to bear in denominal verb conversions: the action schema, the place or motion schema and, in Dirven's words, "the essive schema, or the schema of 'beingness', in which the status of class membership or an attribute is assigned to an entity" (Dirven 1999: 280). I shall not investigate this last type further because it seems less convincing than the other two and in many instances can be interpreted in terms of the action schema. According to Dirven, the basic sources for metonymies are the roles PATIENT, INSTRUMENT and MANNER in action schemas, and principally the GOAL in motion schemas. Examples of these types are compiled in Table 10.2.

Tab. 10.2: Examples of conversions as metonymies adapted from Dirven (1999)

action scene		
PATIENT STANDS FOR ACTION	(10.8)	*He was fishing (salmon)*
INSTRUMENT STANDS FOR ACTION	(10.9)	*He was luring fish.*
MANNER STANDS FOR ACTION	(10.10)	*He was fishing pearls.*
motion scene		
GOAL STANDS FOR MOTION	(10.11)	*The plane landed in Cairo.*

(10.8) illustrates the role of PATIENT, represented by the noun *fish*, which stands for the entire action of fishing; in (10.9) the role INSTRUMENT (*lure*) serves as the source for the conversion. In (10.10) the converted verb *fish* does not simply mean 'to fish', but 'to take something out of the sea in a manner similar to fishing', which explains this being the MANNER type. Finally, in the motion scene in (10.11) the GOAL of the movement is the noun *land*, which stands for the whole scene and motivates the conversion from noun to verb.

What makes Dirven's approach particularly attractive is the fact that the phenomenon of conversion is traced back to a conceptual relationship between the base and the converted form, viz. metonymy, which can be observed in many other contexts in language and is therefore of high explanatory power. The fundamental significance of metonymy for human communication and presumably also human thought can be illustrated by the example of my daughter who, at the age of one and a half years, tapped the floor or the sofa beside her with the palm of her hand, thus asking someone to sit by her. Using non-verbal means she implemented precisely the GOAL-STANDS-FOR-MOTION metonymy mentioned above, by signifying the desired end point in place of the action. In view of the apparent cognitive basicness of the conceptual process of metonymy it seems worthwhile to develop Dirven's model further when we discuss cognitive aspects of conversion in section 10.4.

10.3 Determining the direction of derivation

All the approaches referred to in 10.2 with the exception of the concept of grammatical or conceptual indeterminacy (10.2.1) regard converted elements as the outcome of a process. Consequently, in all these models the question of the direc-

tion of the derivational process arises. Which of the two identical forms in different word classes is the source and which the product of this process? Is the form
aim, for instance, a noun plus denominal verb or a verb plus deverbal noun? Since
the question of derivational direction is not easy to answer, whether in theory or in
the actual practice of analysis – and often very little is said about it in the literature
– we shall briefly discuss the most important criteria for determining the direction
of derivation. In doing so we should keep in mind that historical considerations
about the grammatical function in which a form is first attested – by the OED for
example – should be regarded as irrelevant from a synchronic perspective, while
observations of a semantic, structural, quantitative, distributional and conceptual
nature are significant (cf. Marchand 1963, 1974, Iacobini 2000 and Umbreit 2010
for further criteria).

One important semantic consideration is that the meaning of the derived form
depends on the meaning of the base. This manifests itself on the level of the underlying sentence (see section 5.3.3) and all later levels of analysis in the fact that
the base appears in the paraphrase of the derivation. The deadjectival verb *dry*, for
example, is paraphrased by 'to make dry', the denominal verb *bottle* by 'to put
into bottles'. In each case, the potential bases, i.e. the adjective *dry* and the noun
bottle, occur in the underlying sentences. Unfortunately, the application of this
criterion is not always as simple as it is in these relatively clear examples, which
can even lead to divergent analyses on the part of different linguists. Clark and
Clark (1979: 770), for example, interpret *cover* as a denominal verb ('put cover on
s.th.'), whereas Quirk et al. (1985: 1560) list it under the deverbal nouns as an
'instrument for covering' (cf. p. 188). From a purely semantic standpoint both
analyses are equally plausible. It is especially difficult to come to a decision in the
case of abstract concepts from the mental and emotional field such as *aim, concern, desire, fear, hope, love, plan* and *wish*.

A second semantic criterion is the semantic range of the two lexemes. It is generally assumed that the derivation is semantically more specific than the base. Marchand points out, for instance, that the entry for the noun *look* in the OED only
takes up one column, while that of the homonymic verb fills six columns. This
reflects the greater semantic range of the verb, which is therefore to be regarded as
the base.

For a structural point of view we shall pick up again on Marchand's previously
mentioned requirement that a zero morpheme can only be posited if the same
function is overtly marked morphologically in other cases. Sanders refers to this
as the "overt analogue criterion" (1988: 160 ff.). We can apply this as evidence for
determining the direction of derivation, arguing that in the case of semantically
similar lexemes the derivational direction of conversions is analogous to the direction of comparable suffixations. In the case of forms that denote speech acts such
as *answer, bet, claim, comment, lie, order, protest, remark* and *reply*, for example,
the analogy with a large number of marked suffixations ending in *-(a)tion, -ment*

and *-ance* in the same field (*affirmation, confirmation, contradiction, suggestion*; *announcement, pronouncement, statement*; *assurance, insistence, reassurance*) speaks in favour of their being treated as deverbal nouns. On the basis of the same criterion Quirk et al. (1985: 1559) decide to categorize the mental and emotional concepts named above (*aim, love* etc.) as deverbal nouns.

A comparison of the frequency of both uses can also be a factor in determining the direction of derivation. Marchand (1964: 15) cites the verb *to author*, which is far less common than its nominal base, as an example. We must also take into account whether there are observable differences between the two variants of a form with respect to their prevalence in different types of text and register. The verb *to fedex* meaning 'to send by Federal Express', for example, was originally only found in the language of advertising, but in the meantime has spread into the general vocabulary, at least in the USA.

Finally, considerations about the nature of the underlying concept can also influence the decision on the base and its derivation, this usually being confirmed by semantic dependence. Hence concepts relating to people, animals and objects, such as *father, man, nurse, fish, knife* and *hammer* can be categorized as typical 'nominal' concepts, whereas action and process concepts such as *break, cut, jump, kiss* and *move* are more verbal in character. We will say more about this in 10.4.

In spite of this catalogue of criteria the derivational direction of conversions cannot always be clearly ascertained, mainly because the criteria do not always converge in the outcome. It is not surprising, therefore, that a recent proposal by Umbreit (2010) claims, at least for certain types of conversions, that they are bi-directionally derived, which may be plausible to some extent from a cognitive perspective but is logically somewhat counterintuitive. A fully convincing solution to this problem has thus yet to be found, though it is not unlikely that there is none. Anyone wishing to rise to the challenge would have to address a number of fundamental questions, including the following: can conversions really be analyzed with the help of such generalizations as the *overt analogue criterion* or do they each have their own individual derivational histories as claimed by Štekauer (1996: 46)? If so, then the structural criterion in the form specified, for instance, for the verbs and nouns in the speech act, would be invalid. As I will show later (see p. 199), there is some evidence that conversion and suffixation are not analogous and comparable processes, but rather complementary ones, which operate in different areas. If conversion did indeed take place in a systematic and pattern-like manner, what would the productivity restrictions on this pattern be? Can all cases of potential conversions be measured with the same yardstick or must different groups be differentiated, as was necessary from an historical perspective? While we cannot tackle these question here, the final section in this chapter aims to make a contribution towards distinguishing different types of conversion from a conceptual point of view.

10.4 Considerations on conversion from a cognitive perspective

What can we say about multiple word class membership from the cognitive word-formation perspective introduced in section 5.3.3?

If we consider the different stages of profiling (see pp. 104 ff.), then the first point we can establish is that conceptual profiling – that is the choice of concepts that are overtly highlighted because they are morphologically encoded – is not especially significant in the case of conversion since conversions are morphologically indistinguishable from their bases. In contrast, the profiling of all typical morphemic word-formation patterns (compounding, prefixation, suffixation) involves at least two concepts represented by morphemes. If the base in a conversion is not morphologically complex (as in e.g. *to shoehorn* 'to insert by force' from the noun *shoehorn*), then only one component of the conceptualized scene will be explicitly highlighted. This applies even if one assumes that the highlighted component can stand metonymically for others.

Since only one concept is profiled, the second stage of profiling, the internal figure-ground profiling, does not apply and the figure-ground principle is irrelevant. According to the metonymy approach, it would be plausible to argue that the highlighted scene component is profiled as a figure in front of the ground of the scene, but this would be a different type of figure-ground profiling from that of typical word-formation patterns, in which figure and ground are encoded morphologically within the complex lexeme.

What is, of course, interesting is the stage called concept-type profiling, as it represents the conceptual foundation of word class determination. If we pursue the idea that a zero morpheme is involved, then we can argue that the concept type is profiled by precisely this theoretical construct. However, this contradicts our understanding of profiling, which explicitly relies on the principle that concepts are specifically profiled by the fact that they are expressed by morphological substance, which is not the case with a zero morpheme. This means that the concept type – e.g. PERSON, ACTION, PROCESS etc. – is **not** profiled in conversion.

In short, with regard to profiling, conversion is fundamentally different from the typical morphemic word-formation patterns in that it does not involve the profiling of a new concept, but only a multiple conceptual categorization. (I have specifically avoided the term 're-categorization' used by Štekauer (1996), in order not to imply the existence of a directional process.) Each categorization is determined by the context, since in the end it is only the context that enables us to determine the concept type. In contrast to typical word-formation patterns, the concept type is not overtly marked and is therefore less prominent. This fits in with the impression that the ad-hoc formation of new conversions is frequently more casual than that of compounds, suffixations and prefixations. Speakers are often totally unaware of having produced an ad-hoc conversion when they use a noun as a verb, for instance. Due to the absence of morphological marking and profiling, the novel type of categorization can occur almost unnoticed.

Despite the absence of profiling, both concept types – with the word *clean*, for example, both the quality concept and the action concept – can be institutionalized and entrenched in the same way. However, as pointed out above, this is not necessarily the case. Different concept types expressed by means of the same form can also be established to different degrees. What interests us most of all here is the degree of independent entrenchment in the mental lexicon. According to Ungerer (2002: 560 ff.), different groups can be distinguished, leading to a differentiation of the general term *conversion* from a conceptual perspective.

Group 1: One concept type is entrenched to a noticeably higher degree than the other. This is particularly convincing when the conceptual substance shared by both concept types, in a sense the 'basic concept', can be assigned relatively clearly to a particular concept type. Concepts that fall into this group are typical examples of nominal THING and REGION concepts, verbal EVENT concepts and adjectival QUALITY concepts. Table 10.3 shows examples of these types together with corresponding forms with multiple word class membership (from the MUMC and Marchand 1969):

Tab. 10.3: Concept types with clear basic concepts for words with multiple word class membership

THING and REGION concepts (typically nominal; produce denominal verbs)	
PERSON	*beggar, cripple, dwarf, father, knight*
BODY-PART	*arm, elbow, eye, hand, head, shoulder, thumb*
INSTRUMENT	*comb, filter, knife, hammer, saw, towel*
VEHICLE	*bike, canoe, ship, ski, sledge, taxi*
CONTAINER	*bag, bottle, box, can, pocket*
SUBSTANCE	*butter, cement, grease, milk, oil, pepper, rubber, salt*
PLACE	*bivouac, beach, camp, house, land, nest, room, surface*
EVENT concepts (typically verbal; produce deverbal nouns)	
ACTION	*bite, call, cut, fight, find, kick, laugh, look, play, push, scream, swallow, talk, wash*
MOTION	*lift, move, ride, swim, walk*
PROCESS	*decay, melt, rain, rot, snow*
QUALITY concepts (typically adjectival; produce deadjectival verbs)	
QUALITY	*blind, clean, clear, cool, dirty, empty, faint, foul, humble, narrow, open, secure, sober, thin, warm*

As an explanation for these cases, procedural models such as conversion and zero-derivation work quite well, since the primary concept types can easily be distinguished from the secondary ones. The concepts in this group also have the prerequisites for metonymies because they represent relatively prominent components of comparatively tangible and well definable scenes. As Hansen et al. (1990: 126 ff.) have already explained using different terms, metonymies depend on the nature of the individual concept types. The most important metonymies are compiled in Table 10.4, extending the types in section 10.2.4 taken from Dirven:

Tab. 10.4: Metonymies

metonymies of the type 'THING CONCEPT FOR ACTION CONCEPT'	
AGENT FOR ACTION	*to father* 'to act as father'
AGENT FOR MANNER OF ACTION	*to father* 'to act like a father'
PATIENT FOR RESULT OF ACTION	*to cripple* 'to make a cripple of s.o'
BODY-PART FOR ACTION	*to elbow* 'to use one's elbow for'
INSTRUMENT FOR ACTION	*to hammer* 'to use a hammer for'
INSTRUMENT FOR MANNER OF ACTION	*to hammer* 'to do s.th. as with a hammer'
VEHICLE FOR MANNER OF MOTION	*to canoe* 'to move by means of a canoe'
CONTAINER FOR GOAL OF ACTION	*to bottle* 'to put in a bottle'
SUBSTANCE FOR ACTION	*to pepper* 'to put pepper on'
GOAL OF ACTION FOR MOTION	*to surface* 'to come to the surface'
metonymies of the type 'ACTION CONCEPT FOR THING CONCEPT'	
ACTION FOR RESULT	*a cut* 'result of cutting'
ACTION FOR PERSON	*a cheat* 'someone who cheats'
MANNER OF MOTION FOR ACTION	*a swim* 'act of swimming'
metonymies of the type 'QUALITY CONCEPT FOR EVENT CONCEPT'	
RESULTING QUALITY FOR PROCESS	*to cool* 'to become cool(er)'
RESULTING QUALITY FOR ACTION	*to empty* 'to make empty'

In most of these metonymies, particularly the first type, THING CONCEPT FOR EVENT CONCEPT, the connection between the concepts involved is immediately obvious. It seems entirely reasonable, for instance, that INSTRUMENT concepts can stand not only for the action carried out with their help, but also for the characteristic manner in which they take part in the actions. The variants of the type EVENT CONCEPT FOR THING CONCEPT are to some extent more problematic. It is not entirely clear, for instance, whether the type *cheat* (cf. *bore, coach, flirt, gossip, sneak*) can really be explained by means of the metonymy ACTION FOR AGENT. Kornexl (1998) argues convincingly that in cases of this type it is generally not the action itself that is the basis for the metonymy, but the negatively evaluated inclination to act as indicated by the verb. A *cheat* is thus not 'someone who cheats' but 'someone who shows a tendency to cheat'.

Group 2: Both concepts expressed by the same form could be equally, or at least almost equally, well entrenched in the mental lexicon. This is assumed for concepts such as AIM, LOVE and PLAN, for example. In such cases it is particularly difficult to determine the derivational direction for procedural models, and this problem applies equally to traditional approaches and the metonomy approach. Once more the cause of this conceptual ambiguity can be identified in the nature of the respective concepts which, in contrast to the first group, are not tied to any particular concept type but more open to different ones. The reason for this must be that these concepts come from the mental, emotional and modal domains and are therefore essentially of a more abstract nature than those discussed in the first group. Specifically, the following concept types can be distinguished:

mental states and processes	*aim, believe/f, doubt, guess, interest, plan, view, trust*
emotion concepts	*anger, concern, desire, dread, fear, hate, hope, love, regret, relief, shock, surprise, urge, wish, worry*
modal concepts and action concepts with modal components	*attempt, effort, endeavour, need, risk, test, try*
communicative actions	*account, answer, appeal, call, claim, joke, offer, order, pledge, promise, question, threat, vow*
other abstract concepts	*benefit, challenge, cause, contrast, function, merit, norm, rule*

This list of types and examples leads us to conclude that the reason why it is so difficult to determine which is the primary concept and which is the secondary is that the scenes in which these concepts are embedded are not sufficiently structured, due to their abstractness, to be able to serve as a frame for metonymies. Mental and emotional processes, for instance, comprise essentially the components EXPERIENCER and EXPERIENCED, i.e. the thinking person and the thought, or the feeling and the 'felt' in the broadest sense. This does not leave much room for metonymy and causes problems when determining the derivational direction. *Answer*, for example, could be categorized equally satisfactorily as a deverbal noun ('act of answering') or as a denominal verb ('provide with an answer'), i.e. as a result of the metonymies ACTION FOR OUTCOME or OUTCOME FOR ACTION. The fact that semantically similar material is not always treated analogously from a structural angle can be illustrated using the semantically related example *joke*, which as a verb is not perceived as a base like the other speech act verbs, but as a derivation from the noun *joke*. It is interesting to note that abstract concepts are also explicitly omitted from Clark and Clark's list including 1,300 denominal verbs (1979: 769).

Ungerer's view of the lack of conceptual certainty about these concepts (2002: 562) is that the basic concepts underlying the pairs in group 2 are stored in the mental lexicon in a form that is not profiled with regard to word class. He therefore refers to these concepts as **floating concepts** (2002: 562, Fn. 36). While this conflicts with the reasonably solid findings from psycholinguistics that the storage of word meaning and word class in the mental lexicon are closely linked with each other (Aitchison 2003: 102 ff.), it would be plausible to classify these cases as exceptions. If test subjects were asked for the meaning of words from group 1 such as *hammer* and *father*, they would describe the nominal sense without hesitation. The existence of a verbal use would presumably only occur to them if specifically asked about it. When asked about forms such as *aim*, *love* and *promise* out of context, on the other hand, it is likely that test speakers would firstly wish to clarify whether the nominal or the verbal usage was meant.

In addition to the two groups we have outlined so far, two more possible groups are conceivable, at least in theory. Firstly, the concept type that is not consistent with the basic concept could be more strongly embedded than the 'original' one and could displace it. As examples of this Ungerer (2002: 561) cites the nouns *lay-by*, *drive-in* and *stand-in*, which are far more common than their underlying phrasal verbs *to lay by*, *to drive in* and *to stand in*. Secondly, there is the special case where homonymic verbs and nouns are stored separately as unconnected concepts, e.g. *set* (V 'to arrange s.th.', N 'collection of items').

What can we draw on as empirical support for the claims we are making here, namely distinguishing two fundamental conceptual types of conversion and interpreting conversion as a metonymic process? Firstly, we can invoke correlations with the historical facts, at least to the extent that they can be reconstructed. It is striking, for instance, that – not just in a synchronic analysis but also historically – the person concepts in group 1 have formed denominal verb derivations and not vice versa. Marchand (1963: 178) shows this for *father*, *mother*, *butcher*, *knight*, *lord*, *nurse*, *pirate*, *slave* and a host of other nouns. As for the concepts in group 2 such as *answer*, *anger*, *appeal* and *love*, their multiple word class membership cannot be explained conclusively by means of derivations from a historical perspective, but has to be attributed to other causes such as double borrowing (see section 10.1.2). In order to provide genuine proof of this correlation, a systematic comparison of historical insights and assessments of the concepts involved is required.

Moreover, the distribution of metonymies in group 1 is striking because it could possibly provide an explanation for the above-mentioned observation that denominal and deadjectival conversion to verbs is far more frequent and more productive than deverbal conversion to nouns. From the perspective of the participating metonymies, conversions to a verb generally manifest the classic metonymic type of **synecdoche**, i.e. 'part-stands-for-the-whole' relationships. In each case one component of the scene – AGENT, INSTRUMENT, GOAL etc. – stands for the entire action or the entire event. Contrasting with this, deverbal nouns are based on the relationship 'whole for part', e.g. ACTION for OUTCOME in the case of the noun *cut*. Metonymies based on this relationship are rarely found outside word-formation; they appear to be conceptually less helpful and productive. As we have already suggested, the assumed metonymies in Table 10.4 for *cut*, *cheat* and *swim* are less 'handy' than the denominal and deadjectival metonymies. It could be that the different potential for the formation of metonymic relationships is ultimately responsible for the fact that conversion is basically a process geared to the formation of verbs.

From the perspective of the language system, however, it has to be said that the productivity of conversion to verbs is less impeded by the possible competition from overt suffixations than is the case with conversion to nouns. The reason for this, as we have already observed (see p. 182), is that suffixation is clearly a word-formation pattern orientated towards producing nouns and adjectives, whereas verb suffixation with its small number of suffixes *-en*, *-ify*, *-ize* and *-ate* is restricted almost exclusively to the field of Romance loans and specialist terminology. By contrast conversion, insofar as we restrict ourselves to 'genuine' group 1 conversions, favours the verb as a target word class and affects the entire lexicon with the main focus being on Germanic words and very early borrowings. We could refer to this as a complementary functional distribution or division of labour between suffixation and conversion: suffixation tends to form nouns and adjectives with an abstract content on a formal stylistic level, while conversion tends to form verbs operating in the concrete section of the lexicon in all registers and on all stylistic levels. (What should be kept in mind, however, is that suffixed forms such as *driver* or *agreement* tend of course to be blocked for conversion.)

With regard to the issue of the dubious status of conversion as a word-formation process, this evidence does not enable us to come to an unequivocal conclusion. The idea that conversion is based on conceptual metonymies, which seems plausible at least for the clear cases in group 1, leads us to exclude conversion from word-formation and to treat it as a mild manifestation of figurative language. However, the observation that suffixation and conversion seem to occupy different niches in the (re-)categorization of concepts confirms the impression that, at least from a functional point of view, a relationship seems to exist between these two processes in the language system. The idea underlying the concept of zero-derivation, that conversion is only a formal variant of suffixation, is probably invalidated by such a division-of-labour theory.

Further reading: Cannon (1985), Don, Trommelen and Zonneveld (2000) and **Bauer and Valera (2005a, 2005b).** A now classic, pragmatically orientated approach to the formation of and understanding of new denominal verb conversions, so-called *contextuals*, is adopted by **Clark and Clark (1979).** On the generative approach, see **Lieber (1990: ch. 3)**; on the onomasiological approach:

Štekauer **(1996)**; on conversion from the perspective of cognitive grammar: **Twardzisz (1997), Farell (2001)**; on the metonymy view: **Schönefeld (2005).**

11 Polymorphemic complex lexemes

Up to this point I have restricted my description of English word-formation largely to the idealized case of complex lexemes consisting of two morphemes. Lexemes comprising several morphemes, e.g. *time-consuming* and *post-Freudian* have cropped up in various sections, but the focus there lay to a large extent on the problems involved in the analysis of the morphological structure and/or semantic structure of these lexemes. Regardless of such complications, this chapter will provide a selective discussion of the morphological, semantic and conceptual aspects of complex lexemes consisting of three or more morphemes.

As already explained in section 5.3.1 (see p. 96), it is common practice to split polymorphemic lexemes on the level of morphological structure into hierarchically arranged pairs of modifier and head. This means that the principle of binary branching, i.e. the segmenting into two immediate constituents, is transferred from syntax to complex lexemes comprising several elements. Since polymorphemic affixations and polymorphemic compounds pose different problems for the analysis, the two types will be treated in separate sections (11.1 and 11.2).

11.1 Polymorphemic affixations

Not surprisingly, the simplest and most common type of polymorphemic affixation consists of three morphemes: a simple base (i.e. root), a prefix and a suffix as, for example, in *deformity*, *unsafeness* and *unknowable*. When analyzing lexemes of this morphological form we have to decide which of the two affixes in the morphological structure is attached directly to the root and which to the already affixed base. This decision is influenced by several considerations.

Firstly, we have to weigh up whether the two potential root affixations could ever actually stand alone as English words. In the case of *deformity*, for instance, the suffixation **formity* alone does not exist and can therefore not serve as a base. We can then assume that the prefix is an immediate constituent of the root, generating the verb *deform*, which in turn becomes nominalized by means of the suffix *-ity*. The morphological structure of *deformity* is displayed in Figure 11.1. Instead of using the terms modifier and head, bases and suffixes are labelled with the respective word classes and prefixes as such, depending on the configuration in each case. The abbreviation sfx_N, for example, stands for 'noun-forming suffix'.

Fig. 11.1: Morphological structure of the noun *deformity*

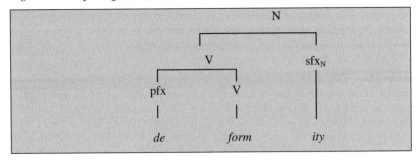

Similarly, the lexemes *irreversible* and *unacceptable* can be clearly segmented but with a different result, since the adjectives *reversible* and *acceptable* exist while the verbs **to irreverse* and **to unaccept* do not (cf. Figure 11.2).

Fig. 11.2: Morphological structure of the adjectives *irreversible* and *unacceptable*

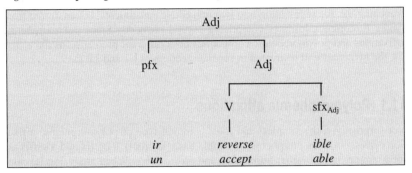

Cases such as the nouns *unsafeness* or *unhappiness*, in which both root affixations yield existing lexemes, are somewhat more problematic. Both *unsafe* and *safeness*, both *unhappy* and *happiness* are established English lexemes. In such cases we have to take into account above all the **distribution** and **productivity** of the prefix, as well as the restrictions on its productivity. Since the negative prefix *un-* in *unsafeness* and *unhappiness* (particularly with the meaning of a polar opposition relevant here) is placed far more frequently before adjectives than nouns, the prefixation must be applied before the suffixation in the morphological structure, as represented in Figure 11.3.

If neither of the two individual affixations constitutes an existing word, as in *unknowable* (**to unknow*, **knowable*), for instance, then we have a case of synthetic prefixation, which will be investigated again briefly at the end of this section.

Fig. 11.3: Morphological structure of the nouns *unsafeness* and *unhappiness*

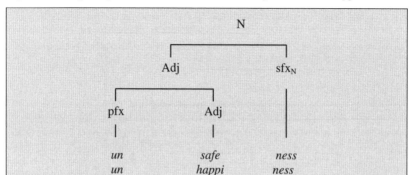

The same two fundamental considerations – the existence of actual lexemes and the distribution and productivity of prefixes – also determine the analysis of more elaborate affixations, whose complexity is more often caused by sequences of several suffixes than several prefixes. Even two prefixes are so rare that no example is documented in the MUMC. Even if we are willing to accept the notorious form *antidisestablishmentarianism* as an example containing two prefixes, it is significant that according to the OED this word is rarely used as a 'normal', i.e. object-linguistic word but is popular as an example of an unusually long English word in meta-linguistic contexts.

The two most complex affixations in the MUMC are the lexemes *reproducibility* and *depolarisation*, consisting of four and five morphemes respectively. In the morphological analysis of both these words it is crucial to take into account that the prefixes *re-* and *de-* are usually placed before verbal bases, as the morphological structures in Figures 11.4 and 11.5 suggest:

Fig. 11.4: Morphological structure of *reproducibility*

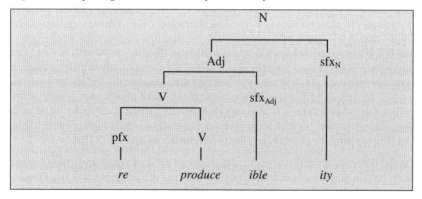

Fig. 11.5: Morphological structure of *depolarisation*

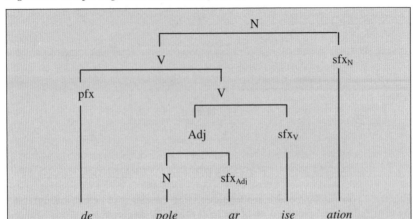

How can these complex morphological structures be analyzed at the cognitive level? It would be plausible to model the internal structure of such lexemes as the hierarchically arranged result of figure-ground profiling by analogy with the morphological structure. At each hierarchical level the base would be interpreted as the ground in front of which the newly-attached morpheme is profiled as the figure. *Reproducible*, for example, would then be the ground for the new profiling as a nominal concept by means of the suffix *-ity* in *reproducibility*. What seems to be clear, however, is that conceptual and morphological structure do not always match, since no matter how complex a given polymorphemic affixation is, its two ends will always have more prominence than the root and the morphemes positioned closer to the root, since the final suffix always determines the concept-type profiling and the (outermost) prefix always has a decisive influence on the conceptual profiling. This seems to be true irrespective of the morphological structure. Intuitively, from a conceptual point of view the prominence of the prefixes *re-* and *de-* in the two lexemes *reproducibility* and *depolarisation* appears to be equal, although in the figures showing the morphological structures, *re-* in *reproducibility* is positioned lower in the tree diagram than *de-* in *depolarisation*. The impression that the two prefixes are nevertheless conceptually equally salient is probably influenced at least partly by the fact that semantically the prefix seems to modify the whole of the rest of the word, irrespective of where it occurs in the morphological structure. It is also supported by the phonological structure of such complex affixations, in which the prefixes can maintain their high prominence as carrying the primary or secondary stress despite the addition of suffixes.

On the other hand, while hierarchically arranged pairs of figure and ground could work in principle, one could also consider relaxing the principle of a strict binary system, at least for conceptual analysis. For words such as *depolarisation*, it would seem sensible to assume that the verb (here *polarise*) represents the conceptual base which is modified by two simultaneous prefixation and suffixation processes, resulting in one step in the form *depolarisation*. Owing to the lack of empirical proof, such considerations are admittedly of a fairly speculative nature at present. Ternary structures – i.e. structures composed of three constituents of equal value – are certainly conceptually by no means unrealistic, as is proved by the countless synthetic prefixations with three morphemes of which neither the prefixation nor the suffixation can stand alone as an actual word (cf. *unknowable – *to unknow* and **knowable*). For these formations, the most viable or maybe even the only representation of the conceptual structure is a ternary constituent structure.

11.2 Corpus study V: polymorphemic compounds

Owing to the fact that compounds are often written as separate words in English, the distinction between polymorphemic compounds and syntactic groups causes notorious demarcation problems for the analysis of the morphological structure (see p. 131). How, for example, can we deal adequately with the noun sequence *mass-market leisure business* in the MUMC? Should it be treated as a compound or as a combination of two compounds (*mass-market* and *leisure business*) or as a noun phrase with two nominal premodifiers, of which one is a compound? We can adopt various positions with respect to questions of this nature. If we assume that word-formation should in principle be restricted to morphologically complex lexical units that are stored in the mental lexicon ready to be recalled, then we are more likely not to interpret such combinations as compounds, because presumably only parts of them are stored as one unit and not the entire construction. If this criterion is not considered to be important, then there is nothing to prevent us from analyzing such expressions as compounds, although we would then have to point out that these compounds have a mainly syntactic function.

This last strategy is adopted, for instance, by Carstairs-McCarthy (2002: 76), who treats the noun sequence *holiday car sightseeing trip* as a compound. In his opinion, proof that this sequence constitutes a compound comes from the intonation pattern, at least if one is willing to modify the basic rule that the constituent on the left should be stressed. In cases where the head of the entire compound is a compound itself, the head is stressed rather than the modifier, he argues. Correspondingly the primary stress in *holiday car sightseeing trip* falls on *sight*.

According to Bauer (1998b: 70–72), not even native speakers agree about the 'correct' stress pattern for polymorphemic N+N-compounds. The criterion is therefore not unproblematic. In any case, noun combinations of this complexity are comparatively rare in spoken English – which is of course decisive for the intonation test – presumably because their advance planning as an integrated concept (with unit intonation and a primary stress) makes too many demands on the mind's processing capacity. When speaking, instead of saying *and then we went on a holiday car sightseeing trip* we would be more likely to say *and then we went on a sightseeing trip in our holiday car.* The same applies to the example *airline cabin crew safety training manual* discussed by Carstairs-McCarthy in his exercises. One can only imagine utterances such as *and then we looked it up in the airline cabin crew safety training manual* occurring in technical jargon, and then one would expect the speaker to use abbreviations or acronyms.

In this book we adopt a relatively narrow cognitive definition of word-formation, which interprets typical compounds as entrenched conceptual gestalts which are stored in the mental lexicon (see p. 142 ff.). Accordingly, word-formations such as those cited in the previous paragraph, which are in all probability assembled by most speakers during speech production, are regarded as falling within the remit of grammar, where they can, of course, be split into their immediate constituents. This applies, for example, to the phrase *local authority social services department* in the MUMC, which can be understood as a syntactically compressed form of *department of social services at the local authorities.* It is of course very likely that speakers who use these forms frequently, e.g. as part of their jobs, and for whom these complex sequences serve a naming function, have an entrenched concept stored in their mental lexicons. This is a good example of how the collective sociopragmatic dimension of institutionalization and the individual dimension of entrenchment (cf. section 4) can diverge.

I have selected the nouns *car boot sale* and *Sunday newspaper* – if we treat *Sunday* as monomorphemic – from the MUMC as examples of units consisting of three morphemes, which fit the concept of compound as represented in this book. Regardless of the intonation, these two expressions seem to be so highly entrenched and lexicalized, that it does not seem plausible not to regard them as compounds. As was the case with polymorphemic affixations, when categorizing the immediate constituents of such compounds we have to bear in mind which elements can actually stand alone as lexemes. Furthermore, the analysis on the semantic level plays a crucial role. The paraphrases 'sale where people sell things from their car boots' and 'newspaper which is published on Sundays' are reflected in the structures shown in Figures 11.6 and 11.7 respectively:

Fig. 11.6 Morphological structure of the compound *car boot sale*

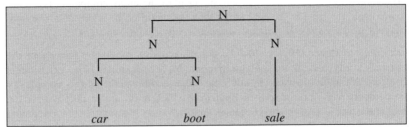

Fig. *11.7* Morphological structure of the compound *Sunday newspaper*

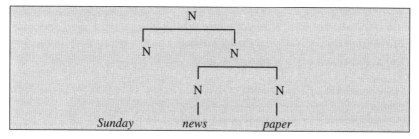

The figures show clearly that the two compounds have differing morphological structures. In the case of *car boot sale* the compound functions as modifier, whereas in *Sunday newspaper* the compound is the head. It is interesting to note that these two competing morphological structures are not found in equal numbers in the MUMC. Table 11.1 lists all the compound combinations in the MUMC of the type N + N + N, arranged according to the two possible patterns of morphological structures.

Tab. 11.1: Combinations according to the pattern N + N + N in the MUMC

[N + N] + N		N + [N + N]
A delta fibres	*home help service*	*childhood girlfriend*
airline group	*honeymoon couple*	*childhood playmate*
Alka Seltzer type	*household help*	*corner newsagent*
all-out strike	*household work*	*government airfield*
back office staff	*housing finance issues*	*guerrilla warfare*
bedroom curtains	*interest rate cuts*	*Gulf deadline*
bedroom window	*land-mine casualties*	*hotel bedroom*
capital investment programme	*mid-afternoon sun*	*hotel car-park*
car boot sale	*muscle fibre disorganisation*	*motor end-plates*
careers information resources	*Myelin sheath disruption*	*school headmasters*
child care concerns	*nerve cell body*	*school timetable*
community care groups	*nerve cell death*	*Sunday newspapers*
community care planning	*nerve conduction velocity*	
community care policy	*Nerve Growth Factor*	
community care provision	*News Corp journalists*	
community care services	*News Corp shares*	
credit quality ratings	*newspaper article*	

credit rating knife	*nursing home care*
Creditweek magazine	*peak flow meter*
dashboard clock	*program-execution stage*
daylight robbery	*race track training*
Degree Presentation Ceremony	*shag-pile carpet*
design-standards committee	*snowcat skiing*
dive store area	*state school heads*
Education Reform Act	*state school students*
Exchange Rate Mechanism	*ten pin bowling*
health care costs	*wartime life*
health care needs	*water-storage tower*

We can see from the table that combinations with a complex modifier (i.e. [N + N] + N: 58 examples) occur almost five times as often as those with a complex head (N + [N + N]: 12 examples). Furthermore, what is also conspicuous is that the complex heads in the right-hand column, apart from one exception which is written with a hyphen (*car-park*), are all written as one word and are highly established compounds consisting of two morphemes. This is not always the case with the complex modifiers in the two left-hand columns. The potential for the formation and syntactic use of polymorphemic compounds whose head is a compound in itself, is obviously more limited. Since the head is the decisive constituent from a grammatical, semantic and conceptual point of view, it seems to be preferred if it is an already established lexeme which most speakers have at their disposal as an entrenched concept in their mental lexicon.

The MUMC contains few word combinations consisting of four elements which could qualify for the status of established compounds. The best example is the lexeme *bank holiday weekend*, which is listed separately in dictionaries such as the OALD and the LDOCE. Owing to its clear semantic structure this compound can be broken down unambiguously into the symmetric structure [*bank + holiday*] + [*week + end*]. The few remaining four-word combinations – *home equity release schemes*, *National Health Service Act*, *postinjury peripheral innervation density*, and *US credit-rating agency* – can scarcely be regarded as established complex lexemes. They are certainly not part of the general vocabulary of English and are very probably only stored as integrated concepts in the mental lexicons of specialists in the particular fields.

This observation brings me to the cognitive perspective. One finding arising from the corpus data is clearly relevant to this perspective: as the morphological complexity increases so the probability of a word combination being stored in the mental lexicon decreases. The reasons for this are presumably cognitive, since it would certainly not be economical if the capacity of the mental lexicon were burdened with a large number of highly complex compounds.[9] It is probably because of this potential mental overload that polymorphemic compounds coined in specialist terminology are usually used in the form of abbreviations or as initials. Syntactically motivated combinations such as *holiday car sightseeing trip* as discussed by Carstairs-McCarthy only occur rarely because of the huge burden placed on on-going speech processing by the complexity involved in planning the utterance. This applies not just to speakers but also to listeners, who are only prepared to be tolerant to a certain extent if the semantic relationships between words are not made clear by means of grammatical or morphological markers, and words are placed next to each other in a form which is typical of compounds but with little connection outwardly.

In contrast to polymorphemic affixations in which the morphological and cognitive analyses appear not to be in agreement, the idea of multi-hierarchical figure-ground relationships in polymorphemic compounds is convincing, since it is analogous to the morphological structure. In *bank holiday weekend*, for example, *bank* functions as the figure in *bank holiday* and *week* as the figure in *weekend*, and on the next level *bank holiday* functions as the figure standing out from *weekend* as the ground. The prominence of the constituents functioning as the ground is lower than that of those profiled as the figure in the given situation.

11.3 Summary

This chapter has not succeeded in achieving much more than to offer a glimpse into some issues pertaining to polymorphemic affixations and compounds. The reason for the limitations we have been facing here lie in the lack of available empirical studies and theoretical discussions. The findings from the corpus suggest that extremely polymorphemic affixations and compounds – which are indeed processed like proper compounds, i.e. as one conceptual unit – are very rarely employed in authentic language. For both structures there are obvious restrictions with regard to the complexity. These could be attributable to the cognitive limitations on capacity when storing established lexemes and when processing established and syntactically motivated combinations. Extremely complex formations of the type *antidisestablishmentarianism*, which are sometimes adduced to illustrate the principle of the recursiveness of word-

---

[9]   Incidentally this aspect of economy was originally also decisive for the transformationalist position in the generative word-formation theory, which claimed that complex lexemes are not stored individually in each case but are derived from sentences by means of transformational rules (see p. 16).

formation processes, are avoided in casual conversation. While similar formations do exist in specialist terminology, they often occur in an abbreviated form.

Important considerations to keep in mind when carrying out analyses of polymorphemic formations include the following:

- Important criteria for the determination of the morphological structures of polymorphemic affixations are the **distribution** and the **productivity** of affixes, as well as restrictions on their productivity, and the question of whether potential bases are existing lexemes or not.
- The conceptual structures of polymorphemic affixations can differ from their morphological structures, since the outermost affixes (i.e. the first prefix and the final suffix) play salient roles irrespective of their place in the hierarchical morphological structure.
- From a conceptual point of view, the existence of ternary constituent structures is possible.
- The compound status of many polymorphemic compound-like combinations is very controversial. If the cognitive criterion demanding storage as an entrenched unit is applied, it is unlikely that there will be a large number of compounds consisting of four or even more word-like constituents in English, which are part of the common core of the lexicon.
- For tripartite compounds, the corpus data suggest a preponderance of the structure [N + N] + N.

12   Non-morphemic word-formation processes

The word-formation processes we will be dealing with in this chapter – **back-formation**, **clipping**, **acronyms**, **blends** and **reduplication** – are fundamentally different in several ways from those we have discussed so far. They do not use morphemes as their basic building blocks and are therefore **non-morphemic**. This raises the question whether they are word-formation processes in the sense that they are predictable on the basis of knowledge of patterns and therefore to some extent regular – a question which is not easy to answer. On the one hand, it cannot be denied that there is a kind of system underlying these processes and that they are indisputably instrumental in the creation of new words (cf. Plag 2003: 116–126, Kemmer 2003). If we assume that word-formation patterns are cognitive schemas for new formations (cf. p. 94), then it would certainly be desirable to identify regularities underlying formation patterns in the non-morphemic processes as well. On the other hand, the products of non-morphemic processes are certainly not predictable (cf. Bauer's term *unpredictable formations*, 1983: 232 ff.) in the same way as those of typical morphemic patterns. Whether a word lends itself to clipping or blending, for instance, can only be described on a very abstract level but cannot be expected, let alone foreseen, on the basis of its form or meaning. For non-morphemic patterns it therefore seems inappropriate to invoke the idea of *productivity* in the sense specified in chapter 6; furthermore, the notion of *possible* or *potential lexemes* introduced in section 6.2 is also not applicable.

With the exception of reduplication all non-morphemic word-formation processes have in common that they result in a reduction of morphological substance. This means they bring about abbreviations, and this indeed seems to be their most important function. Apart from back-formation, which also has some of the characteristics of morphemic processes, none of the patterns we are going to deal with in this chapter changes the word class. From a semantic point of view, it is typical of clippings and acronyms that the full form and the short form have the same meaning, at least with regard to their denotation (if not connotation). Interesting exceptions to this tendency will be dealt with separately in the relevant sections.

Finally – again with the definite exception of back-formation – non-morphemic word-creation processes take place far more consciously than regular morphemic ones. Unintentional ad-hoc formations such as occur in compounding, suffixation and above all in conversion, are scarcely to be expected in clippings, acronyms, blends and reduplications.

12.1 Back-formation

Back-formation (or **back-derivation**) typically deletes morphemes or morpheme-like units at the ends of base-lexemes. We have already had the opportunity to mention a number of examples of the products of back-derivation in the chapter on compounding (see p. 136) because a large number of verbal compounds were created by this process, e.g. *to ghost-write* (from *ghost-writer*), *to sunbathe* (from *sunbathing*), *to baby-sit* (from *baby-sitter*), *to sightsee* (from *sightseeing*) and *to air-condition* (from *air-conditioning*). As these examples show, a suffix is split from a lexeme, leading to a change in word class.

This separation presupposes the morphological analysis of the more complex base. It is interesting to observe that there are cases where this process took place historically even when the source lexemes appeared to be composed of several morphemes but actually were not. Classical examples of this are *to burgle* from *burglar* and *to peddle* from *peddler*, both of which (i.e. *burglar* and *peddler*) are essentially monomorphemic. As a result of what is strictly speaking an 'erroneous' morphological analysis, verbs were formed from these nouns by removing the supposed suffixes. From a purely synchronic perspective, it is almost impossible to identify such cases as back-formations, even more so than in the case of back-formed verbal compounds, since one instinctively assumes that the morphologically more complex word is derived from the simpler one. Attempts at determining the derivational direction synchronically using the catalogue of criteria outlined in section 9.3 (cf. e.g. Kastovsky 1982: 174), are, in my opinion, not always convincing. If we disregard the productive and reasonably systematic area of verbal compounds that are formed or formable by means of back-derivation, then it is without doubt not a typical and productive word-formation process, because there are no systematic underlying regularities and hence it cannot be regarded as a pattern or model for new formations.

Ironically, the phenomenon of back-formation is relevant for a cognitive perspective on word-formation. It demonstrates the confidence speakers have in suffixation, since back-formation processes are based on the assumption that genuinely or supposedly suffixed lexemes have been derived from a base which, of course, must actually exist. Nevertheless, these back-derived concepts cannot be very firmly entrenched in the mental lexicon, particularly in the case of verbal compounds, since we can observe that many of these verbs are **defective**, that is they do not produce forms over the entire verbal inflectional paradigm but only occur, or at least only sound familiar, in the base/infinitive and in participial forms. While the past tense form of *to babysit* does exist, e.g. *I babysat last night at my neighbours' house*, it is not possible to say **We sightsaw in London for a week*. In this instance speakers opt for other ways of expression such as *We spent a week sightseeing in London*.

12.2 Corpus study VI: clipping

In contrast to back-formation, in the case of clipping the word class and the meaning of the original word are preserved. This does not preclude subsequent lexicalization, however. Even completely accepted everyday words such as *car* (from *motor car*), *bus* (from *omnibus*), *pub* (from *public house*) and *flu* (from *influenza*) are the products of clipping.

As these examples demonstrate, words can be clipped at the beginning (**fore-clipping**), at the end (**back-clipping**) or even at both ends (**middle-clipping**). (Note that – somewhat inconsistently – the first element in *fore-clipping* and *back-clipping* refers to the elements being taken away, while in *middle clipping* the *middle* stands for what is retained). Clipping affects not just simple lexemes but also compounds and syntactic groups. Examples of clipped forms in the MUMC are shown in Table 12.1. together with their base words:

Tab. 12.1: Clipped forms in the MUMC with their sources

clipped form	source
ad	*advertisement*
aide	*aide-de-camp*
Aussie	*Australian*
broker	*stockbroker*
bus	*omnibus*
capital	*capital city*
Chris	*Christopher*
civvies	*civilians, civilian clothing*
comprehensive	*comprehensive school*
des.res.	*desirable residence*
disco	*discotheque*
eve	*Evening*
exam	*examination*
fridge	*refrigerator*
Jo'burg	*Johannesburg*
maths	*mathematics*
mini-sub	*mini-submarine*
mo	*moment*
movies	*moving pictures*
News Corp	*news corporation*
Dow	*Dow-Jones average*

par	*paragraph*
phone	*telephone*
photo	*photograph*
piano	*pianoforte*
plane	*aeroplane, airplane*
polytechnic	*polytechnic institution*
Provo	*Provisional* (member of the Provisional IRA/ Sinn Féin)
pub	*public house*
radio	*radiotelegraph*
sax	*saxophone*
semi-detached	*semi-detached house*
Slobo	*Slobodan (Milosevic)*
States	*United States*
vet	*veterinarian, veteran*
zoo	*zoological garden*

This list illustrates further varieties of clipping such as the combination of clipping and suffixation with *-ie* (*Aussie, civvie, movie*), the deletion of the second part of compounds or syntactic groups (*capital, comprehensive, polytechnic, semi-detached*) and, of course, the extremely frequent case of the clipping of proper names (*Chris, Slobo*). The form *Jo'burg* is striking because here the middle section is omitted.

From a semantic perspective it is typical of clippings that the denotative meaning of the full form is identical to that of the shortened form. Nevertheless a difference in meaning can sometimes be observed, particularly in short forms that have been in existence for so long that they are no longer regarded as such: *aide* ('person employed to help a government official') is different from *aide-de-camp* ('officer who assists an officer of higher rank'); *broker* has developed beyond its original meaning of *stockbroker* (cf. also the compound *power broker*), although the primary meaning of *broker* is still dominant.

As for the establishment of clippings, from a sociopragmatic angle we can arrange them on a scale. We have, on the one hand, cases such as *pub, bus, zoo, radio* and *piano*, which are undoubtedly better established than the original forms and are no longer perceived as short forms, being part of the general vocabulary of English with no particular connotations or stylistic characteristics. Occasionally the higher degree of establishment is reflected in the dictionaries in that the short form is not defined as a shortening of the long one but vice versa. In the *Collins Concise Dictionary Plus* (Hanks 1989), for instance, the definition of the lexeme *discotheque* is "the full term for **disco**". Under the entry *soap opera* in the LDOCE4 there is no definition but simply a cross reference to the entry *soap*.

(Interestingly, this has been changed in LDOCE5, where *soap opera* is the main entry, while *soap* is only cross-referenced by "*informal* a SOAP OPERA". At the other end of the scale we find short forms that can only be regarded as institutionalized in certain areas of the speech community or in specialist terminology. The form *des. res.* for a *desirable residence*, for example, comes from estate agents' jargon. As well as being peculiar to the language of specific groups, clipped forms of this type usually have particular connotations for the speakers who are familiar with them. Cases in which the full form and the clipped form can be regarded as being equally established (*exam, plane, sax, vet*), lie between these two poles. In all cases where the full form and the short form are at least partially established, it seems that owing to differences with regard to connotations and associations, clipping is ultimately not a process which fully retains the meaning but that the clipped and the full forms are entrenched as independent though very similar and closely related concepts.

The use of clipped forms – insofar as they are better established than their source words – signals familiarity and closeness in a conceptual as well as a social way. Clipped forms indicate that the speaker is so familiar with the concept that referring to it by its longer form is felt to be unnecessarily complicated. This requires an assumption on the part of the speaker that the listeners are familiar with the clipped form or are at least in a position to understand it. Conversely clipped forms can, of course, also be exploited deliberately as an exclusion mechanism against listeners we know are not familiar with that particular short form. In a colloquial setting this means that speakers make use of short forms that are not as well established as the original words when speaking to people they know. The use of clippings can also indicate social closeness and mutual membership of a group. Against this background it is not surprising that many clipped forms originate from slang and the jargon of social or professional groups (Marchand 1969: 447).

12.3 Corpus study VII: acronyms

Acronyms can be understood as an extreme form of clipping in which only the initial letters themselves or a couple of letters at the beginning of the words remain. This type of short form can only be used with compounds or word groups but not with individual lexemes, since the individual letters are not specific enough even in context to enable one to identify the full form and its meaning reliably. In contrast to abbreviations in writing such as *Mr* for *Mister* and *BBQ* for *barbeque*, the characteristic of acronyms is that they are not just written differently but also pronounced differently. A list of all the acronyms in the MUMC (which of course is itself an acronym) can be found in Table 12.2. Where acronyms have several meanings, the original words relevant to the context are shown first, with the other important ones given in brackets afterwards. Orthographic variants are also noted in brackets.

Tab. 12.2: Acronyms in the MUMC showing pronunciation and original words

acronym	pronunciation	source
AI	/ˌeɪ ˈaɪ/	*artificial intelligence (artificial insemination, Amnesty International)*
ANC	/ˌeɪ en ˈsiː/	*African National Congress*
BBC	/ˌbiː biː ˈsiː/	*British Broadcasting Corporation*
CV (cv)	/ˌsiː ˈviː/	*curriculum vitae*
FORTRAN (Fortran)	/ˈfɔːtræn/	*formula translation*
FTSE	/ˌef tiː es ˈiː/ /ˈfʊtsi/	*Financial Times Stock Exchange*
GCSE	/ˌdʒiː siː es ˈiː/	*General Certificate of Secondary Education*
IRA	/ˌaɪ ɑːr ˈeɪ/	*Irish Republican Army*
M. O. T. (MOT)	/ˌem əʊ ˈtiː/	*Ministry of Transport*
MS DOS	/ˌem es ˈdɒs/	*Microsoft disc operating system*
Nato (NATO)	/ˈneɪtəʊ/	*North Atlantic Treaty Organization*
NCC	/ˌen siː ˈsiː/	*National Curriculum Council (National Computer Conference; Nature Conservancy Council; National Consumer Council)*
NHS	/ˌen eɪtʃ ˈes/	*National Health Service*
Prolog	/ˈprəʊlɒg/	*programming in logic*
QED (q. e. d.)	/ˌkjuː iː ˈdiː/	*quod erat demonstrandum (quantum electrodynamics)*
RNA	/ˌɑːr en ˈeɪ/	*ribonucleic acid*
TNT	/ˌtiː en ˈtiː/	*trinitrotoluene*
TV	/ˌtiː ˈviː/	*television*
UK	/ˌjuː ˈkeɪ/	*United Kingdom*
Unita (UNITA)	/juː ˈniː tə/	Portugese: *União Nacional para a Independência Total de Angola (National Union for the Total Independence of Angola)*
US (U. S.)	/ˌjuː ˈes/	*United States (of America)*
WP	/ˌdʌbljuː ˈpiː/	*word processor (word processing, weather permitting, Warsaw Pact)*

Various types of acronyms can be identified in this list. There are three different types of written form: unseparated capital letters (*BBC, IRA, UK*), capital letters separated by full stops (*M.O.T.*) or one capital at the beginning followed by small letters as in a normal word (*Nato, Prolog, Unita*). As the listed alternatives show, the written form is very inconsistent, particularly with regard to the use of full stops, and partly depends on the in-house style of the publishers. In addition to these three types, there is a small number of highly lexicalized acronyms that do not begin with a capital letter and are not even recognized as acronyms by most people, e.g. *laser* (for *light amplification by the stimulated emission of radiation*) and *radar* (*radio detection and ranging*). These lexemes are comparable with clippings such as *bus* and *pub*, which are also not perceived to be products of word-formation processes.

As regards the pronunciation of acronyms, two basic types can be observed – those pronounced as a series of individual letters (*ANC, BBC, TNT, UK, TV*), and those pronounced like a normal word (*AIDS, FORTRAN, Nato, Prolog, Sars*). Many linguists make a terminological distinction between these two types (e.g. Bauer 1983: 223, Carstairs-McCarthy 2002: 65), describing the *BBC*-type as an **initialism** or **abbreviation** and only the *Nato*-type as an **acronym**. Accordingly the form *MS DOS* would be a combination of an initialism and an acronym; and *FTSE* would have a different designation depending on its pronunciation. It is because of these discrepancies that most linguists use the terms *initialism* and *acronym* synonymously.

The examples *laser* and *radar* also illustrate the variability in the choice of letters that find their way into the acronym. Although the typical case is certainly taking the initial letter of each of the words involved, many of the established acronyms pronounced as words (*laser, UNITA*) omit short function words such as *of, by* and *and* in particular, and/or in addition to the initials use other letters that are constituents of the original word (*FORTRAN, radar*). The key issue with these variants is, of course, that the acronym is pronounceable as a word and therefore compatible with English **phonotactics**, i.e. the rules for the permitted juxtaposition of sounds. The reason for inserting two or even three extra letters is often the need to add vowels in order to make the word pronounceable.

A particularly interesting phenomenon is that of acronyms which are formally identical with (i.e. homonymous with) established words that have a semantic connection with the acronym. While there are no examples of this type in Table 12.2, plenty of instances do exist, e.g. *PEN* (from *Poets, Playwrights, Editors, Essayists, Novelists*), WAR (from *Women Against Rape*), *WASP* (from *White Anglo-Saxon Protestant*) and *STOPP* (from *Society of Teachers Opposed to Physical Punishment*; Ungerer 1991: 137). The semantic connection between the meaning of the acronym and the meaning of the full form serves several purposes. It attracts the attention of other language users, facilitates the interpretation of the acronym, and stimulates thought processes that help to entrench the term in the memory (Ungerer 1991: 139 ff.).

Acronyms of the type *PEN* and *STOPP* are the most striking evidence for the fact that, unlike many products of morphemic word-formation patterns, acronyms are not created randomly or even unconsciously, since the coiner is fully aware of the act of word creation. It is certainly not an exaggeration to claim that in public communications today in the fields of politics, public institutions, the media and the sciences (particularly the natural sciences, technology, information technology and medicine), from which the majority of the existing acronyms originate, complex terms are being coined expressly with an eye to their ability to be reduced to convincing and appealing, or even original-sounding acronyms. Nevertheless, acronyms are, of course, by no means merely gimmicks with no deeper value. On the contrary, without these useful abbreviations communication in these fields would be exceedingly long-winded and laborious. A quick look at the column of the original expressions in Table 12.2 reveals what monstrous constructions one would constantly have to deal with were it not for the availability of acronyms. It is therefore not surprising that the formation of acronyms is probably the word-formation process with the biggest output today. The website www.acronymfinder. com with more than 900,000 entries (as of July 2010, compared to 330,000 entries in 2005) currently claims to be the most comprehensive internet dictionary of acronyms. The *Acronym, Initialisms and Abbreviations Dictionary*, published in 1990, already contained as many as half a million entries. Neither of these acronym dictionaries is restricted to initialisms of the English language, and the overwhelming majority of entries in both consist of names.

Today, apart from the fields already mentioned, the internet and electronic communication by email or in chatrooms is a well-known breeding ground for expressive acronyms with, for example, the numbers *2* and *4* acting as substitutes for the homophonic words *to, too* and *for*, the letter *c* replacing the word *see* and the letter *u* replacing the word *you*. A substantial and reliable list of items of this type can be found in Crystal (2004: 139 ff.). Examples to be found in mobile phone text messages and in various genres on the internet (chatrooms, IRC, ICQ, blogs, social networks, etc.) are the ubiquitous *FAQs (frequently asked questions)* as well as *lol (laughing out loud)*, *mte (my thoughts exactly)*, *myob (mind your own business)*, *weg (wide evil grin)*, *brb (be right back)*, *2g4y (too good for you)*, *j2lyk (just to let you know)*, *awgthtgtata (are we going to have to go through all this again?)*. In these instances the writer has to balance economy of language production with the need to inform and hence the requirement that the signs used can be understood. This both produces and significantly strengthens a feeling of belonging to the culture, of being in the know for insiders.

Further reading: McCully and Holmes (1988), Cannon (1989), Ungerer (1991), Kreidler (2000), Crystal (2004).

12.4 Blending

From a conceptual point of view, **blending** or word mixing as a non-morphemic process comes closest to the morphemic patterns, in particular compounding, since it combines two concepts into one new concept. In contrast to compounding, however, each lexeme is not formally incorporated in unaltered form into the new lexeme but, like the parts of a telescope, they are pushed into each other or shortened in some other way. Some of the most well-known and established examples of this process are the lexemes *smog* (from *smoke* and *fog*), *brunch* (from *breakfast* and *lunch*), *chunnel* (from *channel* and *tunnel*) and *infotainment* (from *information* and *entertainment*), *smog* already having emancipated itself to such an extent from its original bases that it is hardly ever regarded as a blend any more. In typical blends not only have the word-forms merged but the meaning also represents a mixture of both the original concepts: *smog* describes a mixture of smoke and fog, *brunch* is a meal that combines elements of breakfast and lunch. The example *chunnel*, however, which does not really blend two meanings but combines them in a way typical of determinative compounds, shows that there are deviations from typical blends. These can be treated as shortened and merged forms of compounds or compound-like structures.

Blends – in a wider sense, i.e. including semantically non-blending ones – occur in a range of formal variations (cf. Lehrer 1996: 364). Firstly, they can be separated into those derived from overlapping words – e.g. *wintertainment* from *winter* and *entertainment* – and those that do not overlap (e.g. *infotainment*). In each case, the *splinters*, as Lehrer calls the part retained in the blend, taken from the original words are generally preserved unaltered; there are exceptions, however, for which this is not the case, e.g. *enteporneur* from *entrepreneur* and *porn(ography)*. In blends with overlapping lexemes, it is possible for both of the original words to be included in their entirety, as in *sexploitation* (from *sex* and *exploitation*). Blends without overlapping lexemes can consist of a complete original word plus a splinter (*vodkatini* from *vodka* and *martini*) or of two splinters (*Spanglish* from *Spanish* and *English*).

Semantic and cognitive aspects of blends can be explained using a cognitive-linguistic approach called *conceptual blending theory* (cf. Fauconnier and Turner 2002, Ungerer and Schmid 2006: 268–270). Essentially, this theory argues that the source words of blends activate so-called **mental spaces** in the minds of language users, which project selected conceptual content into a blended space. Significantly, this blended space not only receives information from the two input spaces but generates what is called *emergent structure* following certain cognitive principles. On a very mundane level, this explains, for example, why the concept of BRUNCH is not just a mixture of elements contributed by BREAKFAST and LUNCH, but contains 'original' attributes such as 'extends over a fairly long period' or 'people tend to eat a lot'. The funny side of some blends is accounted for by emergent structure as well, since the conceptual blending of highly disparate mental spaces, as e.g. in *entreporneur*, has a humorous effect. Conceptual blending theory is particularly suitable for the analysis of novel blends, but also novel compounds (Benczes 2011, Schmid 2011).

According to Kemmer (2003), blends are also involved in a process similar to secretion (see p. 130), in which new meaningful elements with morpheme-like character are formed. An example of the starting point of such a process is the blend *glitterati* (from *glitter* and *literati*, "people who are rich, famous, and fashionable"; LDOCE5). Based on this lexeme and others exhibiting a similar syllable structure such as *chatterati*, formations like *luncherati* and *Britpoperati* are created. In these, the splinter *-terati* has lost its initial /t/ sound and the remaining form *-erati* (also *-ati*) has taken on a meaning of its own, described as "a class of people believed to be expert in what is denoted by the first part of the combination" by Stein (2007: 16). Apparently, a transition to a new suffix-like element has taken place. Kemmer explains this phenomen as being facilitated by a **cognitive schema**, in which a single example serves as a starting-point of a schema which acts as a model for deriving further formations. The overriding aim of this approach is to recognize that there is some degree of regularity in what is normally regarded as an unsystematic and irregular process, allowing lexical blending to be described as a mental pattern for the formation of new lexemes.

With regard to the current 'productivity' of blending, Lehrer (1996: 385) claims that this morphological process is a common and important source of new words. Quirk at al. (1985: 1583) also state that "[b]lending is a very productive process, especially in commercial coinages, which suggests that its rather daring playfulness is popular". Twenty-five years later, not only does this still seem to be true, but the trend has certainly gained further momentum in the meantime, partly pushed by the "daring playfulness" of the language use found on the internet. Recent blends found on the web – which may not manage to catch on – are listed in Table (12.3) together with their sources and glosses of their meanings.

Tab. 12.3: Recent blends taken from the internet

blend	source	gloss
bankster	*bank(er?) + gangster*	'a person in the financial service industry who grows rich despite the continued impoverishment of those who depend on their services' (http://www.urbandictionary.com)
diabesity	*diabetes + obesity*	'obesity caused by diabetes'
ethonomics	*ethics + economy*	'the study of ethics in the marketplace' (Wikipedia)
globesity	*global + obesity*	'the idea that obesity has become a global problem'

meaniac	mean + maniac	'a person that is simultaneously mean and a maniac'
radiculous	radical + ridiculous	's.th. so rad (i.e. incredible) that it is ridiculous'
wellderly	well + elderly	'elderly people who are in good health'

Blending certainly enjoys a considerable amount of popularity as a means of expressing creativity and originality, especially in computer-mediated communication but also in private everyday life, and of course in the press. Whether a new blend has the potential to become recognized, correctly interpreted and finally established – aside from general extralinguistic factors – depends on how common the original words are, how easy to identify they are, how large the splinters are, and how pronounced the phonetic similarity and the shared characteristics in the syllable structure are with the original words (Lehrer 1996: 385, Kemmer 2003: 81 ff., Gries 2004).

Further reading: Hansen (1963), Cannon (2000), Kemmer (2003), Gries (2004), Lehrer (2007).

12.5 Reduplication

Reduplication refers to a group of word-formation processes in which one word – or word-like sequence of sounds – is repeated either unchanged (**full reduplication**, e.g. *hush-hush, girly-girly*), with a different vowel (**ablaut reduplication**, e.g. *singsong, hip-hop*) or with a different consonant (**rhyme reduplication**, e.g. *boogie-woogie, walkie-talkie, bow-wow*). We should make a distinction here between formations that consist of already established words (such as *singsong* and *walkie-talkie*) and those that are composed of expressive or onomatopoeic elements which do not have the status of words or morphemes.

In the so-called *new varieties* of English spoken in Africa and Asia, under the influence of indigenous languages, reduplication is used grammatically to express intensification (*big big* 'very big') or a larger quantity (*money money* 'a lot of money'), whereas in the native varieties it primarily has an expressive function. Several of the established formations, e.g. *tick-tock, puff-puff* and *bow-wow* (i.e. words imitating the sounds made by a clock, train engine and dog, respectively) originate from child language. Others denote contrasts or alternating movements or rather their associated sounds in a more or less onomatopoeic form e.g. *click-clack, ding-dong, criss-cross, zigzag*. Many reduplications express a derogatory attitude towards what is being denoted, for instance, *chitchat, tittle-tattle, mishmash, wishy-washy, singsong*, or the more recently created *Aga saga* which is "a form of popular novel typically set in semi-rural location and concerning the domestic and emotional lives of middle-class characters" (Knowles 1997) and *happy-clappy* "an informal and mildly disparaging name for a member of a Christian group whose worship is marked by enthusiasm and spontaneity" (Knowles 1997).

Further reading: Hansen (1964), Marchand (1969: 429 ff.), Hansen et al. (1990: 140 ff.), Baldi and Dawar (2000: 970 ff.), Adams (2001: 127 ff.).

12.6 Summary: borderline cases and problems of classification

The discussion in this chapter has shown that back-formation, which is in a sense clearly the odd man out, cannot be regarded as a morphemic word-formation process. While the fact that genuine or supposed morpheme boundaries are taken into account moves back-formation closer to the domain of morphemic patterns, the very lack of the potential to form paradigms indicates that it also belongs with the other unpredictable processes discussed in this chapter.

These other non-morphemic processes are functionally similar to each other in important respects:

- They result in abbreviations and thereby contribute to the economy of speech production.
- Partly as a result of the formal abbreviation, one could say that they all obscure meanings. This has several social consequences. For the initiated they reflect a sense of belonging and identification with social groups or discourse domains, whereas for people who are not acquainted with them, they create the effect of exclusion.
- Furthermore, many of the formations discussed in this chapter take on a more or less distinctive expressive character. Particularly compared to the corresponding full forms, many short forms acquire connotative and associative semantic elements. In contrast, many acronyms originate from the rather prosaic area of public and institutional communication in which they are also predominantly used.
- Finally, the non-morphemic patterns are characterized by a relatively high degree of awareness on the part of the speaker of being engaged in the process of word-formation. Linguistic originality and creativity are employed to an even greater extent in non-morphemic formations than in morphemic ones.

Borderline cases and classification problems occur amongst the various non-morphemic word-formation processes as well as between them and the morphemic patterns. For the last two lexemes mentioned, *Aga saga* and *happy-clappy*, for example, the rhyming argues for treating them as reduplications. However, in each of these cases two established lexemes with completely different meanings contribute to the overall meaning of the new lexeme, which in turn is more typical of compounding than reduplication, and suggests that it would be better to treat both forms as special cases of composites marked by an internal rhyme.

The lexemes *entreporneur* and *infotainment* illustrate cases where blends and clipped forms are combined, since both *porn* and *info* occur as abbreviations for *pornography* and *information* independently of their appearance in the blends. The established lexeme *sitcom* (from *situation comedy*) stands at the interface between acronym-formation, clipping and compounding. The established lexemes *e-mail*, *e-commerce* and *e-learning* as well as the recently coined *e-tailer*, *e-tivity* and *e-waste* demonstrate that unpredictable processes also occur in combination with morphemic patterns.

13 Summary and conclusion

The main purpose of this book has been not only to describe the morphology and word-formation patterns of English from a structural viewpoint but also to emphasize the need to do justice to the sociopragmatic and cognitive aspects of this area. The corpus adopted has proved to be a useful and reliable aid on the path to this goal. In several chapters – on prefixation, suffixation, polymorphemic compounds, clipping and acronyms – we have managed to derive a structural description more or less directly from the corpus data. The insights on the frequency of morphological phenomena obtained from analyzing the corpus were also instrumental in forming and supporting hypotheses from the sociopragmatic and cognitive perspectives.

From a structural perspective it was firstly essential to take stock of the fundamental morphological building blocks of English in a precise and theoretically consistent way. This step was already based on empirical observations, since the postulated elements were derived from the analysis of the corpus. The central concepts *word* and *morpheme* were defined as categories that manifest themselves in a range of prototypical, typical and less typical examples. This has the advantage that morphological units such as *bound roots* or *combining forms* are not regarded as troublesome exceptions but, on the contrary, can be characterized in a prototype-theoretical framework as absolutely normal variations of typical morphemes. An overview of inflectional morphemes in contemporary English and their allomorphs, as well as a look into the historical development in this field, were also part of the structure-oriented account.

The structural description of English word-formation profited considerably from the morphological, syntactic and semantic analyses achieved by structuralist and generative approaches. Based on the existing literature and the corpus analyses carried out here, the previous chapters have provided a detailed overview of the inventory of forms and processes that English speakers employ to form complex lexemes. The formation processes that have been identified have not been formulated here as rules with as few exceptions as possible, but as patterns or models that are used by speakers as blueprints, moulds or guidelines for new formations. For this reason the exceptions to a rule or special cases of the basic patterns of compounding, prefixation or suffixation have also been explained as variants and slight deviations from typical patterns. The degree to which a word conforms to the rules only partly determines its chances of establishing itself in the word stock; the reaction of members of the speech community is just as important a factor in determining the extent to which it will spread and catch on.

This takes us to the sociopragmatic perspective, which deals with the use of in-flectional morphemes and complex lexemes in social contexts. The corpus was of huge significance in this respect, since all examples were taken from authentic linguistic situations and social contexts. Five different types of texts or registers were differentiated systematically. It was shown even in the distribution of mor-pheme types that the relative frequency of inflectional morphemes such as {ed$_1$} correlate with user intentions and functions of texts such as narration or exposi-tion. The data collected on the distribution of derivational suffixes and the analy-sis of prefixations and suffixations have shown that both forms of affixation occur with disproportionate frequencies in the more formal and abstract text types of press texts and scientific texts. On the other hand, conversion is employed primar-ily in other stylistic areas. These findings were interpreted as representing a com-plementary division of labour between suffixation and conversion in the recatego-rization of concepts.

The sociopragmatic perspective is of key importance for investigating the diffu-sion and establishment of new complex lexemes and the productivity of the under-lying patterns. In this respect one must judge *inter alia* whether a speaker is using an ad-hoc formation with a naming function, which then possibly serves as the starting point for its spread and institutionalization, or merely with a context-specific syntactic or pragmatic function.

The sociopragmatic viewpoint proved to be particularly productive when working with non-morphemic shortening processes, several of which do not lead to an obvious conceptual change of the original word. In this case, interpersonal, social and expressive motives are frequently decisive for the coining or use of a new form.

Cognitive considerations could not be supported to the same extent by available insights from structuralist approaches. Precursors of cognitive-linguistic claims were found in the fields of concept-formation and information distribution particu-larly within compounds, and in the notion that complex lexemes are based on underlying scenes against whose background they emphasize certain semantic roles or concepts.

Building on this basis and using recent contributions to the study of word-formation from the field of cognitive linguistics, a set of analytical tools was developed for the cognitive perspective that looks closely at the cognitive func-tions of word-formation in general and of individual word-formation patterns, as well as their multifacetted potential to allocate attention by means of profiling. Here it was crucial to investigate the effects of word-formation patterns on en-coded concepts and to draw conclusions from this about the cognitive mechanisms involved. In this context, quantitative findings from the corpus analyis played an important role, too. For example, based on frequency analyses of the corpus data, the shared cognitive function "other than X" was attributed to the various models of prefixation. Suffixation and conversion were portrayed as mechanisms that generate a new or additional conceptual profiling in largely complementary areas of the lexicon. The complementarity refers not only to the stylistic differences that have already been mentioned, but also to a conceptual division of labour. Suffixation is a predominantly nominal, i.e. reifying process, whereas conversion frequently leads to the dynamization of object or quality concepts. With regard to conversion, a cognitive-linguistic model based on Dirven's approach (1999) was developed which explains this extraordinarily common phenomen as a form of metonymic transfer, and is thus based on a process that transcends word-formation and is of fundamental cognitive significance.

In this book morphology and word-formation have been portrayed as aspects of the English language that can be described systematically with regard to their structure, are relevant for the general cognitive system or influenced by it, and subject to sociopragmatic influences. Speakers coin and use complex lexemes as a result of immediate cognitive, social and pragmatic needs – because they want to encapsulate a complex fact, state of affairs or social practice; because they want to pick up on something that has been said previously; because they wish to express themselves in a particularly original, familiar, elevated or secretive way; because they want to convey feelings and mental attitudes; because they wish to throw new light on a well-known concept; and for many other reasons that have not yet been clarified. Since the structural aspects of morphology and word-formation have already been described fairly extensively in the existing literature, this book has been an attempt to encourage future research into morphology and word-formation which concentrates rather on the language users themselves and their thinking and actions than was the custom in the past.

References

Adams, Valerie (1973): *An introduction to modern English word-formation*, London etc.: Longman.

Adams, Valerie (2001): *Complex words in English*, Harlow: Pearson Education Limited.

Aitchison, Jean (2003): *Words in the mind. An introduction to the mental lexicon*, 3rd ed., Oxford: Blackwell.

Aitchison, Jean (2005): "Speech production and perception". In: Booij et al. (2005), 1778–1788.

Algeo, John (1978): "The taxonomy of word making". *Word* 29, 122–131.

Algeo, John (1980): "Where do all the new words come from?". *American Speech* 55, 264–277.

Anderson, Stephen R. (1982): "Where is morphology?". *Linguistic Inquiry* 13, 571–612.

Aronoff, Mark (1976): *Word formation in generative grammar*, Cambridge /MA – London: MIT Press.

Aronoff, Mark (2000): "Generative Grammar". In: Booij, Lehmann and Mugdan (2000), 194–209.

Baayen, Harald (1994): "Derivational productivity and text typology". *Journal of Quantitative Linguistics* 1/1, 16–34.

Baayen, Harald and Rochelle Lieber (1991): "Productivity and English word-formation: a corpus-based study". *Linguistics* 29, 801–843.

Baldi, Philip and Chantal Dawar (2000): "Creative processes". In: Booij, Lehmann and Mugdan (2000), 963–972.

Barker, Chris (1995): "Episodic -*ee* in English: Thematic relations and new word formation". In: Mandy Simons and Teresa Galloway, eds., *Proceedings from semantics and linguistic theory V. Papers presented at the conference on semantics and linguistic theory, 1995*, Ithaca/N.Y.: Cornell University, 5–18.

Barnhart, C. L., S. Steinmetz and R.K. Barnhart, eds. (1973): *A dictionary of new English words*, London: Longman.

Bauer, Laurie (1979): "On the need for pragmatics in the study of nominal compounding". *Journal of Pragmatics* 3, 45–50.

Bauer, Laurie (1983): *English word-formation*, Cambridge: Cambridge University Press.

Bauer, Laurie (1988): *Introducing linguistic morphology*, Edinburgh: Edinburgh University Press.

Bauer, Laurie (1994): "Productivity". In: R. E. Asher, ed., *Encyclopedia of language and linguistics, Vol. 7*, Aberdeen, Aberdeen University Press, 3354–3357.

Bauer, Laurie (1998a): "Is there a class of neoclassical compounds in English and is it productive?". *Linguistics* 36, 403–422.

Bauer, Laurie (1998b): "When is a sequence of two nouns a compound in English?". *English Language and Linguistics* 2(1), 65–86.

Bauer, Laurie (2000a): "Word". In: Booij, Lehmann and Mugdan (2000), 247–257.

Bauer, Laurie (2000b): "System vs. norm: coinage and institutionalization". In: Booij, Lehmann and Mugdan (2000), 832–840.

Bauer, Laurie (2001): *Morphological productivity*, Cambridge: Cambridge University Press.

Bauer, Laurie and Rodney Huddleston (2002): "Lexical word-formation". In: Rodney Huddleston and Geoffrey K. Pullum, *The Cambridge Grammar of the English language*, Cambridge etc.: Cambridge University Press.

Bauer, Laurie and Salvador Valera, eds. (2005a): *Approaches to conversion/Zero-derivation*, Münster et al.: Waxmann.

Bauer, Laurie and Salvador Valera, eds. (2005b): "Conversion or zero-derivation". In: Bauer and Valera (2005), 7–17.

Benczes, Réka (2006): *Creative compounding in English. The semantics of metaphorical and metonymical noun-noun combinations*, Amsterdam – Philadelphia: John Benjamins.

Benczes, Réka (2011): "Blending and creativity in metaphorical compounds: A diachronic investigation". In: Sandra Handl and Hans-Jörg Schmid, eds., *Windows to the mind. Metaphor, metonymy and conceptual blending*. Berlin – New York: de Gruyter Mouton, 247–267.

Bergenholtz, Henning and Joachim Mugdan (2000): "Nullelemente in der Morphologie". In: Booij, Lehmann and Mugdan (2000), 435–450.

Biber, Douglas (1988): *Variation across speaking and writing*, Cambridge: Cambridge University Press.

Biber, Douglas, Susan Conrad, Geoffrey Leech, Stig Johannson and Edward Finegan (1999): *Longman grammar of spoken and written English*, London etc.: Longman.

Biese, Y. M. (1941): *Origin and development of conversion in English*, Helsinki: Annales Academiae Scientiarium Tennicae.

Bloomfield, Leonhard (1933): *Language*, London: Allen & Unwin.

Booij, Geert (2000): "Inflection and derivation". In: Booij, Lehmann and Mugdan (2000), 360–369.

Booij, Geert (2007): *The grammar of words. An introduction to morphology*, 2nd ed., Oxford: Oxford University Press.

Booij, Geert (2010): "Constructions and lexical units. An analysis of Dutch numerals". *Linguistische Berichte*, Sonderheft 17 (ed. by Susan Olsen), 81–99.

Booij, Geert, Christian Lehmann and Joachim Mugdan, eds. (2000): *Morphology: An International Handbook on Inflection and Word-Formation, Vol. I*, Berlin – New York: Walter de Gruyter.

Booij, Geert, Christian Lehmann, Joachim Mugdan and Stavros Skopeteas, eds. (2005): *Morphology: An International Handbook on Inflection and Word-Formation, Vol. II*, Berlin – New York: Walter de Gruyter.

Brunner, Karl (1965): *Altenglische Grammatik*, 3rd ed., Tübingen: Niemeyer.

Bybee, Joan (1985): *Morphology: A Study of the Relation between Meaning and Form*. Amsterdam – Philadelphia: Benjamins.

Bybee, Joan (1995): "Regular Morphology and the Lexicon." *Language and Cognitive Processes* 10/5, 425–455.

Bybee, Joan (2000): "Lexical, morphological and syntactic symbolization". In: Booij, Lehmann and Mugdan (2000), 370–377.

Bybee, Joan (2006): "From usage to grammar: the mind's response to repetition. *Language* 82.4, 71 711–733.

Cannon, Garland (1985): "Functional shift in English". *Linguistics* 23, 411–431.

Cannon, Garland (1987): *Historical Change and English Word-Formation. Recent Vocabulary*, New York etc.: Peter Lang.

Cannon, Garland (1990): "Abbreviations and acronyms in English word-formation". *American Speech* 64, 99–127.

Cannon, Garland (2000): "Blending". In: Booij, Lehmann and Mugdan (2000), 952–956.

Carstairs-McCarthy, Andrew (2000): "Lexeme, word-form, paradigm". In: Booij, Lehmann and Mugdan (2000), 595–607.

Carstairs-McCarthy, Andrew (2002): *An introduction to English morphology. Words and their structure*, Edinburgh: Edinburgh University Press.

Carter, Ronald (1987): *Vocabulary*, London etc.: Allen & Unwin.

Chomsky, Noam (1970): "Remarks on nominalization". In: Roderick A. Jacobs and Peter S. Rosenbaum, eds., *Readings in transformational grammar*, Waltham/Mass. etc.: Ginn and Company, 184–221.

Chomsky, Noam and Morris Halle (1968): *The sound patterns of English*, New York: Harper and Row.

Clark, Eve (1981): "Lexical innovations: How children learn to create new words". In: W. Deutsch, ed., *The child's construction of language*, London: Academic Press, 299–328.

Clark, Eve and Herbert H. Clark (1979): „When nouns surface as verbs". *Language* 55, 767–811.

Croft, William (2000): "Lexical and grammatical meaning". In: Booij, Lehmann and Mugdan (2000), 257–263.

Crowther, Jonathan, ed. (1995): *Oxford advanced learner's dictionaryof current English*, 5th ed., Oxford: Oxford University Press. (= OALD5)

Crystal, David (2004): *A glossary of netspeak and textspeak*, Edinburgh: Edinburgh University Press.

Dalton-Puffer, Christiane and Ingo Plag (2000): "Categorywise, some compound-type morphemes seem to be rather suffix-like: On the status of *-ful*, *-type* and *-wise* in Present Day English". *Folia Linguistica* XXXIV/34, 225–244.

Dirven, René (1999): "Conversion as a conceptual metonymy of event schemata". In: Klaus-Uwe Panther and Günter Radden, eds., *Metonymy in language and thought*, Amsterdam – Philadelphia: Benjamins.

Di Scullio, Anna-Maria and Edwin Williams (1987): *On the definition of word*, Cambridge/MA – London: MIT Press.

Don, Jan, Mieke Trommelen and Wim Zonneveld (2000): "Conversion and category indeterminacy". In: Booij, Lehmann and Mugdan (2000), 943–952.

Downing, Pamela (1977): "On the creation and use of English compound nouns". *Language* 53, 810–842.

Dressler, Wolfgang U. (1989): "Prototypical differences between inflection and derivation". *Zeitschrift für Phonetik, Sprachwissenschaft und Kommunikationsforschung* 42, 3–10.

Dressler, Wolfgang U. (1990): "Sketching submorphemes within natural morphology". In: Julian Mendez Dosuna, ed., *Naturalists at Krems*, Salamanca, 33–41.

Faiß, Klaus (1978): *Verdunkelte Compounds im Englischen*, Tübingen: Narr.

Faiß, Klaus (1989): *Englische Sprachgeschichte*, Tübingen: Francke.

Farell, Patrick (2001): "Functional shift as category underspecification". *English language and linguistics* 5, 109–130.

Fauconnier, Gilles and Mark Turner (2002): *The way we think. Conceptual blending and the mind's hidden complexities*, New York: Basic Books.

Fillmore, Charles J. (1968): "The case for case". In: Emmon Bach and Robert T. Harms, eds., *Universals in linguistic theory*, London etc.: Holt, Rinehart & Winston, 1–88.

Fillmore, Charles J. (1977): "The case for case reopened". In: Peter Cole and Jerry M. Sadock, eds., *Syntax and semantics, Vol. 8: Grammatical relations*, New York etc.: Academic Press, 59–81.

Fillmore, Charles J. (1985): "Frames and the semantics of understanding". *Quaderni di Semantica* VI, 222–254.

Fischer, Roswitha (1998): *Lexical change in present-day English. A corpus-based study of the motivation, institutionalization and productivity of creative neologisms*, Tübingen: Gunter Narr.

Fleischer, Wolfgang (2000): "Die Klassifikation von Wortbildungsprozessen". In: Booij, Lehmann and Mugdan (2000), 886–897.

Fleischer, Wolfgang and Irmhild Barz (1995): *Wortbildung der deutschen Gegenwartssprache*, 2nd ed., Tübingen: Niemeyer.

Fries, Charles C. (1952): *The structure of English*, London: Longmans, Green and Company.

Geeraerts, Dirk and Hubert Cuyckens (2007): T*he Oxford handbook of cognitive linguistics*, Oxford etc.: Oxford University Press.

Gerdts, Donna B. (1998): "Incorporation". In: Andrew Spencer and Arnold M. Zwicky, eds., *The handbook of morphology*, Oxford: Blackwell, 84–100.

Gläser, Rosmarie (1986): *Phraseologie der englischen Sprache*, Leipzig: VEB Verlag Enzyklopädie.

Görlach, Manfred (2002): *Einführung in die englische Sprachgeschichte*, 5th ed., Heidelberg: Winter.

Gries, Stefan Th. (2001): "A corpus-linguistic analysis of -*ic* and -*ical* adjectives." *ICAME Journal* 25, 65–108.

Gries, Stefan Th. (2004): "Shouldn't it be *breakfunch*? A quantitative analysis of the structure of blends." *Linguistics* 42/3, 639–667.

Gussmann, Edmund and Bogdan Szymanek (2000): "Phonotactic properties of morphological units". In Booij, Lehmann and Mugdan (2000), 427–435.

Halle, Morris (1973): "Prolegomena to a theory of wordformation". *Linguistic Inquiry* 4, 3–16.

Hanks, Patrick, ed. (1989): *Collins concise dictionary plus*. Glasgow: William Collins Sons & Co.

Hansen, Klaus (1963): "Wortverschmelzungen". *Zeitschrift für Anglistik und Amerikanistik* 11, 117–142.

Hansen, Klaus (1964): "Reim- und Ablautverdoppelungen". *Zeitschrift für Anglistik und Amerikanistik* 12, 5–31.

Hansen, Klaus (2001): "Review of Štekauer (1998)". *Zeitschrift für Anglistik und Amerikanistik* 48, 173–176.

Hansen, Barbara, Klaus Hansen, Albrecht Neubert and Manfred Schentke (1990): *Englische Lexikologie*, 2nd ed., Leipzig: VEB Verlag Enzyklopädie.

Hay, Jennifer (2002): "From Speech Perception to Morphology: Affix-ordering Revisited." *Language* 78, 527–555.

Hay, Jennifer (2007): "The phonetics of '*un*'". In: Munat (2007), 39–57.

Hay, Jennifer B. and Ingo Plag (2004): "What constrains possible suffix combinations? On the interaction of grammatical and processing restrictions in derivational morphology." *Natural Language and Linguistic Theory* 22, 565–596.

Herbst, Thomas, Rita Stoll and Rudolf Westermayr (1991): *Terminologie der Sprachbeschreibung. Ein Lernwörterbuch für das Anglistikstudium*, Ismaning: Hueber.

Heyvaert, Liesbeth (2003): *A cognitive-functional approach to nominalization in English*, Berlin – New York: Mouton de Gruyter.

Heyvaert, Liesbeth (2009): "Compounding in cognitive linguistics". In: Lieber and Štekauer (2009), 233–254.

Hockett, Charles (1958): *A course in modern linguistics*, New York: MacMillan.

Hohenhaus, Peter (1996): *Ad-hoc-Wortbildung. Terminologie, Typologie und Theorie kreativer Wortbildung im Englischen*, Frankfurt/M. etc: Peter Lang.

Hohenhaus, Peter (2005): "Lexicalization and institutionalization". In: Štekauer & Lieber (2005), 353–373.

Hughes, Arthur and Peter Trudgill (1987): *English accents and dialects. An introduction to social and regional varieties of British English*, London etc.: Edward Arnold.

Iacobini, Claudio (2000): "Base and direction of derivation". In: Booij, Lehmann and Mugdan (2000): 865–876.

Jespersen, Otto (1942): *A modern English grammar. On historical principles. Part VI Morphology*, London – Copenhagen: George Allen & Unwin Ltd.

Käsmann, Hans (1992): "Das englische Phonästhem *SL-*". *Anglia* 110, 307–346.

Kastovsky, Dieter (1982): *Wortbildung und Semantik*, Düsseldorf.

Kastovsky, Dieter (1985): "Deverbal nouns in Old and Modern English: from stem-formation to word-formation". Jacek Fisiak, ed., *Historical semantics. Historical word-formation*, Berlin etc.: Mouton, 221–261.

Kastovsky, Dieter (1986): "The problem of productivity in word formation". *Linguistics* 24, 585–600.

Kastovsky, Dieter (1999): "English and German morphology: a typological comparison". In Wolfgang Falkner and Hans-Jörg Schmid, eds., *Words, lexemes, concepts – approaches to the lexicon. Studies in honour of Leonhard Lipka*, Tübingen: Narr, 1999, 39–51.

Kastovsky, Dieter (2005): "Conversion and/or zero: word-formation theory, historical linguistics, and typology". In: Bauer and Valera (2005a), 31–49.

Kemmer, Suzanne (2003): "Schemas and lexical blends". In: Cuyckens, Hubert, Thomas Berg, René Dirven and Klaus-Uwe Panther, eds., *Motivation in language: Studies in honor of Günter Radden*, Amsterdam: Benjamins, 69–97.

Knowles, Elizabeth, ed. (1997): *The Oxford dictionary of new words*, Oxford – New York: Oxford University Press.

Kornexl, Lucia (1998): "Nomina agentis und die sog. agentiven Nullableitungen im Englischen: eine semantisch-kognitive Neubewertung". *Rostocker Beiträge zur Sprachwissenschaft 5. Kognitive Lexikologie und Syntax*, 49–75.

Koziol, Herbert (1937): *Handbuch der englischen Wortbildungslehre*, Heidelberg: Winter.

Kreidler, Charles W. (2000): "Clipping and acronymy". In: Booij, Lehmann and Mugdan (2000), 956–963.

Kruisinga, Etsko (1932): *A handbook of present-day English*, Groningen: Noordhoff.

Kubrjakova, Elena S. (2000): "Submorphemische Einheiten". In: Booij, Lehmann and Mugdan (2000), 417–426.

Lampert, Martina and Günther Lampert (2010): "Word-formation or word formation? The formation of complex words in Cognitive Linguistics". In: Onysko and Michel (2010), 29–73.

Langacker, Ronald W. (1987a): *Foundations of cognitive grammar, Vol. I: Theoretical prerequisites*, Stanford/CA: Stanford University Press.

Langacker, Ronald W. (1987b): "Nouns and verbs". *Language* 63, 53–94.

Langacker, Ronald W. (1991): *Foundations of cognitive grammar, Vol. II: Descriptive application*, Stanford/CA: Stanford University Press.

Langacker, Ronald W. (2008): *Cognitive Grammar. A basic introduction*, Oxford: Oxford University Press.

Lass, Roger (1992): "Phonology and morphology". In: Norman Blake, ed., *The Cambridge history of the English language. Volume II 1066-1476*, Cambridge: Cambridge University Press.

Leech, Geoffrey N. (1981): *Semantics. The study of meaning*, 2nd ed., Harmondsworth: Penguin.

Lees, Robert B. (1966): *The grammar of English nominalizations*, 4th ed., The Hague: Mouton.

Lehnert, Martin (1971): *Rückläufiges Wörterbuch der englischen Gegenwartssprache*, Leipzig: Verlag Enzyklopädie.

Lehrer, Adrienne (1996): "Identifying and interpreting blends: An experimental approach". *Cognitive Linguistics* 7 (4), 359–390.

Lehrer, Adrienne (2007): "Blendalicious". In: Munat (2007), 115–133.

Leisi, Ernst (1975): *Der Wortinhalt. Seine Struktur im Deutschen und Englischen*, 5th ed., Heidelberg: Winter.

Leisi, Ernst (1985): *Praxis der englischen Semantik*, 2nd ed., Heidelberg: Winter.

Leisi, Ernst and Christian Mair (1999): *Das heutige Englisch*. 8. Aufl. Heidelberg: Winter.

Lenker, Ursula (2002): "Is it, stylewise or otherwise, wise to use *-wise*?". In: Teresa Fanego, María José López-Couso and Javier Pérez-Guerra, eds., *English historical syntax and morphology*, Amsterdam – Philadelphia: Benjamins, 157–180.

Libben, Gary and Gonia Jarema, eds. (2007): *The representations and processing of compound words*, Oxford: Oxford University Press.

Lieber, Rochelle (1990): *On the organization of the lexicon*, New York – London: Garland Publishing.

Lieber, Rochelle (2005): "English word-formation processes". In: Štekauer & Lieber (2005), 375–427.

Lieber, Rochelle (2009): "IE, Germanic: English". In: Lieber and Štekauer (2009), 357–369.

Lieber, Rochelle and Joachim Mugdan (2000): "Internal structure of words". In: Booij, Lehmann and Mugdan (2000), 404–416.

Lieber, Rochelle and Pavol, Štekauer, eds. (2009): *The Oxford handbook of compounding*, Oxford: Oxford University Press.

Lipka, Leonhard (1977): "Lexikalisierung, Idiomatisierung und Hypostasierung als Probleme einer synchronen Wortbildungslehre". In: Dieter Kastovsky and Herbert E. Brekle, eds., *Perspektiven der Wortbildungsforschung. Beiträge zum Wuppertaler Wortbildungskolloquium vom 9.-10. Juli 1976*, Bonn: Bouvier, 155–164.

Lipka, Leonhard (1981): "Zur Lexikalisierung im Deutschen und Englischen". In: Leonhard Lipka and Hartmut Günther, eds., *Wortbildung*, Darmstadt: Wissenschaftliche Buchgesellschaft, 119–132.

Lipka, Leonhard (1983): "A multi-level approach to word-formation: complexe lexemes and word semantics". In: S. Hattori and K. Inoue, eds., *Proceedings of the XIIIth international congress of linguists, Tokyo 1982*, Tokyo, 926–928.

Lipka, Leonhard (1987): "Word-formation and text in English and German". In: B. Asbach-Schnitker and J. Roggenhofer, eds., *Neuere Forschung zur Wortbildung und Historiographie der Linguistik. Festgabe für Herbert E. Brekle zum 50. Geburtstag*, Tübingen: Narr, 59–67.

Lipka, Leonhard (1992): "Lexicalization and institutionalisation in English and German or: Piefke, Wendehals, smog, perestroika, AIDS etc.". *Zeitschrift für Anglistik und Amerikanistik* 40, 101–111.

Lipka, Leonhard (1994): "Wortbildung und Metonymie – Prozesse, Resultate und ihre Beschreibung". *Münstersches Logbuch zur Linguistik* 5, 1–15.

Lipka, Leonhard (2000): "English (and general) word-formation – The state of the art in 1999". In: Reitz and Rieuwerts (2000), 5–20.

Lipka, Leonhard (2002): *English lexicology. Lexical structure, word semantics & word formation*, Tübingen: Narr.

Lipka, Leonhard (2007): "Lexical creativity, textuality and problems of metalanguage". In: Munat (2007), 3–12.

Luschützky, Hans Christian (2000): "Morphem, Morph und Allomorph". In: Booij, Lehmann and Mugdan (2000), 451–462.

Lyons, John (1968): *Introduction to theoretical linguistics*, Cambridge: Cambridge University Press.

Marchand, Hans (1963): "On a question of contrary analysis". *English studies* 44, 176–187.

Marchand, Hans (1969): *The categories and types of present-day English word-formation. A synchronic-diachronic approach*, 2nd ed., München: Beck.

Marchand, Hans (1974): "A set of criteria for the establishing of derivational relationship between words unmarked by derivational morphemes". In: Dieter Kastovsky, ed., *Studies in syntax and word-formation. Selected articles by Hans Marchand*, München: Wilhelm Fink Verlag, 242–252. (Originally published in *Indogermanische Forschungen* 69, 1964, 10–19.)

McArthur, Tom (1988): "The cult of abbreviation". *English Today* 15, 36–42.

McCully, C.B. and Martin Holmes (1988): "Some notes on the structure of acronyms". *Lingua* 74, 27–43.

McQueen, James M. and Anne Cutler (1998): "Morphology in word recognition". In: Spencer and Zwicky (1998), 406–427.

Mel'čuk, Igor (2000): "Suppletion". In: Booij, Lehmann and Mugdan (2000), 510–522.

Mettinger, Arthur (1994): "*Un*-prefixation in English: Expectations, formats, and results". *Münstersches Logbuch zur Linguistik* 5, 17–31.

Mitchell, Bruce and Fred C. Robinson (1992): *A guide to Old English*, 5th ed., Oxford/U.K. – Cambridge/MA: Blackwell.

Mugdan, Joachim (1986): "Was ist eigentlich ein Morphem?". *Zeitschrift für Phonetik, Sprachwissenschaft und Kommunikationsforschung* 39, 29–43.

Munat, Judith, ed. (2007): *Lexical creativity, texts and contexts*, Amsterdam – Philadelphia: John Benjamins.

Muthmann, Gustav (1999): *Reverse English dictionary. Based on phonological and morphological principles*, Berlin – New York: Mouton de Gruyter.

Neef, Martin (2000a): "Morphologische und syntaktische Konditionierung". In: Booij, Lehmann and Mugdan (2000), 473–48.

Neef, Martin (2000b): "Phonologische Konditionierung". In: Booij, Lehmann and Mugdan (2000), 463–473.

Obst, Wolfgang and Florian Schleburg (1999): *Die Sprache Chaucers. Ein Lehrbuch des Mittelenglischen auf der Grundlage von Troilus and Criseyde*, Heidelberg: Winter.

Olsen, Susan (2000): "Composition". In: Booij, Lehmann and Mugdan (2000), 897–916.

Onysko, Alexander and Sascha Michel, eds. (2010a): *Cognitive perspectives on word-formation*, Berlin etc.: Mouton de Gruyter.

Onysko, Alexander and Sascha Michel (2010b): "Introduction: Unravelling the cognitive in word-formation". In: Onysko and Michel (2010a), 1–25.

Panther, Klaus-Uwe and Linda Thornburg (2001): "A Conceptual Analysis of -er Nominals." In: Susanne Niemeier and Martin Pütz, eds., *Applied Cognitive Linguistics II: Language Pedagogy*, Berlin – New York: Mouton de Gruyter, 149–200.

Pennanen, Esko V. (1971): *Conversion and zero-derivation in English*, Tampere: Tampereen Yliopisto.

Pfeffer, Alan J. and Garland Cannon (1994): *German loanwords in English. An historical dictionary*, Cambridge etc.: Cambridge University Press.

Plag, Ingo (1997): "The polysemy of *-ize* derivatives: On the role of semantics in word formation". In: Geert Booij and Jaap von Marle, eds., *Yearbook of morphology 1997*, Dordrecht etc.: Kluwer, 219–242.

Plag, Ingo (1999): *Morphological productivity. Structural constraints in English derivation*, Berlin etc.: Mouton de Gruyter.

Plag, Ingo (2003): *Word-formation in English*, Cambridge: Cambridge University Press.

Plag, Ingo (2006): The variability of compound stress in English: structural, semantic, and analogical factors. *English Language and Linguistics* 10, 143–172.

Plag, Ingo, Christiane Dalton-Puffer and Harald Baayen (1999): "Morphological productivity across speech and writing". English *Language and Linguistics* 3, 209–228.

Plag, Ingo and Harald Baayen (2009): "Suffix ordering and morphological processing." *Language* 85, 109–152.

Plank, Frans (1981): *Morphologische (Ir-)Regularitäten. Aspekte der Wortstrukturtheorie*, Tübingen: Narr.

Plank, Frans (1994): "Inflection and derivation". In: R. E. Asher, ed., *The encyclopedia of language and linguistics, Vol. III*, Oxford: Pergamon Press, 1671–1678.

Quirk, Randolph, Sidney Greenbaum, Geoffrey Leech and Jan Svartvik (1985): *A comprehensive grammar of the English language*, London – New York: Longman.

Raffelsiefen, Renate (2010): "Idiosyncracy, regularity, and synonymy in derivational morphology: Evidence for default word interpretation strategies". *Linguistische Berichte*, Sonderheft 17 (ed. by Susan Olsen), 173–232.

Rainer, Franz (2000): "Produktivitätsbeschränkungen". In: Booij, Lehmann and Mugdan (2000), 877–885.

Reitz, Bernhard and Sigrid Rieuwerts, eds. (2000): *Anglistentag 1999 Mainz. Proceedings*, Trier: Wissenschaftlicher Verlag Trier.

Ryder, Mary Ellen (1994): *Ordered chaos. The interpretation of English noun-noun compounds*, Berkeley etc.: University of California Press.

Ryder, Mary Ellen (1999): "Bankers and blue-chippers: an account of -er formations in present-day English". *English Language and Linguistics* 3, 269–297.

Sanders, Gerald (1988): "Zero derivation and the overt analogue criterion". In: Michael Hammond and Michael Noonan, eds., *Theoretical morphology: Approaches in modern linguistics*, New York: Academic Press, 155–178.

Scheler, Manfred (1977): *Der englische Wortschatz*, Berlin: Schmidt.

Schmid, Hans-Jörg (2000): *English abstract nouns as conceptual shells. From corpus to cognition.* Berlin etc.: Mouton de Gruyter.

Schmid, Hans-Jörg (2007): "Entrenchment, salience and basic levels". In: Geeraerts and Cuyckens (2007), 117–138.

Schmid, Hans-Jörg (2008): "New words in the mind: Concept-formation and entrenchment of neologisms". *Anglia* 126 (1), 1–36.

Schmid, Hans-Jörg (2011): "Conceptual blending, relevance and novel N+N-compounds". In: Sandra Handl and Hans-Jörg Schmid, eds., *Windows to the mind. Metaphor, metonymy and conceptual blending*, Berlin – New York: de Gruyter Mouton, 219–245.

Schneider, Klaus Peter (2003): *Diminutives in English*, Tübingen: Niemeyer.

Schönefeld, Doris (2005): "Zero-derivation – functional change – metonymy". In: Bauer and Valera (2005), 131–159.

Schröder, Anne (2008): "Investigating the Morphological Productivity of Verbal Prefixation in the History of English". *Arbeiten aus Anglistik und Amerikanistik* 33 (1), 47–69.

Schröder, Anne and Susanne Mühleisen (2010): "New ways of investigating morphological productivity". *Arbeiten aus Anglistik und Amerikanistik* 35/1, 43–58.

Selkirk, Elisabeth (1982): *The syntax of words*, Cambridge/MA.: MIT Press.

Siemund, Peter (2008): *Pronominal gender in English*, London: Routledge.

Simpson, John and Edmund Weiner, eds. (1989): *Oxford English dictionary. Second edition*, 20 vols., Oxford: Oxford University Press. (= OED)

Spencer, Andrew and Arnold M. Zwicky (1998): *The handbook of morphology*, Oxford: Blackwell Publishers.

Stegmayr, Susanne, Daphné Kerremans and Hans-Jörg Schmid (forthcoming): "The NeoCrawler: Identifying and retrieving neologisms from the Internet and monitoring ongoing change". In: Kathryn Allan and Justyna Robinson, eds., *Current methods in historical semantics*, Berlin etc.: Mouton de Gruyter.

Štekauer, Pavol (1996): *A theory of conversion in English*, Frankfurt/M: Peter Lang.

Štekauer, Pavol (1998): *An onomasiological theory of English word formation*, Amsterdam – Philadelphia: John Benjamins Publishing Company.

Štekauer, Pavol (2000): *English word formation. A history of research*, Tübingen: Narr.

Štekauer, Pavol and Rochelle Lieber, eds. (2005): *Handbook of word-formation*, Dordrecht: Springer.

Štekauer, Pavol (2000): "Onomasiological approach to word-formation". In: Štekauer and Lieber (2005), 207–232.

Stemberger, Joseph P. (1998): "Morphology in language production with special reference to connectionism". In: Spencer and Zwicky (1998), 428–452.

Stein, Gabriele (2007): *A dictionary of English affixes*, Munich: Lincom.

Stein, Gabriele (2009): "Classifying affixes and multiple affixations in Modern English". *Zeitschrift für Anglistik und Amerikanistik* 57.3, 233–253.

Stockwell, Robert and Donka Minkowa (2001): *English words. History and structure*, Cambridge etc.: Cambridge University Press,

Summers, Della, ed. (2003): *Longman dictionary of contemporary English*, 4th ed., Harlow: Pearson Education. (= LDOCE4)

Summers, Della, ed. (2009): *Longman dictionary of contemporary English*, 5th ed., Harlow: Pearson Education. (= LDOCE5)

Sweet, Henry (1900): *A new English grammar. Logical and historical*, Oxford: Clarendon Press.

Szawerna, Michal (2007): *A corpus-based study of nominalizations predicated by English deverbal nouns in* -tion, Frankfurt/Main: Peter Lang.

Szymanek, Bogdan (1988): *Categories and categorization in morphology,* Lublin: Redakcja Wydawnictw, Katolickiego Uniwersytetu Lubelskiego.

ten Hacken, Pius (2000): "Derivation and compounding". In: Booij, Lehmann and Mugdan (2000), 349–360.

ten Hacken, Pius (2010): "Synthetic and exocentric compounds in a parallel architecture". In: Olsen (2010): 233–257.

Tournier, Jean (1985): *Introduction descriptive à la lexicogénétique de l'anglais contemporain,* Paris – Genève: Champion-Slatkine.

Tournier, Jean (1988): *Précis de lexicologie anglaise,* Paris: Nathan.

Tuggy, David (2005): "Cognitive approach to word-formation". In: Štekauer and Lieber (2005), 233–265.

Twardzisz, Piotr (1997): *Zero derivation in English. A cognitive grammar approach,* Lublin: Wydawnicto UMCS.

Umbreit, Birgit (2010): "Does *love* come from *to love* or *to love* from *love*? Why lexical motivation has to be regarded as bidirectional." In: Onysko and Michel (2010), 301–333.

Ungerer Friedrich (1991): "Acronyms, trade names and motivation". *Arbeiten aus Anglistik und Amerikanistik* 16/2, 131–158.

Ungerer, Friedrich (2002): "The conceptual function of derivational word-formation in English". *Anglia* 120/4, 534–567.

Ungerer, Friedrich (2007): "Derivational morphology and word-formation". In: Geeraerts and Cuyckens (2007): 991–1025.

Ungerer, Friedrich and Hans-Jörg Schmid (1998): "Englische Komposita und Kategorisierung: eine empirische Untersuchung". *Rostocker Beiträge zur Sprachwissenschaft 5. Kognitive Lexikologie und Syntax,* 77–99.

Ungerer, Friedrich and Hans-Jörg Schmid (2006): *An introduction to cognitive linguistics,* 2nd ed., London etc.: Longman.

Warren, Beatrice (1978): *Semantic patterns of noun-noun compounds,* Göteburg: Acta Universitas Gothoburgensis.

Warren, Beatrice (1990): "The importance of combining forms". In: Wolfgang U. Dressler, Hans Christian Luschützky, Oskar E. Pfeiffer and John R. Rennison, eds. *Contemporary morphology,* Berlin – New York: Mouton de Gruyter, 111–132.

Welna, Jerzy (1996): *English historical morphology,* Warschau: Wydawnictwa Uniwersytetu Warszawskiego.

Zirkel, Linda (2010): "Prefix combinations in English: Structural and processing factors". *Morphology* 20, 239–266.

Subject and author index

Index of prefixes, suffixes and combining forms